PRINCE  ON PRINCE

PRINCE ON PRINCE

INTERVIEWS AND ENCOUNTERS

EDITED BY ARTHUR LIZIE

CHICAGO
REVIEW
PRESS

ISBN 978-1-64160-715-5

Library of Congress Control Number: 2022940145

A list of credits and copyright notices for the individual pieces in this collection can be found on pages 263–265.

Cover design: Jonathan Hahn
Front cover image: Steve Parke / Iconic Images
Interior layout: Nord Compo

Printed in the United States of America
5 4 3 2 1

CONTENTS

ACKNOWLEDGMENTS

I want to thank:

All the contributing writers, many of whom went beyond the call of duty with their generosity toward me.

Kara Rota and the team at Chicago Review Press for all their support and encouragement during the writing process.

Michael "Princeologist" Robertson for access to his impressive Prince archives.

The Minnesota Historical Society for their archival support.

Susan, Eloise, and Orson for enduring the writing of another Prince book.

PREFACE

Prince interview (prins in-ter-vyoo) *noun.* A journalist's information-gathering discussion with one of the greatest entertainers of the twentieth century that may or may not actually take place, and, when taking place, is often conducted via phone or fax and without the usual tools of the trade such as an audio recorder and, often, without even a pen and paper.

After God, and maybe after music, what Prince seemed to care most about was control. The type Janet Jackson sang about in Jimmy Jam and Terry Lewis's "Control," but even more so. Or, without pushing metaphors about his regal name too far, what Prince sought was sovereignty—the ability to craft his world without outside interference.

We can see this need for control early on with his insistence on an unprecedented debut recording contract that allowed him the right to play all the instruments and produce his own work. We can see it in his behind-the-scenes string-pulling with bands such as the Time and Vanity 6. We can see it with his autocratic record label Paisley Park. We can see it in his battle with Warner Bros. over musical output and master recordings, a battle that saw him change his name to an unspeakable glyph. And we saw it with his direct-to-consumer marketing, pioneering use of the Internet, and lucrative, ad hoc approach to touring in the latter part of his career. And we saw it in his interviews.

Unlike paid advertising and news reports, entertainment interviews are a wholly transactional business exchange: the artist gets to share their ideas and promote their product while the interviewer gains professional status and their media outlet acquires sellable content. As such, for an artist, it can be thought of as a necessary price of doing business. Prince probably learned this much in his Bryant Junior High Business of Music class with teacher Jimmy Hamilton and, if not there, from his first manager Owen Husney, who, when speaking of the music business, said, "Prince really wanted to know every aspect of it himself."

But, for whatever cognitive understanding Prince had of the importance of interviews to a music career, at the beginning of his career he didn't engage with interviewers, who early on described him as aloof, quiet, and shy, and interaction with him "like trying to pry open a clam." And when he did engage, he often fed false information, such as telling one interviewer that he used the name Prince since his real name was "too hard to remember" (he'd return to this joke on 1994's "Now": "Don't worry about my name, it's too long to remember / I could tell you now but we'd be here 'til next September"). Eventually, his reluctance to be interviewed and the hoop-jumping process of interviewing him became part of almost every published interview.

The aloof/difficult narrative was fueled by Prince's first national interview outside a handful conducted with Black-culture magazines such as *Black Stars* and *Right On!*, his January 1980 appearance on *American Bandstand*. The interview is less than two minutes, but it feels like a thousand as Prince rebuffs host Dick Clark with a series of brief, evasive responses, an interchange that TV veteran Clark admitted was among his most difficult. There are differing theories as to why the interview unfolded this way (shyness, stage fright), but band members say Prince chose this approach backstage after meeting Clark. If it was a tactical business-of-music move, then it paid off with instant press coverage, however off-putting some found it.

From here on, Prince's willingness to be interviewed would be most tactical. In late 1980 he and publicist Harold Bloom met to figure out ways for Prince to cross over (a term Prince hated) to White rock audiences, specifically punk and new wave fans. Part of the strategy was a flurry of early 1981 interviews with both the mainstream press, such as the *Los Angeles Times* and *Rolling Stone*, and quasi-underground rock publications such as *Boston Rock* and *Boston Real Paper*. He sidled up to the press when necessary.

Immediately after this group of interviews, which coincided with the end of the *Dirty Mind* tour, Prince mostly let the music and movies do the talking, conducting fewer than a dozen interviews over the next decade. He only reemerged with a handful of interviews for 1991's *Diamonds and Pearls*, which found him reenergized with the newly minted New Power Generation and in need of some positive press after the critical and commercial failure of the *Graffiti Bridge* project. This pattern would generally hold for the rest of his life—lots of talking when he needed a win in the marketplace, such as with his 1996 self-released *Emancipation*, his 1999 move to Arista Records, and 2004's *Musicology* album and tour. Highly transactional.

It's at this point, 1991, that the process of interviewing Prince perpetually becomes part of the story of the interview: Arriving in Minneapolis only to wait a week before Prince will speak . . . by phone. Getting a call in the middle of the night with directions to meet the next day . . . on a different continent. Talking and hanging out with the band for days hoping for a few minutes with Prince. Interviews without any recording device, even pen and paper. Six-question interviews by fax. Five-question e-mail interviews. And, in 1994 and for six subsequent years when he was no longer calling himself Prince, he decided he wasn't even going to talk about Prince. Prince-controlled chaos and disorder for every no-name (and name) reporter.

So what did he talk about over the course of his career? Or, rather, what was he asked about that he decided whether or not he'd respond to? About his solitary recording process. About the inaccuracy of people's ideas about him. About the music that made him. Religion and spirituality and God. Nasty lyrics and swearing. His personal concepts about freedom, oppression, and race. His battles with the music industry and his projects meant to wrestle control from the industry. How to get through this thing called life.

The rich group of interviews collected here spans from early 1978, when Prince's debut *For You* was released, to late 2015, when he was promoting his last two studio albums, *Hitnrun Phase One* and *Phase Two*, and an association with the Tidal streaming service. Attention has been given to offering pieces from diverse sources, both large and small media outlets and domestic and international sources, that have not been anthologized. Prince's memoir was left incomplete, but this volume offers a different type of autobiography in his own words.

Note: Errors in the source material, such as Prince's pliable age, have not been corrected, but some minor textual changes have been made (such as the use of American spelling) for the sake of clarity and consistency.

PRINCE: A TOUCH OF MAGIC

Jeff Schneider | May/June 1978 (No. 3, Vol. 11) | *Insider: The Midwest Magazine of Music News, Arts and Lifestyles*

For all of Prince's early disparaging of his hometown, the community featured a vibrant music press that helped promote both Prince's Minneapolis Sound and the area's influential rock scene, including such legendary bands as the Replacements and Hüsker Dü. Most of Prince's first half-dozen interviews were with Minneapolis-area publications, including high school and university newspapers he spoke with prior to signing his 1977 three-album contract with Warner Bros. The debut LP, *For You*, released April 7, 1978, found Prince talking with larger publications in the Twin Cities area and making inroads with national, Black-oriented publications such as *Black Stars* and *Right On!*

This interview, which bears more than a passing resemblance to a contemporaneous one in the *Minneapolis Tribune*, appeared in the last edition of the much-loved *Insider* magazine. *Insider* was a major supporter of the Minnesota arts scene from 1966 until founder Connie Hechter's untimely death in early 1978. The magazine's void was filled by *Sweet Potato* and *Twin Cities Reader*. *Sweet Potato* subsequently morphed into the Prince-supporting weekly *City Pages*, which shut down in 2020 as a result of the global pandemic; *Twin Cities Reader* shut down in 1997 after being acquired by *City Pages*. For all their proximity, coverage, and cheerleading, and at times unwanted attention, Prince spoke sparingly with these publications during his career.

Jeff Schneider's interview covers the musical side of Prince's backstory, with Prince chiming in on his school days, the search for a record deal while hanging out in New York City with his sister Sharon Nelson, and his comparison of working in the studio to painting. Manager Owen Husney dishes on the process that led to the $180,000 debut contract.

1

At this point we can only dream about finding a recording of Prince clacking the keys on an old-school Magnus Chord Organ. —Ed.

Prince believes in magic—the kind you work at because it's laying there inside you like a wand without an arm to wave it—and he's been busy practicing his magic since he was seven, banging out Jazz and Blues songs on the piano. He was raised in South Minneapolis with his three brothers and four sisters. His dad, billed as Roger Prince, was a swing-band leader. His mother worked on and off as the band's lead singer. When he was in the seventh grade at Bryant Junior High he joined a local dance band called Grand Central. Around the time he and the rest of the members were ready for a change of schools (Central High) they changed the band's name to Shampayne.

By the time Prince was 13 he was comfortable with a bass or a lead guitar. A year later he began working on the drums with a Magnus Chord Organ, a clavinet, and an array of synthesizers following the beat of his magic in the making. A formal musical education didn't have much influence in that magic. Prince says as he recalls his school days, "I took one piano and two guitar lessons while I was in school. I wasn't really a model student. I didn't want to play the funky stuff music teachers used and I couldn't read music. It would always end up that the teacher would go through his thing, and I'd end up doing mine. Eventually they just gave me an A and sent me on my way.

"By the time I was a sophomore, school had gotten to be a real drag. I was getting further and further into making music. The more I found myself entertaining at local gigs during the night, the more I hated the thought of going to school in the morning."

"But later on, there I was seventeen, a graduate and still frustrated. I felt that I had to keep going after the music but didn't know how long I'd be able to do it and eat too. I did know that I wanted something more than nine to five."

Frustration and the going-nowhere-in-a-hurry blues trapped Prince in a case of the "Midwest Lethargism" syndrome. He was struck with the affliction's common symptoms. First you begin viewing the scene as lethargic. This lethargy soon spreads to *your* scene until you just know that the only way anything's gonna pop is if you get the hell out to where the action is. Destination choice is another predetermined characteristic of the affliction. You only see apples or oranges in your dreams. Prince chose the Big Apple because an older sister, Sharon, lived there.

"The only way I can relate to that period, is that it was part of a search," Prince admits.

"While I was living with Sharon I got hooked up with a woman producer who was always busy pitching her own angles. She was only looking at me as a singer, the kind that opts for the silk capes, high heeled shoes and white Cadillacs. You know, somebody who dresses and sings the same part—a nice dresser and a sweet singer. I tried to explain that even though I didn't have the key to the recording industry, that I knew myself and that I knew for sure what I would and wouldn't do for that key. I told her I never considered myself a singer. I saw myself as an instrumentalist who started singing out of necessity. I don't think I ever got through, but I tried explaining, that to me, my voice is just like one of the instruments I play. It's just one thing I do."

Two years ago Prince was just another 16-year-old musician with a band. The drummer's mother managed it, arranging as many school gigs and club appearances as she could. Today he's an 18-year-old studio soloist who just may be sitting on the largest debut recording offer ever to be approved by Warner Brothers Records. Direction from Prince's new manager, Owen Husney, a three-song demo tape and an awe-inspiring amount of talent landed a bottom line that reputedly ran into six figures.

The debut LP entitled *Prince—For You* established enough firsts in its own right to humble a limo-load of market-proven recording artists. *For You* is the first debut album ever to be completely controlled by the artist and his management. Prince was granted control of production, performance, composition and arrangement. On the LP, the Minnesota artist practiced what the contract preached. He arranged the material which—with the exception of "Soft and Wet"—he had created. In Warner Brothers' Record Plant located in Sausalito, California, this 18-year-old, 16-track neophyte stepped in and put down nine solid tunes—single handed. A previous studio merger had yielded the demo which had stimulated his lenient agreement. This time a developed conception emerged. Nine major league tunes—with lush instrumentation and enough multitrack voice dubbing to prompt the Divine Miss M into polishing her bugle.

Ironically, while Prince was in New York unsuccessfully explaining the magic he wanted to come across in a production to an unyielding producer, some of that same magic he'd left behind in Minneapolis was casting spells and lighting up wands on its own.

Before his eastern migration, Prince had gotten a call from Chris Moon, the owner of Moon Sound Inc., a recording studio in South Minneapolis. Moon had remembered the black dude on piano who had played with Shampayne in a previous session. Now he had a demo tape that needed a solid piano track for icing. He knew Prince could easily handle the job and that he'd get an economical billing to boot.

After the pianist had added the keyboards he picked up a bass and suggested that it would also be an asset to the tapes' sound. Moon agreed, but added that he hadn't planned on paying for a bass player too. While a mesmerized Moon sat behind the control panel, the kid from Shampayne laid down a tight bass line. Then he put the bass aside and pounded out a drum track, added an electric guitar lead line and finished by feeding the studio's recorders with multiple backup vocal tracks.

A short while after Moon had edited the tape, he asked the proprietor of The Ad Company at 430 Oak Grove to give it a listen. The agency's owner, Owen Husney, had been through the corridors of the music industry. He'd done everything from local and national promotion to artist management over the years, and Moon was sure he'd recognize Prince's unlimited potential when he heard the tape.

"That's pretty good, who are they?" was Owen's initial response. While Moon explained that the "they" being referred to was one, and that the "one" hadn't any positive commitments for the future, Owen's eyes grew the size of record discs (color them platinum).

A phone call later and Prince was on his way back to the city of lakes; without the company of his silk pitching New York manager . . .

Owen and Prince became fast comrades. As it became apparent to Prince that he'd finally found a manager who would work with him instead of against him, the music began to flow. "I knew whatever had to be done for Prince had to be first class," Owen stated. "If we went to L.A. or anywhere else to score a recording deal, we weren't just going to go out there and phone record execs from our hotel room."

"The best support I could offer was to give Prince the confidence he needed to keep on doing it."

A demo tape was cut at Sound 80 studios. The event, the young artist's first long-term studio stay, created a bond between man and music-machine that isn't likely to be broken. "For me, there's nothing like working in a recording studio. It's satisfying. It's like painting. You begin with a conception and keep adding instruments and laying tracks down. Soon, it's like the monitors are canvas. The instruments are colors on a palette, the mikes and board are brushes. I just keep working it until I've got the picture or rather the sound that I heard inside my head when it was just an idea."

Owen admits that Warner Brothers had a slight edge in negotiations due to friendships he had cultivated at the Southern California base. "But we were approached by everybody, and we considered each proposal." Owen goes on to explain that although A+M and Columbia were more than a little interested in the 18-year-old Minnesota virtuoso, Warner Brothers showed the most positive interest in Prince's music itself.

"We were wined and dined by a lot of companies. but when everybody else was talking gifts and bonuses, the people at Warner Brothers were actually listening to the demo."

Owen also recalls an incident in the negotiations during which the duo demanded the unprecedented latitude that the final agreement outlined. "Naturally, their first reaction was 'sure, doesn't everybody nowadays want to have complete control?'"

After a visit to a studio where Prince displayed his creative expertise first hand, Warner Brothers was convinced. Complete control *could* be granted on the debut disc. A three-year, three-album contract was signed.

Owen says, "I made a point of not hassling Prince while he was working at the Record Plant. They'd go in at 7:00 P.M. and usually end up staying until sunrise. He kept the pace, five, sometimes six days a week for five months. Periodically he'd give me a tape so I could keep abreast of his progress, but otherwise he handled it himself."

Currently, Prince is back in the Twin Cities, working on soundproofing his basement so the neighbors aren't bothered as he jams the night through. He's not star-struck over the recent airplay he's been getting all over the country, but confesses that hearing one's own tunes on the radio is altogether another kind of adventure.

"I was driving down the street in my Datsun the first time I heard it," he says. "It wasn't that I couldn't believe it, it's simply that my heart dropped to my knees."

He's also enthusiastic about taking his show on the road. That is, as soon as he assembles it. "Andre is a musician friend of mine from the days of Shampayne. He's the only definite member of my touring group so far. Andre is a lot like me; he eats and sleeps his music and that's the only kind of people I want with me on that stage. I'm planning to add 6 or 7 people, a couple of keyboardists, a rhythm player and a percussionist. I'm looking for a big stage sound so I'd like to find people who can sing, too. During the performances I guess I'll play guitar because that will allow me to move. It would be great if I could strap a piano around me too."

THAT MYSTERIOUS PRINCE: HE TALKS ABOUT HIMSELF!

J. Randy Taraborrelli | March 1980 | *Soul Teen*

Released October 19, 1979, Prince's eponymous sophomore effort was the twenty-one-year old's commercial breakthrough. On the back of the LP's success and the number-one soul hit "I Wanna Be Your Lover," Prince made his first American national TV appearance on *Midnight Special* and embarked on his first American tours, headlining a score of club dates before hitting the arena trail in February 1980 opening for highly competitive funk star Rick James.

This interview was published while Prince was busy upstaging James, surfacing in *Soul Teen*, a Black-oriented music and entertainment magazine on the shelves from 1974 to 1983. Think covers with Stevie Wonder, lots of Jacksons, and the occasional Kim Fields. Steven Ivory's 1992 interview on page 96 of this volume digs a bit deeper into Prince's relationship with Black publications.

This piece finds Prince hyping his live band and wondering if he wants to stay in the music business, the latter a common early concern, one which might be as much about deflecting questions as his intentions. It also features Prince's mischievous side, as he claims to use his last name Prince because his first name is too long (he returns to this idea after his name change in the song "Now": "Don't worry about my name, it's too long to remember / I could tell you now but we'd be here 'til next September").

What's not here is something that would later become a standard part of most interviews: The unusual circumstances of the interview itself. Taraborrelli recalled the Hollywood interview in 2021:

"It took place in a restaurant on Sunset and Vine, top floor with a view of the city, called 360.

"Prince was young and very unsure of himself. After maybe a half hour, he excused himself and went to the men's room. Guess what? He never returned. He left the restaurant.

"His PR guy from Warners and I sat at the table for a half hour before we realized he wasn't coming back.

"I was fine with it. He was young, so was I. But I did think, 'this kid's not going to make it in this business if he can't even get through an interview for a teen magazine.'

"About three days later, my phone rang and it was Prince. 'Sorry, man . . . I just couldn't do it. It's not me, this press business. Hope you understand.' I did. I thought, wow . . . what a nice thing to do, to call me and apologize.

"So . . . I changed my mind. I figured, OK, maybe he'll make it, after all." —Ed.

"I don't know why so many people think I'm trying to be so mysterious," says Prince innocently. "I'm really not into mysteries. I'm just into my music . . . that's all."

Maybe that's why he seems so mysterious. Since bursting on the music scene just last year with the album *For You*, many have wondered just where this young guy they call Prince was coming from.

First of all, what kind of name is "Prince," anyway?

Secondly, why don't we ever see any pictures of the guy? All we see is the same ol' publicity shot over and over again.

Well, the mystery is beginning to unfold. Prince is beginning to open up and there've been plenty of new photos in circulation. Prince (who simply goes by his last name because, he claims, the first is "too long"), has scored with a triple-sized hit, "I Wanna Be Your Lover."

To backtrack a little of his history, the young, 19-year-old singer/ musician was born and raised in Minneapolis. He's the son of a jazz band leader and at the age of 12, Prince fronted his own band and called it Champagne.

After about five years of local struggle, the group disbanded and, recalls Prince, "I figured that if I was going to get serious about a career in music, I better start getting busy."

And that's exactly what he did.

A friend of his worked as an engineer in a recording studio. This came in mighty handy when Prince decided to cut some demos (demonstration tapes to take to record companies for possible contractual talks). Prince played all of the instruments on the tape and produced it as well.

With demo in hand he went to New York to find his deal. He returned to Minneapolis two months later with two possible contracts. He turned both deals down however because neither record company was interested in having him produce himself. They'd rather he be assigned a producer—which didn't sit well with Prince.

Warner Brothers, though, saw the natural talent so obvious in Prince's music and decided that, yes, he was certainly able to produce his own recordings. Prince signed a deal with the company and, last year at 18, the young mastermind released his *For You* album.

Needless to say, the record was vinyl-magic. "Soft and Wet," a smash single release, brought Prince into the public eye and, from there, it's been smooth sailing all the way.

Well, now the man's reached the ripe ol' age of 19 and rode the charts with "I Wanna Be Your Lover." Again, he produced, arranged and played all of the instruments.

Many have criticized the young wizard with assaults on his ego. What kind of entertainer wants to do everything on his session and not have other musicians involved? Is Prince, in fact, ego-tripping?

"No, I don't think so," he says softly (Prince says everything "softly," by the way). "It's just that when I was putting those two albums together, I didn't have a band. The ideal situation would have been to have a band back me but I didn't have one so I did it all myself."

"I've got one now," he smiles, "and they are really hot! In fact, we've been out on the road and it's been a great experience for all of us. If everything goes all right then I may use them on my next album."

Prince recalls the years when his father called his piano playing "banging on the keys." He adds, "No one really paid much attention to my playing when I was a kid. It was just a phase, maybe that's what they thought."

But that "phase" mushroomed into a spiraling recording career more astronomical than anyone would have dreamed, including Prince himself.

"It's been great in a lot of ways," he related, "but I just don't know if this is what I want to do. Sometimes I think it is . . . other times I don't."

One thing, however, is pretty certain and that's the fact that Prince does not want to be a so-called "teen idol." In fact, he goes so far as to say that "if it ever gets to the point where I can't concentrate on my music because I'm always dodging crowds, then I'll quit."

But meanwhile, his career steadily progresses. Prince doesn't listen to much music outside of his own recordings.

Why? "Because if I listen to other people's stuff I think of how I would have done it differently," he explains.

"I begin changing the whole song around in my head and that's not really fair. Whoever recorded the tune probably worked very hard on it."

"So rather than be critical, I just don't listen to anyone except myself. When I feel like I want to hear music, I rehearse."

Prince's current album has done quite well on the national charts and consists of nine of the 20 tunes he wrote for the project. His stage act is quite dynamic.

Along with five powerhouse musicians, including a female keyboardist, Prince performs with more stage energy than one would ever dream possible.

He's an introvert in many ways and doesn't say a great deal. But he thinks a lot and manages to convey those thoughts through his music. When on stage under those hot lights, Prince really comes alive.

"I live for my music," he says, "for the time being. But there's no telling what I might do if I get bored with it. Maybe I'll go into art. Who knows? Or I might do just about anything," he shrugs.

Actually, one can't imagine Prince being involved in anything but his music. But one thing is certain and that is, in Prince's words:

"Whatever I do is gonna be good. It'll be the best I have to give . . . whether it's in music or something else. I always do the ultimate to make sure that I always come across positively. All the time . . . "

PRINCE: MORE THAN JUST A "DIRTY MIND"

Dennis Hunt | December 21, 1980 | _Los Angeles Times_

Prince's third album, _Dirty Mind_, was released October 8, 1980. It was expected to better the chart success of the previous year's _Prince_, but the stark collection of would-be demos about, broadly, sex, sex, and more sex (with some partying and romantic pining thrown in) sputtered on its way up the charts. Spurred on by his management team (perhaps the last time they told him what to do rather than vice versa), Prince entered a brief period of interview glasnost, talking with more than a half-dozen publications through the middle of 1981. When asked about his decision to talk with the media in this _Los Angeles Times_ article, conducted by phone from Charleston, North Carolina, around December 11, 1980, Prince declared, "It's time I step forward and started making myself heard."

Of course, making himself heard didn't necessarily mean being factually accurate, in spite of his concern here that, in the absence of other information, people "start making things up" about him. This widely syndicated interview includes Prince's contention that his father is "black and Italian" and his mother is "a mixture of a bunch of things." In a February 1981 _Rolling Stone_ interview, this would morph into the author identifying Prince as "the son of a half-black father and an Italian mother." Although Prince probably benefited in the long run from the confusion of making his background more mysterious and exotic (at the very least he got the lyrics to "Controversy"), this misinformation would follow him his entire life; the _New York Times_ published the following correction to his obituary six days after his death in April 2016: "Although the character, known as the Kid, is biracial, Prince himself was not. (Both his parents were African-American.)" —Ed.

When he was a precocious 9-year-old in Minneapolis, Prince, pop music's new boy wonder, used to sneak into his mother's bedroom and read her spicy novels. "They were underneath the *Better Homes and Gardens* and places like that," recalled the 20-year-old pop/rhythm and blues musician.

Soon, reading such novels wasn't enough for him: "Once I got tired of reading those stories, I wrote my own. For a while I thought that's what I wanted to do in life. But I realized as I got a little older I wasn't going to make any money writing those novels. I think I would have been a failure at writing them."

Being a prepubescent porn addict left its mark on him: "I think reading those novels has a lot to do with my sexuality and my openness about it. I think it affects you when you have a very early awareness about sexual issues."

Prince's interest in the subject, which may be a byproduct of an erratic home life, didn't lead to a writing career but it influenced his music. A sexual thread runs through his three Warner Bros. albums. The first two—*For You* and *Prince*—are merely suggestive. However, certain songs on his latest album, appropriately titled *Dirty Mind*, are as seamy as anything in those novels he used to read. For one, "Sister" is about an incestuous relationship between a teen-ager and a sister twice his age: "It's part of life. It's something that's inside of all of us to some degree, whether we like it or not. We may think about it or encounter it in some form or other."

It's rare to see an album from a major label by a well-known artist that is littered with such sexually explicit lyrics. Other artists, Prince observed, are just too timid to roam in this range. "They bypass a lot of heavy things, particularly sexual things," he said. "I'm not about to do that."

There's more to *Dirty Mind* than X-rated lyrics. It's exceptional in every area—vocals, instrumentation, production, arrangement, and composition. Remarkably, Prince, a one-man studio gang, does all these things by himself.

Prince, in Charleston, S.C., at the time, did the interview by phone. Unlike just about every other artist, he prefers phone interviews. "No one can see me on the phone," he explained.

His problem has always been extreme shyness: "I would wonder what it would be like if you were sitting here with me?" he inquired. "I don't seem shy now but I would if you were here. I'm really shy when I meet someone for the first time. I like to listen. I think other people are more interesting than I am. An interview means I have to do all the talking."

Until the last few weeks, he had done very few interviews. As a result a Prince mystique sprang up. "When people couldn't talk to me or find out much about me, they start making things up," he said. "I'm supposed to be a mysterious person but I'm not mysterious."

But now he's talking to the media mainly to help people understand his album: "My first two albums were self-explanatory but this one isn't," he said.

Skeptics, of course, are saying he isn't so much interested in explaining *Dirty Mind* as he is in bolstering its lagging sales. The album, stalled at No. 46 on the Billboard chart, does need a boost because most of it, no matter how excellent, is unsuitable for radio. If fans don't hear it often on the radio, they are less likely to buy it. Media attention could prod some stations to play the album.

"That's not the idea behind me talking to the media," he insisted. "I never thought the album would get a lot of airplay. Maybe I can help those who buy it to understand it better. Anyway, it's time I stepped forward and started making myself heard."

Prince may be sorry: "I've been spilling my guts more to the media then I ever have to my friends," he admitted. "They'll find out things from these interviews they didn't know about."

One reason Prince is so dedicated to music is that as a child in Minneapolis singing and playing piano was his refuge against unhappiness. His boyhood chronicle belongs in a primer on how not to raise a child.

"I have four brothers and sisters by different fathers and mothers," he said. "We were never an immediate family. When I was 12 I ran away for the first time because of problems with my stepfather. I went to live with my real father but that didn't last too long because he's as stubborn as I am. I lived with my aunt for a while. I was constantly running from family to family. It was nice on one hand because I always had a new family, but I didn't like being shuffled around. I was bitter for a while but I adjusted."

Prince looks black but that's only a fraction of his heritage. "My dad is black and Italian," he explained. "My mom is a mixture of a bunch of things. I don't consider myself part of any race. I'm just a human being, I suppose."

Prince is his real first name but he won't reveal his last name. He speculated he was named Prince—the stage name of his father, a jazz band leader—for an odd reason: "I think my father was kind of lashing out at my mother when he named me Prince."

He felt he was ridiculed by his mother for getting into music. "I was into it a little too much for her," Prince recalled. "My father left home when I was 7. That's when I got into music. She didn't like that because music is what broke up her marriage. My father was too serious about music.

"I was considered strange. I recall having a lot of strange dreams. I spent a lot of time alone. I turned to music. In some ways it was more important than people."

Prince started his own band at 12 and by the time he was out of high school was a good enough musician to be signed to a Warner Bros. contract. A self-taught musician, he plays every instrument on his albums—keyboards, drums, guitar and bass. "I learned how to play so many things out of boredom," Prince said. "I got bored with one and then I'd go on and learn something else." His musical expertise is all the more remarkable considering he doesn't read music.

Prince is one of those Jekyll-and-Hyde types. Offstage he's shy; on stage he's a torrid performer who even strips down to his bikini underwear. However, he doesn't regard these personas as being all that different: "I don't say that much on stage. I'm still shy on stage. But it's easy because it's music. I'm just interpreting music, which is still the one thing in life I feel good about."

PRINCE IN THE AFTERNOON

Gene Kalbacher | February 25–March 4, 1981 (Issue 356) | *Aquarian—Night Owl*

In Matt Thorne's unfairly maligned biography *Prince: The Man and His Music*, public relations guru Harold Bloom discusses the strategy he and Prince's management team, primarily Bob Cavallo, helped devise to cement Prince's public persona and turn around sagging *Dirty Mind* sales. Meeting with Prince in Buffalo during *Dirty Mind* tour rehearsals in late fall 1980, Bloom settled on two "imprinting points" from Prince's youth that would humanize him for the press and fans. First, they would focus on Prince's wonder at seeing his father onstage. Second, they'd publicize when he left his own home to live in bassist Andre Cymone's basement with his surrogate mom, Cymone's mother Bernadette Anderson. He may have been an overtly erotic creature who sang about having sex with his sister, but in the end he could be packaged as a good son.

The promotional strategy also included continuing to expand Prince's musical appeal beyond his solid Black fan base to rock, punk, and especially new wave audiences. This was achieved on the *Dirty Mind* tour through the choice of both performance venues (e.g., the Agora Ballroom in Atlanta and Metro in Boston) and press interactions (e.g., Boston's *The Real Paper* and *New York Rocker*). Prince never wanted to be understood as simply a "Black" artist. These promotional efforts, and his overt appeal to rock and pop fans on *Purple Rain*, went a long way to insuring he wasn't pigeonholed by race.

This article was part of those diversification efforts, appearing in the northern New Jersey alternative weekly *The Aquarian Weekly*. The publication was founded in 1969, went through a spell as *East Coast Rocker*, and survives independently more than a half century later in print and online as *The Aquarian*.

Prince is particularly effusive in this interview, working to make sense of the differences between developing his craft in Minneapolis and performing for increasingly diversified audiences, questioning the value of money (a continual theme over the course of his career), and thinking about how the next LP (which would turn up as *Controversy*) will be different and more expansive than *Dirty Mind*. —Ed.

"I don't care what people expect," proclaims Prince, the provocative 20-year-old musician who has emerged as perhaps the most versatile and engaging performer on the pop/soul scene. "They don't expect me to wear what I wear; they don't expect me to say what I say—but I'm doing it."

Indeed. One must expect the unexpected from Prince. Onstage, Prince is a brash, flamboyant, scantily clad guitarist/vocalist, singing about such unholy subjects as "Head" (not the anatomical part of the human body atop the spinal column, but the intimate human activity) and incest, throwing barbs at and catching return volleys from his audience, and leading an oddly attired band that is racially and sexually mixed (blacks and whites, men and women).

But offstage, curled up in an armchair in his suite at the Malloran House, Prince is as reserved in repose as he is frenetic in action. A visitor half expects to encounter Prince sprawled across an unmade bed, wearing nothing but the bandana and bikini briefs he favors onstage. But that's not the case; he's wearing dark, straight-legged trousers, white shirt and black vest.

Where the onstage Prince is brash and saucy, the offstage Prince is composed and polite. And while his statement "I don't care what people expect" is declarative in content, it is subdued in tone. His smile is benign, almost meek, beneath his wispy black mustache.

His smile may be shy but his music is outspoken and his credits astonishing. His three albums for Warner Bros. have sold close to three million copies. Moreover, he not only wrote, arranged and produced every song, but played virtually every instrument as well. At this stage of his career it would not be an exaggeration to say he is the most prodigiously talented black youngster to bask in the bright lights since Little Stevie Wonder.

But even more impressive than his blend of sultry, throbbing funk and sweet soul, however, is his resolve to speak his piece without pulling any punches.

"I Wanna Be Your Lover," from his second album, was a platinum smash single and a radio mainstay in 1979. His most recent effort, last year's *Dirty Mind*, has sold rather briskly but flunked on the radio. The warning label on the album jacket reads: "Programmers please audition prior to airing."

Songs about incest, oral sex and homosexuality aren't your standard broadcast fare, and Prince remains philosophical about the cool radio reception. His record company, his management and he himself were mindful of the eventual outcome, but, he points out, "everyone felt it was probably more an extension of me and my audience than anything I've ever done."

Prince is quick to point out that the album started as a series of demo tapes, "not all of which I intended on using." Unlike his two earlier efforts, *Dirty Mind* was sequenced according to the order in which the songs were recorded.

"On the other albums," he says, "I used to sit down and say, 'What's gonna sound best?' I'd make sure it was in a relative key and things like that. I'd try to do it from an intellectual point of view, and I don't think that was so wise. Now I tend not to analyze my own stuff. I just do it!"

Does he have any regrets about having released such controversial songs when he could have taken a safer route? "No," he answers decisively. "Only because it's real to me.

"I knew I was going to get in trouble for them, and I subsequently did. I knew it then, but I didn't know whether or not I was ready to stand up for them. Now I feel strongly about them after listening to them."

Although he refuses to restrict the subject matter of his songs, Prince admits that, for now, he is restricting the lengths of his songs. He credits his former manager for convincing him that he "couldn't continue writing 'seven-minute terror songs.'"

Explains Prince: "I wrote a lot of strange things. I'll probably start again when I'm accepted for what I am rather than for how much money I make. See, what I do now is try to give a piece of myself in three minutes. That way I know it can be a single and it'll be on the radio. Otherwise, no one will give you the time of day.

"I'm trying to look at it realistically," he says. "In time I'll be able to do exactly what I want to do."

Considering the controversy already stirred up by "Head," "Sister" and "Uptown" (a national rock-concert TV program deleted the word "gay" from Prince's performance of the song), how much more expressive can he be?

"'Head' was a **lot** longer," he answers. "When I first cut it, it went on and on. See, well," he proceeds, laughing and then stopping himself. "I was trying to take a real-life experience—there are parts of the longer version that are sometimes shocking to **me**.

"That would never have made it on an album. No one would ever put it out. It ('Head') doesn't get on the radio now. All I'm saying is that now I'm trying to condense everything a little bit more only so that—I don't want to be stupid about it; I don't want to make so many songs that are so long that they never get heard at all.

"I want to be listened to first. Then I can give longer, detailed versions of things."

For a musician who describes his childhood as "depressing," his music is anything but. The son of a jazz bandleader, Prince taught himself to play the piano at age seven and led his first band, Champagne, by 12.

By the time he was a teenager, he had run away from home and picked up the guitar, the instrument with which he feels more comfortable. Although he describes his native Minneapolis as a musically circumscribed market, Prince maintains that the competitiveness among the local bands not only fostered but mandated originality.

"Have you ever been to Minneapolis?" he asks. "It's a really small joint and if you really dig country & western music, that's the place to go. The radio stations don't play any new-wave music; they only play country & western music. The clothes, the dance, the music—everything is so behind.

"I'd call my sister, who lives here (in Manhattan), and ask her what was going on. I was shocked because we got everything (in Minneapolis) she talked about six months later."

As a teenager, Prince attended very few concerts and listened to few records. How, one wonders, did he develop such an understanding of and proficiency with so many different instruments and styles of music?

"We jammed a lot with other bands," Prince recalls. "There was a lot of competition around '75. It was a time when there was a lot of spirit. It was nice back then.

"I think that helped me come out of myself," he continues. "We got in a lot of trouble from other band members if we copied anything (from them), and we gave them a lot of trouble if they copied anything (from us), so it was a real competitive thing. You had to be as out as you could and as different, and as much **you** as possible."

After playing original material with the group Champagne for five years, Prince left the fold to follow his own career.

Deciding that he needed to make a demo, but having no backup band to work with, Prince took matters into his own hands—writing all the songs, playing all the instruments and producing all the tracks. Several major labels expressed interest in his work, but Prince held back until he landed a deal with a company (Warners) that would enable him to produce his own records.

Upon the release of his debut effort, *For You*, Prince assembled a touring band. His current road group (Andre Samone [*sic*], bass; Dez Dickerson, guitar; Gail [*sic*] Chapman, keyboards; Matt Fink, keyboards; and Bobby Lee [*sic*], drums) is pictured on the sleeve of *Dirty Mind*, but played a very insignificant role in the actual record-ing of the LP. Fink is credited as the co-writer of "Dirty Mind" and as the synthesizer player on the title track and "Head." Lisa Coleman contributes backing vocals on "Head," but that's the extent of the members' musical input. Does Prince plan to employ these musicians on his fourth album?

"It's hard to say," he replies. "They're on this record because they're my friends. I see my band differently than most bands, I guess.

"They're just my friends," he adds obliquely. "I think maybe I might meet new friends sometime, so maybe I'll get new band members. They all have aspirations of being big in their own right; they want to do other things, so it's hard to say."

Prince may be uncertain about the recording status of his road band, but he's positive that listeners are looking for something new.

Asked if the racial and sexual composition of his band reflects the nature of his audience, Prince responds, "It's basically the same. They're real loud, they make a lot of noise, they shout a lot of obscenities and good things.

"It's a free crowd," he adds. "They're ready for change. I can sense it."

For what change is the audience ready?

"Change in music, change in lifestyle. They want to be open and they want to dress anyway they want to at the gigs and stuff like that," he remarks.

"Tradition at black concerts a lot of times wants to wear your best clothes, to come looking really dapper. It's not like that at our concerts. There are a lot of black kids out there, but they're like open-minded and free, and they want to have a good time . . .

"Especially where I lived, there were very few events that you got to go to. So any chance you got to show off your best clothes, you did. It was basically for ego."

When asked how the record business differs in actuality from the way he'd envisioned it when he began his career, Prince reveals the motivation behind his music.

"I imagined more **spirit** overall. I guess I got even more hip to it once I got into it and started talking to people who'd been through all the things that happened before me—like Woodstock and all the festivals they used to have.

"That's kind of what I envisioned," he points out, leaning forward in his chair. "I always wanted to do outdoor gigs. But they don't do that so much anymore, only the big, giant groups. It's hard for upcoming groups to get breaks like that."

Prince laments his discovery that many musicians are trying to make money "rather than doing what they feel inside and speaking for their time."

"That's the way I always thought it was supposed to be. See, we didn't hear (in Minneapolis) about all the money that was to be made. We just heard about acts that were being followed. We all knew we wanted to be an act that people followed. We don't talk a lot about material things—we talk about people we meet."

Prince claims that he spends most of his money on himself. "I give away a lot of my money to friends," he notes. "So you might say I spend it on myself."

At what point did he feel he had made his mark in the record business? Did any particular instance drive that point home?

"You can never really tell," he muses. "Records are like writing letters to somebody, and doing a gig is like talking to the person face to face. The difference is that you feel the response right away when you're in concert. I think that when you get your first fan letter, you start thinking you're reaching somebody, and it makes you want to keep going."

Besides spending money on his friends (and thus, he avows, on himself), Prince derives the most satisfaction from "just knowing that somebody is listening." He may not care what people expect from him, "and I don't care if they don't like it," he contends, but adds: "I just want them to hear it and know that I have the privilege of telling them."

PRINCE: MOM'S FAVORITE FREAK

Ed Ochs | June 1981 | *Rock & Soul Songs*

Rock & Soul Songs was a Black-oriented music magazine published from the late 1960s through the 1980s. Its target audience tended to skew a bit older than that of Black teen publications that had previously talked with Prince.

Although conducted earlier than the one in the previous chapter, this interview didn't appear in print until four months later, by which time Prince had moved on to his first European performances. It's interesting not only for an unfiltered if somewhat sensationalized look at how media outlets were discussing Prince at the time, but also for the letter-perfect execution of public relations consultant Harold Bloom's "imprinting points"–Prince seeing his father perform and living in Andre Cymone's basement. There's a paraphrase of a Shakespeare *Twelfth Night* quote that says, "Be not afraid of greatness. Some are born great, some achieve greatness, and the rest hire PR firms." Prince was on his way to greatness in all three ways. –Ed.

Who is this charismatic, elfin performer who confronts audiences, inspires laughter, good feeling and dancing in the aisle?—and who used to answer the question with, "Who am I? I'm just my mother's favorite freak."

But if it's true that clothes make the man, then what can be made of a talented singer/songwriter/musician/producer who calls himself Prince and wears onstage what could be either the Emperor's new clothes or the Empress' old undies?

(a) That Mr. Prince is a screaming queen?

(b) That he is no man at all, but a woman with a peachfuzz moustache?

(c) That he has forsaken clothes onstage because he does not wish to be judged by what he wears?

(d) *All* of the above?

If you selected answer (c) you are correct. Prince doesn't wish to be judged by what he wears either, which, by the way, isn't very much. One look inside his wardrobe locker tells the tale. Let's see: one pair purple tights; black thigh-high tights; one pair black leather briefs; one pair leopard skin bikini briefs. This Prince could catch a cold and die!

By way of partial explanation, the 20-year-old Minneapolis-born and bred wonderboy would probably like us to peep into his *Dirty Mind*, not just coincidentally the title of his third Warner Bros. album and second single release. And although the words to many of his funk-disco songs may not be dirty on the dance floor, don't expect to hear it on the radio. Prince has been sentenced to twenty years at hard rock somewhere in the underground of total orgasm, lesbianism, incest, sodomy, anarchy, revolution—and more than a dash of tender love and care, just to confuse things more.

Using sex to sell records predates Elvis Presley, who twitched, quivered and shook himself to fame and beyond. But you'd have to go back to Little Richard and, later, Jimi Hendrix, to find a black rocker whose sheer outrageousness could mesmerize both black and white, male and female, the way Prince does. With softer sounds filling the black music mainstream, the electronic roar of Prince's '80s-style loin-shaking punk-funk has made him a champion of the people. While other black artists thrive on bleaching funk for the middle of the road, Prince is getting *raunchier*.

Musically, it might be easier to simply dismiss him as a sicko, if it weren't for the fact that he also happens to be a multidimensional artist who has welded well-crafted R&B songs to hard-edged rock— the Motown falsetto of Smokey, Kendricks and the young Jacksons to heavy new-wave rhythms. The result, a sophisticated, uptown sound both strikingly original and stunningly perverse, is dirtier than Donna Summer, raunchier than Sly Stone. Along with the Bus Boys, Prince stands in the vanguard of a wave of black rock and roll that has not yet arrived.

The leaping legend of Prince starts in the refrigerator of America, Minnesota, where the population is only one percent Black and Hispanic, and rock is plowed under the fields or crushed into gravel.

Prince's father was the leader of a jazz group, the Prince Rogers Band (so Prince is really Prince II). When he was five, Prince got a chance to see his father in action. The sights and sounds of his father's music filled him with excitement, the effects of which still reverberate through Prince's music, whatever direction it may take.

Prince wanted to bask in the same musical glow, perform the same musical miracles, and when his father went out of town again, he sat at his father's piano and taught himself to play by ear the themes from *Batman* and *Man from U.N.C.L.E.* It wasn't too much longer before he began entering talent contests, playing for people, and writing songs he spun from his childhood fantasies.

Sexual awareness dawned early and rudely. Doctor Freud would have had a field day. For Prince, though, it marked the beginning of an odyssey that would take him down the trail of loneliness, poverty and awakening.

Rock and Soul spoke to Prince recently in Buffalo, New York, where he was about to embark on his second extensive national tour within a year. In early 1980, he'd upstaged the act he opened for—Rick James. This time Prince was the headliner.

"My mom used to leave trashy pornography around, and I used to sneak them out of her room when I was eight years old. Then I got sick of those and started writing my own. I didn't write risque lyrics. I didn't know the two went together: people's feelings and music."

Prince's preference for sexy lyrics never wavered. Even when he began to play (top 40) for money, he'd sneak in one of his own songs whenever he got the chance. Once he was old enough, Prince moved in with his friend and bass player on the road, Andre Cymone, whose father played in Prince's band.

"When I was sixteen," said Prince, his shyness dissolving as he warmed to the subject. "I lived in Andre's basement. It was a turning point for me. I wrote a ton of songs, my brain was free of everything, I didn't have anything to worry about. That's when I realized music could express what you were feeling, and it started showing up in my songs.

"One night Andre's mother said, 'Prince, is that girl still down there?' I got nervous but said 'Yes.' She said, 'Okay, just lock the door when she leaves.' After that, I knew things weren't forbidden anymore."

By the time Prince was 17, he already had five years as a professional musician under his belt, played in groups and written some solid songs. He then went to New York City and, with studio time exchanged for arranging chores, recorded demos of "Soft and Wet" (on *For You*), "Aces" and "Machine," all with sexual lyrics. Prince received offers from one record and one publishing company, but none to produce his own music. A management dispute followed, and Prince was forced to return home, but not without new enthusiasm.

"I went back to Minneapolis and back to Andre's basement," he said candidly. "I could deal with the centipedes and poverty better because I knew I could make it. I'd proven it to myself and that's what really mattered."

When Prince signed with Warner Bros., the headlines of strait-laced Minnesota newspapers were rife with rumors of a vulgarian given a six-figure contract to fill the airwaves with raw, sweaty sex. And when his first album was followed by a second, *Prince*, and a hit single, "I Wanna Be Your Lover," the scalphunters were not disappointed.

"Sex is always the most interesting thing to write about," he says. "It's the one subject people can't talk about without losing their cool. Have you ever noticed people can talk about Iran, they can talk about JFK being shot, but as soon as you bring up their sex life they start stuttering? My family, my father and my mother, life and death, are far more personal to me than sex."

Printed lyrics are not included in *Dirty Mind*, Prince's breakthrough rock and roll LP. Even though you need a headset to hear the lyrics, the music still kicks up a storm of rhythm and kink. The album cover is stickered with the warning: "Album contains language which may be unsuitable for some listeners." The sticker does not however obstruct the cover photo of Prince in the royal bikini. Obviously, Prince's kingdom has come.

Prince's five-piece band is tight and crisp, and, as a result, an undercurrent of energy gets audiences jumping to their feet. Pretty soon he has everybody singing the chorus to "Head" without any help from the band. The Prince's sparkling green eyes dart and dash as he writhes and moans in ecstasy. All of a sudden clothes start coming off, the audience goes berserk. Is this any way for a real Prince to behave?

STRUTTING WITH THE NEW SOUL MONARCH

Chris Salewicz | June 6, 1981 | *New Musical Express*

Winding down the *Dirty Mind* era and drumming up business for his three-date debut European tour and UK-only single "Gotta Stop (Messin' About)," Prince met with European reporters in New York in late spring 1981. The results included a few one-off articles on the continent and June 6 feature interviews in the top UK music weeklies, *Sounds*, *Melody Maker*, and *New Musical Express*.

Musical biographer Chris Salewicz's tone here is more playful and less sanctimonious than contemporaneous American interviews. A similar tone would return in many later interviews, especially after Prince changed his name to an unpronounceable glyph and the arcane and often humorous process of interviewing Prince became as much a part of the story as the Prince interview itself.

This interview finds Prince talking about music genres (disco—bad; new wave—good) and digging deeper into the *Dirty Mind* dynamics between his management and his label. He also fleshes out his political opinions more than usual. After recounting the "gonna have to fight your own damn war" sentiment in "Partyup," he "rather startlingly" offers support for recently elected US president Ronald Reagan (especially startlingly for a member of the then left-leaning UK music press). This endorsement, which, in context, might have just been an excuse to mention Reagan's "bigger balls," didn't negatively impact Prince's reputation the way Reagan support did for other musicians in the 1980s, such as Neil Young. However, unlike Young, Prince never incorporated this support into his persona and rarely shared his political opinions.

For those keeping tabs, his mom is Black here and his father is now Italian-Filipino. —Ed.

This fellow sitting across the table from me in an uptown Manhattan Holiday Inn room may be a Prince but he ain't no Charlie.

On the other hand, this 20-year-old Prince is just as much a lad with the ladies as is our prospective monarch: In the musicality of his speaking voice, which is much lower in tone than the high pitch you'd expect from listening to his records, there is a slur that comes from lack of sleep.

"I haven't been to sleep for a couple of nights . . . Well, I've been to bed, but not for sleeping," he adds meaningfully.

"Ho-ho-ho!" I spontaneously chuckle with disrespectful satire, miming macho ribnudging.

Such lack of awe for the Big Willie talk that is such an essential part of Prince's everyday mood and music obviously pisses him off a bit. But, really, what does he expect? Still, not a bad lad when all's said and done . . . .

Prince has flown in to New York from his home-town of Minneapolis, Minnesota, for this interview. This is just the beginning of a lot of mileage he's going to be putting under his belt. This week he also jets to Europe for a series of dates that includes one London show, at the Lyceum.

In the jargon of the trade, Prince is "working" his *Dirty Mind* album, released at the end of last year. Like his first two Warners LPs, *For You* and *Prince*, *Dirty Mind* was produced, arranged, written and almost entirely performed by Prince alone.

In America, *Dirty Mind* is an "underground" hit—which means that via word of mouth and exceptionally favorable press coverage it has notched up a more than healthy half-million sales. Radio play has been virtually nil, this being due to much of the subject matter of the LP, which contains the kind of lyrics that might have come out of a few heavy sessions of Freudian dream analysis. Amongst other topics, the album deals with oral sex, troilism and incest. It also concerns itself with direct political matter, however; *Dirty Mind* climaxes with the song "Partyup," and an atmosphere of militant defiance that insists "You're gonna have to fight your own damn war, 'cos we don't wanna fight no more."

There is a weird mist about the body music made by the green-eyed, sensually slack-jawed Prince, as there is also about the multi-instrumentalist himself. An academic analysis of his intensely immediate sounds indicate their origins lie in areas as far apart (and as close together) as pre-Disco Philly, Eddie Cochran's primal rock 'n' roll rhythms, The Beatles, and the inevitable Jimi Hendrix, who seems to have provided much of the spiritual source material for the notoriously lascivious, wild spectacular which Prince enacts every time he steps out onstage. Yet the hypnotic accessibility of this compound belies a mysterious, vinegary cold within the cool of its core.

Whatever, Prince dislikes suggestions that he is re-defining R&B. Or that his first two, less cohesive LPs were an interpretation of disco in rock terms.

"To me disco was always *very* contrived music. It was all completely planned out for when the musicians were recording it in the studios. Basically, what *I* do is just go in and play.

"It's easy for me to work in the studio, because I have no worries or doubts about what the other musician's going to play because that other musician is almost always me! All the other musicians on the record are me. Disco music was filled with breaks that a studio musician would just play and fill up when his moment came. But I don't do that at all—I just play along with the other guy."

Prince's voice, which lies in a region occupied by Michael Jackson and Smokey Robinson, also has its curious edge. *Too* much that of a beautiful young boy, it is like the silky near-castrato of a choirboy beneath whose starched, spotless surplice is a body crawling with crabs.

Maybe that's what Prince is about—the twin sides of human nature. "Sin and salvation," says the man who dedicates to God *Dirty Mind*, a record that promises "incest is everything it's meant to be."

But Prince has a lot more going for him than the majority of his compatriot contemporaries who have experienced any measure of significant success.

"All the groups in America seem to do just exactly the same as each other—which is to get on the radio, try to be witty, say the most sickening things they can think of and gross out the interviewer. They think that's going to make them big and cool.

"They're a little too concerned," says the man who claims he's given away most of the cash he's made to friends and acquaintances in need, "with keeping up the payment on the Rolls Royce when really they should be busying themselves with doing something that's true to their own selves. Obviously the new wave thing has brought back a lot of that greater reality. There are so many of those groups that there is just no way many of them can make it in those vast commercial terms. So they have no choice but to write what's inside of them.

"I think it's all getting better, actually."

Such a subdued, low-key character offstage that one feels it certainly must be his alter ego that takes over in performance, Prince all the same remains always a natural communicator. He waxes warm and cold, though—just like his two-edged music. But it's his prerogative; he's very much his own man, working on *his* terms in a similar manner to that insisted on by other of black America's genuine musical artists like Marvin Gaye and Stevie Wonder.

He dislikes being considered a prodigy: "I don't even know what the word really means," he shrugs. "I'm just a person."

Prince also bristles uncomfortably at PR descriptions of his fluency with 27 separate instruments.

"That came about because that was the exact number of instruments I played on the first album. But actually there are a lot of instruments which if you can play you can also play another six related ones."

The black and white front cover shot on *Dirty Mind* is an exact representation of the persona Prince presents onstage—the army surplus flasher's mac (which he is wearing in the Holiday inn at this very moment: "It's the only coat I've got"), the dark jockstrap-like underpants. The photograph has been cropped at pubis level, missing out the bare thighs and leg warmers that complete Prince's androgynous stage-wear.

This image, though, is far from the soft-focus colour job of the horseman astride his winged white steed that graced the rear of *Prince*. Pretty dodgy stuff—enough to make a strong man weep.

It was his need to extend the autonomy he'd already gained in production and arrangement terms that led to Prince breaking with his

Minneapolis-based management following the release of *Prince*, and signing a deal with the former managers of Little Feat.

"I think I've always been the same. But when you're in the hands of other people they can package it in a way that is more . . . uhhh acceptable. All along I've had the same sort of ideas that came out on this record. It's just that my former management had other thoughts about it all." His voice curls downwards.

"The songs on *Dirty Mind* were originally just some demo tapes that I recorded and took to LA to play to my new management. Even they weren't too happy with them. We also had long talks about what I felt was me getting closer to my real image, and at first they thought that I'd gone off the deep end and had lost my mind. Warners basically thought the same, I think.

"But once I told them that this was the way it was, then they knew they had no choice and they'd have to try it, because they weren't going to get another record out of me otherwise.

"I know that *I'm* a lot happier than I was. Because I'm getting away with what I want to do. With the other two albums I feel I was being forced to suppress part of myself—though also I was younger."

This grabbing of greater control of his own destiny was probably inevitable, considering the production and arrangement autonomy Prince already had.

"I just turned down all the producers that Warners suggested to me for the first album. Even when they finally agreed to let me produce myself they insisted I had to work with what they said was an Executive Producer, who was really just an engineer. And that caused a whole lot of other problems, because he was versed in shortcuts and I didn't want to take any—though (*laughs*) that *was* why it took five months to make.

"The recording's become a little easier these days. I used to be a perfectionist—too much of one. Those ragged edges tend to be a bit truer."

Prince is the third youngest in a family of four brothers and four sisters. They are not all of the same blood: "There was a lot of illegitimacy—different fathers, different mothers."

Prince's father, who obviously christened him as he did because he knew he'd need to learn how to fight, was an Italian-Philipino leader of a mid-west pro jazz band. He left his son's black mother when the boy was seven.

"That's when I first started playing music," he says. "He left the piano behind when he left us behind. I wasn't allowed to touch it when he still lived with us."

His background, he says, was "essentially middle-class, though our financial position took a big down swing when he went."

Around the age of nine, Prince started spending much of his out-of-school hours in his mother's bedroom, poring over her substantial porn collection. "She had a lotta interesting stuff. Certainly that affected my attitude towards my sexuality."

His mother's choice of replacement for his father also affected him. At the age of 12 Prince moved out of the family home and into that of one of his sisters. "It's very difficult having a step-father—basic resentment all the way around. Nobody belongs to anybody."

During this time, up until when he graduated from high school at 17, Prince played in a succession of high school bands, notably one called Champagne.

"It was all Top 40 stuff. The audiences didn't want to know the songs I was writing for the group. They'd just cover their faces largely because of the lyrics. I remember I had this song called 'Machine' that was about this girl that reminded me of a machine. It was very explicit about her, urrhhh parts. People seemed to find it very hard to take.

"There was quite a lot of Sly Stone stuff we used to do. I really liked it when he'd have a hit, because it would give us an excuse to play them."

It was also this spell of living with his sister that was to inspire the "incest is all it's meant to be" line.

"I write everything from experience. 'Dirty Mind' was written totally from experience . . . "

So he's experienced incest?

"How come you ask twice?" (chuckles)

Oh well, one often hears it's far more common than is popularly imagined . . .

For someone who is sold heavily as a primal black artist, Prince visually is hardly black at all.

"Though they say that even if you've just got one drop of black blood in you it makes you entirely black. But in fact I don't necessarily look on myself as a member of the black race—more a member of the human race . . . "

The perspective on the apparently obsessive sexuality of *Dirty Mind* is shifted by the non-specific politics of "Partyup": "I was in a lot of different situations when I was coming up to make that record. A lot of anger came up through the songs. It was kind of a rough time. There were a few anti-draft demonstrations going or that I was involved in that spurred me to write 'Partyup.'

"Really, that song is just about people who'd rather have a good time than go and shoot up one another. That's all—it's pretty basic. I just seem to read about a lot of politicians who're all going to die soon and I guess they want to go out heavy, because they're prepare to make a few mistakes and end up starting a war that they don't have to go out and fight.

"I just think the people should have a little more to say in some of these foreign matters. I don't want to have to go out and die for their mistakes.

"Thank God we got a better President now," Prince continues, rather startlingly, "with bigger balls"—the reader may note the recurrent sexual imagery—"than Carter. I think Reagan's a lot better. Just for the power he represents, if nothing else. Because that also means as far as other countries are concerned.

"He also has a big mouth, which is probably a good thing. His mouth is his one big asset."

Perhaps this is Prince's Minneapolis background coming out. Who else has Minnesota turned up in recent years? Only Prince, Bob Dylan, Walter Mondale and Hubert Humphrey. Which is at least a healthy bit of yin and yang.

Prince says he still lives in the city in which he was born precisely *because* it is so isolated. Ask Prince about his musical influences and he'll go all coy on you. You don't hear *anyone*, he'll claim, if your home is in Minnesota. All the radio stations play is C&W music, he says. In fact, he genuinely doesn't appear to have heard, or even heard of, a large percentage of acts with whom one might assume he would be familiar.

"Listening to the radio there," he insists, "really turned me off a lot of things that were supposedly going on. If they did pick up on something they'd just play it to death, and you'd end up totally disliking it. So I missed out on a lot of groups."

There was a certain amount of deliberate choice operating here.

"When I started doing my own records I really didn't want to listen to anybody, because I figured I should just disregard what anybody else might be doing. Though I suppose subconsciously I might have been influenced just by the mood that was going on around me. I can only be a product of my time . . . unless I cut myself off totally. Though that," he adds, purposely enigmatic, "is soon to come."

From what's he going to cut himself off?

"The world."

What does he intend to do? "Just write music, and things like that. Hang around in my head. And just make records. I don't think I'll perform anymore. I don't want to do this too much longer."

Is it stopping being fun?

"It's still fun. But I get bored real fast. Yeah, it's still fun. But I can't see it going on for too much longer in the same fashion."

And so Prince strides off into the sunlit Manhattan streets, heading for that last plane to Minnesota.

THE RENEGADE PRINCE

Robert Hilburn | November 21, 1982 | *Los Angeles Times*

Nature abhors a vacuum. As do entertainment journalists.

Interpersonally shy and often reluctant to engage, and further stung by inaccurate information, gossip, and outright lies, Prince all but stopped speaking to the press by summer 1981, granting about a dozen interviews over the subsequent decade. Of course, it's not surprising he didn't waste time talking to the press at a time he was so consumed with recording, rehearsing, performing, and later filming that he barely ate or slept. Or relaxed, as shown by his failed mid-1980s attempt at a vacation in Rio de Janeiro that's detailed in Duane Tudahl's masterful *Prince and the* Parade/Sign o' the Times *Sessions: 1985–1986*.

This article starts with the well-worn "I saw my father" talking point and later returns to some of the "when I was a kid" tropes, but expands with Prince's version of his disastrous 1981 Rolling Stones opening gig, some thoughts on *Prince*, and observations of today's music being too easy. For an article promoting *1999*, there's very little promoting *1999*.

Of course, for all his concern about inaccurate information, he's not above spreading it. He claims to clear up three rumors, but one is a denial that he's Jaime Starr, the pseudonym he used while working with the Time, Apollonia 6, Vanity 6, and Sheila E. As he later sang in "The Truth," "Everybody's got a right to lie." And he took advantage of that right when necessary. —Ed.

Prince seemed to cringe as the door swung open at his West Hollywood hotel room. On stage, he's a boldly aggressive performer whose teasingly sensual stance challenges sexual and social norms in the classic pop-rock manner of Elvis Presley, Jimi Hendrix and David Bowie. His frequently

X-rated themes include incest and masturbation. But away from the spotlight he can be painfully shy.

As an aide from Prince's management company ushered a reporter into the room, the young singer's doleful eyes suggested the sad resignation of a fugitive cornered after a long chase. It was Prince's first interview in more than a year and—as it turned out—perhaps his only one for another year.

Prince, 23, had reluctantly agreed to do four interviews to promote his new Warner Bros. album. After this first interview, however, he canceled the others, rushing home to Minneapolis, where he feels most comfortable in the isolation of a recording studio. Using other musicians only on stage, Prince writes, produces, sings and plays all the instruments on his albums. He doesn't even permit an engineer in the studio with him.

Sitting on the floor in the semidark hotel room, Prince was giving one- or two-word answers. He didn't exhibit a trace of his performance passion until the discussion wound around to his earliest memories of wanting to be on stage. Then he began to open up.

Lifting his gaze from the floor, he said, "My dad was in a jazz band, and I went to watch one of his gigs when I was about 5. We were supposed to stay in the car, but I snuck out and went into the bar. He was up on stage and it was amazing. I remembered thinking, 'These people think my dad is great.' I wanted to be part of that."

But Prince doesn't see much of his father anymore. "I think he's confused about a lot of what is happening," he explained. "When I first played the *Dirty Mind* album for him, he said, 'You're swearing on the record. Why do you have to do that?' And I said, 'because I swear.'

"We got into this whole big thing about what you can and can't do on record. The point for me is that you can do anything you want. My goal is to excite and to provoke on every level."

Prince's father isn't the only one confused by his son's steamy music and renegade image.

The young singer/songwriter has been called too extreme by both mainstream black and rock audiences. Frequently dressed on stage in little more than bikini bottoms, Prince deals so explicitly with sexual taboos that Warner Bros. put stickers on the album covers which warn about some of his language.

But there's more to Prince's music then its superficial naughtiness. He's a serious artist and a skilled craftsman who may become the biggest black star in rock since Sly Stone. Prince certainly has the charisma and vision. His sound confidently mixes the heat of post-disco funk, the drive of hard-line rock and the melodic flow of pop.

Prince also weaves a liberating message into a colorful pop-rock vocabulary which gives a modern, urban edge to the ribald blues tradition. His *Controversy* album last year sold nearly a million copies, and his new *1999* is a more accessible collection that should attract an even wider audience.

Like the most important figures in rock, from Presley and Dylan to Sly Stone and Bowie, Prince challenges listeners to examine their lives rather than accept what has been outlined for them. In "Sexuality" from last year's *Controversy* album, he urges:

Stand up everybody, this is your life,
Let me take you to another world, let me take you tonight
You don't need no money, you don't need no clothes.
The second coming, anything goes
Sexuality is all you ever need, sexuality let your body be free.

While he sometimes worries that the eroticism overshadows other aspects of his music, Prince refuses to tone down his imagery, insisting that the emphasis on sex is an honest rather than calculated reflection of his own creative instincts.

"Sex is something we can all understand. It's limitless. But I try to make the songs so they can be viewed in different ways. I know some people will go right through those (message) elements in a song, but there are some who won't. If you make it too easy, you lose the point. Most music today is too easy. People just come out and do the same old same olds over and over. . . . All people care about nowadays is getting paid so they try to do just what the audience wants them to do. I'd rather give people what they need rather than just what they want."

Who is this guy who thinks he knows what pop fans *need*?

"Well," he said early in the interview, "let me clear up a few rumors while I have the chance. One, my real name is Prince. It's not something I made up. My dad's stage name was Prince Rogers and he gave that to me: Prince Rogers Nelson.

"Two, I'm not gay. And three, I'm not Jamie Starr."

Because Prince discovered the Time and Vanity 6, two other R&B-shaded Minneapolis acts, it has been widely assumed that name "Starr" after production credits on the two albums was simply a playful pseudonym for Prince. But Starr is a producer-engineer in Minneapolis, Prince said. The gay rumors grew out of his stage manner, which often reflects the ambisexual tendencies associated with Jagger in the late '60s and Bowie in the early '70s.

"There's a certain type of people who may dig what we're doing, but they won't even listen to it because of the stereotypes or whatever," Prince continued. "I'm real proud of the new album, and I'd hate to have things get in the way of it."

Still, he's not about to back away from the sexual imagery. One of the jacket sleeve photos in the new album shows him lying nude, barely covered by a sheet, looking seductively at the camera.

"The most important thing is to be true to yourself, but I also like danger," he continued. "That's what is missing from pop music today. There's no excitement and mystery—people sneaking out and going to these forbidden concerts by Elvis Presley or Jimi Hendrix. I'm not saying I'm better than anybody else, but I don't feel like there are a lot of people out there telling the truth in their music."

Prince started playing piano when he was 7, tinkering at first with TV themes like *Batman* and *The Man From U.N.C.L.E.* By the fourth grade, he was dancing and playing piano in talent shows. At 12, he put together a band, but he was too shy to sing, something he didn't overcome until high school. Part of his motivation by the time was to get out of the shadow of an older brother.

"My older brother was the basketball and football star," Prince said. "He always had all the girls around him and stuff like that. I think I must have been on a jealous trip because I got out of sports . . . . I wasn't bad at basketball, but my brother was better and he wouldn't let me forget it. There were other guys like that, too.

"I just wanted to do something else and when I did get a band, the first thing you did was bring it to school and play the homecoming dance and say, 'Look at that.' It was something they couldn't do."

Because he didn't get along with his stepfather, Prince spent a lot of time away from home during his early teens, staying with his father, his aunt, a friend's parents and, eventually, his sister in New York. He was 17 when he cut the demo tapes that led to a much publicized six-figure contract with Warner Bros. Records. The word soon shot through the industry that another Stevie Wonder had arrived.

"Prince was totally absorbed with his music," said Owen Husney, who was Prince's manager at the time of the Warners signing. "He always has been. There's nothing else that goes on in his life. Though he was still in his teens when I met him, he was amazing. He knew exactly the sound he wanted. That's why we felt it was essential that he produce his own records. But I knew it would be hard convincing a record company to let someone that young go into the studio and do everything himself.

"So we developed this first-class campaign that left very little for the record company to do: press kits that cost $100 each, a marketing campaign, everything. It was a very convincing package. We got offers from Columbia and A&M, but we went with Warners because they were willing to give Prince the most leeway."

Prince's 1978 debut album was a polished but rather conventional affair which sold 100,000 copies. But his second LP, *For You*, thanks to the hit single "I Wanna Be Your Lover," almost hit the million mark. By this time, Prince's management had been taken over by the high-powered L.A. firm of Cavallo, Ruffalo and Fargnoli (among its other clients: Earth, Wind & Fire) and the Wonder comparison became even more common.

Just when Prince's commercial direction seemed firmly set in saccharine-flavored pop/R&B mode, however, the young man had second thoughts. His third album, *Dirty Mind*, was a stunning departure which was filled with sassy vocals, an insistent rock tinge and—oh yes—those *adult* themes.

"The second album was pretty contrived," Prince said in an almost confessional tone as he sat in the West Hollywood hotel room. "I had put myself in a hole with the first record because I spent a lot of money to make it. I wanted to remedy that with the second album. I wanted a 'hit' album. It was for radio rather than for me, and it got a lot of people interested in my music. But it wasn't the kind of audience you really want. They only come around to check you out when you have another hit. They won't come to see you when you change directions and try something new. *That's* the kind of audience I wanted."

The *Dirty Mind* album began as experimental demo tapes, he said. "They were just like songs inside that I wanted to hear. When I took them to Steve (Fargnoli), he said, 'This should be your album.'"

Warner Bros. executives, however, weren't so sure about Prince's controversial new direction. Explained Fargnoli in a separate interview, "I thought *Dirty Mind* was an album that deserved to be made. But Warner Bros., understandably, didn't know how to react. The last record had sold almost a million, and they expected something with the same sound. They were very negative at first—about the music and the (seminude) cover—but they eventually got behind it."

Dirty Mind sold only about half as many records as *For You*, but it established Prince as a far more arresting figure. The LP was voted one of the year's 10 best in the *Village Voice*'s annual poll of the nation's leading rock and pop critics. Last year's *Controversy* was an even bolder, more eclectic collection that reached out to a rock audience, nearly doubling the sales of *Dirty Mind*.

The new *1999* lacks some of the experimental edge of *Controversy*, but the two-record set is a dance-floor marvel that offers an even more assured-blend of Prince's rock and R&B instincts. The tunes from the lustful celebration of "Little Red Corvette" and the jaunty infatuation of "Delirious" to the chilling emotional exorcism of "Lady Cab Driver" and the sly sarcasm of "All the Critics Love U in New York."

"I didn't want to do a double album, but I just kept writing and I'm not one for editing," Prince said. "I like a natural flow. I always compare songwriting to a girl walking in the door. You don't know what she's going to look like, but all of a sudden she's there."

For the nearly 100,000 people who were on hand and the thousands of others who heard about it, Prince may be best known in Los Angeles as the guy who was booed off the stage when he opened last year for the Rolling Stones at the Memorial Coliseum.

Rock-oriented radio stations avoid playing records by black artists, even if the records have a rock slant, because they feel rock fans associate any black artist these days with the dreaded disco. This *black*-out has only reinforced the rock audience's intolerance for contemporary black music.

Though the almost exclusively white audience at the Stones show listened to the nostalgic strains of Jimi Hendrix records during intermission, many near the front of the stage hurled paper cups and shouted obscenities when Prince began playing, eventually driving him from the stage briefly.

"When we first went on the stage, a lot of people were throwing things and making noises," Prince recalled. "At first, I thought it was funny. I figured 'We'd better just play.' When I looked up a bit later, it had simmered down and a lot of people seemed relaxed. But there was this one dude right in front, and you could see hatred all over his face.

"What was really strange was there was two of them. We kept playing and the one of them noticed that everyone else (in the crowd) had cooled out. So he tried to stop this other dude, but the guy wouldn't stop. The reason I left was because I didn't want to stay anymore. I just wanted to fight—to fight *him*. I was really angry."

Smiling for one of the few times in the interview, Prince added that if he had been able to reach the heckler, "They wouldn't have found him. He just didn't want to see me. I was thinking, 'Look. I've only got 20 minutes up here. If you can't deal with that, we've got to go outside and work it out.' But I couldn't get at him and I was frustrated."

But what about reaching that rock audience?

Prince's new album has entered the pop charts nicely, and the single is a hit on pop, dance and black music charts. But neither is on the list of Top 50 records on *Billboard* magazine's check of rock radio playlists.

Steve Fargnoli, Prince's manager, is disappointed by rock radio's resistance to black artists. "To me, tracks like 'Little Red Corvette' and 'Delirious' are classic rock 'n' roll records. I just think stations are more concerned with what they think the image of an artist is than with what the music is. Those few rock stations who have played Prince have gotten good response. I don't know what the alternative is other than to keep doing what we're doing. Slowly and surely, the demographics are shifting every tour. White kids are beginning to pick up on what's happening."

Though some of Prince's uneasiness melted away during the interview, he slipped back into his shell after the final questions. Rather than engage in the usual small-talk, he simply faded across the room with the quiet of a man entering a church confessional as the aide reappeared to usher the reporter out of the room.

Of the contrast between the public flamboyance and the offstage shyness, Fargnoli suggested a few days after the interview, "That's just how he is. I've never seen an artist totally consumed to the level of Prince. It pretty much excludes everything else. He has very little to say about what he's doing other than what's in his music, but he has a clear perception of what he's done and what he wants to be. He's not afraid to follow his own instincts."

About those instincts, Prince explained in the hotel room, "When I first got started in music, I was attracted by the same things that attract most people to this business. I wanted to impress my friends and I wanted to make money. For a while, I just did it as a hobby. Then it turned into a job and a way to eat. Now I look on it as art. I realized after *Dirty Mind* that I can get away with anything I want to get away with. All I have to do is be true to myself. I can make the records I want to make and still be OK. I feel free."

MIXED EMOTIONS:
PRINCE ON THE MUSIC

Robert Hilburn | September 1983 | *Musician*

This brief collection of questions and answers was included as a sidebar within the longer *Musician* article by Barbara Graustark that appears in the next chapter. In a 2021 e-mail exchange, esteemed critic and biographer Hilburn couldn't recall the circumstances of writing this article, but it includes some duplicate material from his *Los Angeles Times* article of the previous chapter, along with some interview "outtakes." These outtakes are slightly less biographic and music-oriented than other interviews of the time. Think of this article as a remix of the previous, with some unreleased bonus tracks thrown in. —Ed.

MUSICIAN: *I liked your first two albums, but it seemed to me that the third record,* Dirty Mind, *was really a growth...*

PRINCE: Yes. The second record (*For You*) was pretty contrived. After the first record, I put myself in a hole, because I'd spent a lot of money to make it. With the second record, I wanted to remedy all that, so I just made it a "hit" album. I usually write hits for other people, and those are the songs I throw away and don't really care for. *Dirty Mind* started off as demo tapes; they were just like songs inside that I wanted to hear. So I took it to my manager and he said, "This is the best stuff I've heard in a long time. This should be your album." The drag is that I don't know how I could make another album like that. I usually change directions with each record, which is a problem in some respects, but rewarding and fulfilling for me. I have mixed emotions.

MUSICIAN: *The fourth record,* Controversy, *sounds more new wave.*

PRINCE: It depends a lot on what instrument I write on. When I write on guitar, I come up with songs like "When You Are Mine [*sic*]" and "Ronnie Talks To Russia [*sic*]." When I start with drums, I get "Controversy." *Controversy* is a little erratic. I'm really proud of this new album (*1999*).

MUSICIAN: *How did "Little Red Corvette" come about?*

PRINCE: That song was a real life incident. A girl in a little red Corvette . . . .

MUSICIAN: *Did you resist the idea of* 1999 *being a double album?*

PRINCE: Yes. I didn't want to do a double record, but I just kept on writing. Of course, I'm not one for editing. I did try to shorten things.

MUSICIAN: *How do you prepare to go into the studio? Do you have rough ideas . . . ?*

PRINCE: I don't plan or anything like that. When I record, I find if I usually just sit down and do something, I'll gradually come up with something. Sometimes it starts with a lyric.

MUSICIAN: *Is it easier to work alone rather than with others?*

PRINCE: Oh, much easier. I have a communication problem sometimes when I'm trying to describe music.

MUSICIAN: *Were you always a musical loner?*

PRINCE: When I first started, I always had buddies around me. I never wanted to be a front man. It felt spooky to be at the mike alone. I had a bad habit of just thinking of myself—if I just moved constantly, then people would think I was comfortable. But that wasn't right.

MUSICIAN: *When did you finally become comfortable performing?*

PRINCE: Last year, on the *Controversy* tour. There was something about coming down the pole and going out in front. I felt real comfortable.

MUSICIAN: *What was the incident at the Stones' Coliseum show when you left the stage early?*

PRINCE: When we went onstage, there were a lot of people throwing things and making noises and stuff. At first I thought it was fun, okay, and then I thought, "Well, we just better play." Dez, my guitar player, is just a rock 'n' roller at heart and he said, "Show 'em we can play, and then it'll simmer down." But there was this one dude right in the front and I looked down at him—you could see the hatred all over his face. He wouldn't stop throwing things. And the reason that I left was I didn't want to play anymore. I just wanted to fight him. I got really angry. It's like I'm feeling, "Look, I got twenty minutes. If you can't deal with that, well, we'll have to go outside and work it out." You know? How dare you throw something at me?

MUSICIAN: *Many songwriters use the word "love" to mean other things such as ambition or goal or talent. Is the word "sex" almost interchangeable sometimes?*

PRINCE: Yes, I think everything basically is. Like in "Lady Cab Driver," for example, "sex" is used in two different contexts. One is anger.

MUSICIAN: *Does that imply an S & M kind of thing? A lot of people might perceive that from the record.*

PRINCE: Well, that's up to them. I don't want to burst anybody's bubble, but the idea was that a lot of people make love out of loneliness sometimes.

MUSICIAN: *And they want to be touched in reassurance?*

PRINCE: Yes, exactly. It just went from anger and you start saying, "Well, how long can this go on? This is a person here. I have to be human." The right spot was hit so . . .

MUSICIAN: *Do you enjoy being in the studio?*

PRINCE: Yes. There's nothing like the feeling after you've done something and play it back and you know that you'll never hear anything like it and that they'll never figure it out—I'm sorry, I know what that sounds like. When I say "figure it out," I mean something like I'll try to go so high and so jagged with my voice that if anybody tries to do it their tonsils will fall out. I don't try to trick people. Life is too confusing itself, and I wouldn't put any more on anybody else. Now everybody's worried about the fact that I can't use engineers.

MUSICIAN: *You can't use engineers?*

PRINCE: No, they drive me crazy. It's because they're so technical. Everything just got so esoteric, "We've got to do this a certain way," when you're ready to play. The engineer I use and give credit to on the album, she sets everything up for me, most of the time before I come in. And then I just do what I have to do and split. She puts things together afterward.

MUSICIAN: *I once heard you described as a child prodigy.*

PRINCE: Don't. That's all fabricated evidence that the management did to make it happen. I don't want to say that I was anything less than what they thought, but I just did it as sort of a hobby, and then it turned into a job and just a way to eat, and now I do it as art.

PRINCE: STRANGE TALES FROM ANDRE'S BASEMENT . . . AND OTHER FANTASIES COME TRUE

Barbara Graustark | September 1983 | *Musician*

By word count, this solitary 1983 interview is among the longest of Prince's career. So long, in fact, that when it was over, he told writer Barbara Graustark, "That was the longest I've ever talked." But, for all its length, there are no headline-worthy revelations here. Instead, we're treated to a more personal side of Prince, with unusual depth and nuance on multiple common topics as Prince is pushed to think beyond simple answers by the skillful interviewer Graustark. The biggest revelation here is probably an extended version of his pre-label New York City adventures with his sister and "Danielle."

Ultimately, what's most remarkable is what's not here, an example of Prince's ability to compartmentalize different aspects of his personal and professional life. Just as his public face at press interactions and performances in fall 1996 offered no clue that he had just lost a newborn son, there is little here to indicate all the amazing activity that enveloped him at the moment of the interview, which took place around the time of his March 21 show at Radio City Music Hall. No bragging about the wildly successful *1999* album and related Triple Threat Tour (Vanity 6 and the Time) that had just installed the legendary Alan Leeds as road manager. Nothing about discussions the previous week for a fiction film that would morph into *Purple Rain*, nor about being named *Rolling Stone*'s artist of 1982. And, without the ability to see into the future, nothing about the failure of Jimmy Jam and Terry Lewis to show up at the next gig in San Antonio, leading to the demise of the Time as a functioning band and inadvertently freeing the duo to become one of the top R&B production teams of all time. —Ed.

Sure he's a weird kid. For Prince Rogers Nelson, a man whom Henry Miller and Howard Hughes are undoubtedly behavioral models, the two S's of sex and secrecy are paramount. His reluctance to talk to the press is well established and his role as a beacon of sexual controversy is past legendary. Jimi Hendrix may have helped open the floodgates when he asked an innocent generation, "Are you experienced?" But Prince didn't have to ask. His sexual excesses in a dank, dark Minneapolis basement with his confidant and companion Andre Cymone and a host of neighborhood girls shaped the values of his earliest songs and mirrored the experiences and insecurity of a liberated generation.

His first albums were full of funky innuendo. *For You* established him as a poetic prince of love, with a mission to spread a sexy message here on earth—a message reinforced by his "special thanks to God" credit on the LP's jacket. Prince had heard the call, all right, but it wasn't the Lord's sermon that he was preaching, and with his next album, *Dirty Mind*, he catapulted out of the closet and into the public eye as a raunchy prophet of porn.

That album established Prince in rock critical circles as a truly special case. He created his own musical world in which heavy-metal guitars crashed into synth-funk rhythms, where rockabilly bounced off rapid punk tempos, all of it riding under lyrical themes of incest, lost love, sexual discovery and oral gratification. It was then that I became interested in talking to this elusive boy genius.

His concerts that fall had been a hot, erotic blast of wind through the chilly Northeast, and I was primed to meet a proper, swaggering conqueror—"The leader of a pack in a brave new world without rules or categories or any limitations," as Boston critic Ariel Swartley had extravagantly described him. What I found facing me that sleepy-eyed morning was shockingly different: a man-child in the promised land. Despite the studded trenchcoat, the leather jock bikini and the blatant bare chest, he was a shy and unsure creature, small as a leprechaun and just as elusive.

The interview became a lengthy excursion into Prince's pained past and through songs that had a purpose beyond the titillating of fantasies, as I was soon to learn. Prince's preoccupation, disclosed between the lines of the interview, was loneliness, which in the world had become painfully interwoven with sexuality. His own childhood was something else. Multiracial, one of nine children of a hard-working Italian mother and a half-black father—a struggling musician who was mostly absent during his youth—Prince was a veteran of foster homes and a chronic runaway.

At the time of our interview, he was proud and hurt, contemplating ending interviews altogether. He communicated with the gravity of a crestfallen child, speaking in short grudging bursts of words that nevertheless revealed a great deal more than he wanted anyone to know. At the end of our long visit, he gave an eloquent summation: "That was the longest I've ever talked," he said with a child's awe. He gave me an uncertain grin and, as he trudged off into the New York rain, wobbling a bit on his high-heeled cobra boots, I liked him immediately and had the feeling that Prince would survive his current bout with success.

MUSICIAN: *Let me start off with* the *question, to me at least. Dirty Mind seems to be the antithesis of what sex should be. Or is it? Why was that album called* Dirty Mind?

PRINCE: Well, that was kind of a put-on . . . I wanted to put it out there that way and in time show people that's *not* what sex was about. You can say a bad word over and over again and sooner or later it won't be bad anymore if everybody starts doing it.

MUSICIAN: *Are songs like "Head" and "Sister" serious or satiric?*

PRINCE: "Sister" is serious. "Head" could be taken as satire. No one's laughing when I'm saying it so I don't know. If people get enjoyment out of it and laugh, that's fine. All the stuff on the record is true experiences and things that have occurred around me and the way I feel about things. I wasn't laughing when I did it. So I don't suppose it was intended that way.

That's why I stopped doing interviews. I started and I stopped abruptly because of that. People weren't taking me seriously and I was being misunderstood. Everything I said they didn't believe anyway. They didn't believe my name. They didn't believe anything.

MUSICIAN: *Your father's stage name was Prince Rogers. Was that his real name?*

PRINCE: That wasn't his real name. He made it up.

MUSICIAN: *And what's your last name? Is it Nelson?*

PRINCE: I don't know.

MUSICIAN: *Your point about being misunderstood is kind of important. We should try and be as straight as possible with each other so I know that what you're saying is being interpreted correctly.*

PRINCE: Okay. I tell the truth about everything but my last name. I just hate it. I know how it's just the name that he had to go through life with, and he hated it too. So that's why he gave me this name and that's why he changed his when he went onstage. I just don't like it and I just really would rather not have it out. It's just a stupid name that means nothing to my ancestry, my father and what he was about.

MUSICIAN: *Was your father very much there when you were growing up?*

PRINCE: Well, up until the time I was seven he was very much there. Then he was very much away. Then I went to live with him once . . . I ran away the first time when I was twelve. And then he worked two jobs. He worked a day job and then he worked downtown playing behind strippers. So he was away and I didn't see him much then, only while he was shaving or something like that. We didn't talk so much then.

MUSICIAN: *Did he have any feelings about you being a musician? Was he a supportive person?*

PRINCE: I don't think so because he didn't think I was very good. I didn't really think so either. When I finally got a band together he used to come and watch us play every once in a while. But he finds it really hard to show emotion. I find that true of most men and it's kind of a drag, but . . . .

MUSICIAN: *Is your father a good musician? What does he play?*

PRINCE: Piano. The reason he's good is that he's totally . . . he can't stand any music other than his. He doesn't listen to *anybody*. And he's really strange. He told me one time that he has dreams where he'd see a keyboard in front of his eyes and he'd see his hands on the keyboard and he'd hear a melody. And he can get up and it can be like 4:30 a.m. and he can walk right downstairs to his piano and play the melody. And to me that's amazing because there's no work involved really; he's just given a gift in each song. He never comes out of the house unless it's to get something to eat and he goes right back in and he plays all the time. His music . . . one day I hope you'll get to hear it. It's just—it sounds like nothing I've ever heard.

MUSICIAN: *How did* you *get into music? Where were you? What were you doing?*

PRINCE: I was at home living with my mother and my sister, and he had just gone and left his piano. He didn't allow anybody to play it when he was there because we would just bang on it. So once he left then I started doing it because nobody else would. Everything was cool I think, until my father left, and then it got kinda hairy. My step-dad came along when I was nine or ten, and I disliked him immediately, because he dealt with a lot of materialistic things. He would bring us a lot of presents all the time, rather than sit down and talk with us and give us companionship. I got real bitter because of that, and I would say all the things that I disliked about him, rather than tell him what I really needed. Which was a mistake, and it kind of hurt our relationship.

I don't think they wanted me to be a musician. But I think it was mainly because of my father, who disliked the idea that he was a musician, and it really broke up their life. I think that's why he probably named me what he named me, it was like a blow to her—"He's gonna grow up the same way, so don't even worry about him." And that's exactly what I did.

I was about thirteen when I moved away. I didn't really realize other music until I had to. And that was when I got my own band and we had to play top forty songs. Anything that was a hit, didn't matter who it was. We played everything because we were playing for white and black audiences at the time. Minneapolis is mostly white anyway.

MUSICIAN: *Do you feel a strong identification with anything . . . anybody?*

PRINCE: No. I think society says if you've got a little black in you that's what you are. I don't.

MUSICIAN: *When you moved away, did you move in with your father?*

PRINCE: Well, that was when I went to live with my aunt, also in Minneapolis, because I couldn't stay at my father's. And my father wouldn't get me a piano, it was too much or whatever, so . . . he got me a guitar. I didn't learn to play the *right* way, because I tuned it to a straight A chord so it was really strange. When I first started playing guitar, I just did chords and things like that, and I didn't really get into soloing and all that until later, when I started making records. I can't think of any foremost great guitarist that stuck in my mind. It was just solos on records, and it was just dumb stuff; I hated top forty. Everybody in the band hated it. It was what was holding us back. And we were trying to escape it. But we had to do it to make enough money to make demo tapes.

MUSICIAN: *How'd you get to Andre Cymone's cellar?*

PRINCE: Andre Cymone's house was the last stop after going from my dad's to my aunt's, to different homes and going through just a bunch of junk. And once I got there, I had realized that I was going to have to play according to the program, and do exactly what was expected of me. And I was sixteen at the time, getting ready to turn seventeen.

MUSICIAN: *Were you still in high school?*

PRINCE: Mm-hm. And, that was another problem. I wasn't doing well in school, and I was going to have to. Otherwise the people around me were going to get very upset. I could come in anytime I wanted, I could have girls spend the night, and it didn't make a difference. I think it had a great deal to do with me coming out into my own, and discovering myself. I mean, the music was interesting at that time, once I got out of high school. And I got out of high school early, when I was like sixteen.

MUSICIAN: *Did you finish?*

PRINCE: Yeah. Because I got all the required credits. And that's relatively early. In about two and a half years, or something like that. It was pretty easy and stupid. To this day, I don't use anything that they taught me. Get your jar, and dissect frogs and stuff like that.

MUSICIAN: *How'd you support yourself?*

PRINCE: Well, that was the problem. Once I got out of high school it was interesting for a while because I didn't have any money, I didn't have any school, and I didn't have any dependents, I didn't have any kids, or girlfriends, or anything. I had cut myself off totally from everything. And that's when I really started writing. I was writing like three or four songs a day. And, they were all really long. Which is interesting for me as a writer, because it's hard to just take a thought, and continue it for a long period of time without losing it. And it's harder for me now to write than it was back then, because there's so many people around me now. I wrote a lot of sexual songs back then, but they were mainly things that I *wanted* to go on, not things that *were* going on. Which is different from what I write about now.

MUSICIAN: *You mean, what you were writing about then was just a fantasy of women?*

PRINCE: All fantasies, yeah. Because I didn't have anything around me . . . there were no people. No anything. When I started writing, I cut myself off from relationships with women.

MUSICIAN: *Did you ever have a relationship?*

PRINCE: Several solid relationships (laughs). When you're broken, and poor and hungry, you usually try to find friends who are gonna help you out.

MUSICIAN: *Who are rich and things?*

PRINCE: Yeah. And successful. And have a lot of food in their fridge. I don't know.

MUSICIAN: *Did you ever do anything that you're embarrassed about?*

PRINCE: Mmm . . . no . . . well . . . .

MUSICIAN: *Were you doing drugs?*

PRINCE: No. One thing that turned me off to that was seeing my brother get high. At first we all thought it was funny, but then I started asking him questions and he couldn't answer 'em, you know. So I felt it was kinda stupid. And I didn't want my mind all cloudy at any time, because I always felt . . . I don't know, maybe it was a basic paranoia or something about me, but I didn't want anybody sneaking up behind me, and doing me in, or taking my money, or tricking me in any way. So I never wanted to get high.

MUSICIAN: *How does Andre Cymone fit into all of this? Was he there at the beginning, and then you went to New York and came back, and resumed the friendship?*

PRINCE: Well. what happened was, before I went to New York we lost our friendship, because he was in the band with me at the time, and I asked them all what they wanted to do, "Do you want to stay here, or do you want to go to New York?" And Andre didn't speak up, but everyone else was against it. No one wanted to do it. They liked their lifestyle, I guess. I don't think they really liked the idea of me trying to manipulate the band so much. I was always trying to get us to do something different, and I was always teamed up on for that. Like, in an argument or something like that, or a fight, or whatever . . . it was always me against them. That's when I wrote "Soft And Wet," which was the first single I put out. I really liked the tune, but everyone thought it was filthy, and "you didn't have no business doing stuff without us, anyway." I just did what I wanted to. And that was it.

MUSICIAN: *When did you realize that?*

PRINCE: When I was in Andre's basement. I found out a lot about myself then. The only reason I stayed was because of Andre's mother. She would let me do anything I wanted to, but she said all I care about is you finishing school. *Anything.*

MUSICIAN: *How much can you do in a basement?*

PRINCE: Well, it depends on how many people are there! (laughs) You know, one time she came down and saw a lot of us down there, and we weren't all dressed, and stuff like that. It kind of tripped her out, and we got into a semi-argument, and whatever, but it, was . . . you know . . . .

MUSICIAN: *Was the scene back then in the basement a heterosexual scene? Was it homosexual?*

PRINCE: No, everything was heterosexual. I didn't know any homosexuals, no. There was one guy who walked around in women's clothes, but we didn't know *why* he did it, we just thought it was funny, and that was that. Some things don't dawn on you for a long time. And now I hear, like . . . Minneapolis is supposed to be like . . . the third largest gay city in the country, or whatever. Huge.

MUSICIAN: *Were you ready for New York when you came?*

PRINCE: Yeah. I was ready for anything. I felt disgusted with my life in Minneapolis.

MUSICIAN: *What'd you do when you got here? Did you know you were gonna live with your sister?*

PRINCE: Mm-hm. When I called her and told her what had happened, she said, well come here and I'll help you. And I came. She had a great personality. You know, all my friends were girls, okay? I didn't have any male friends, because they were just cheap, all of 'em were just cheap, so I knew then that if she used her personality and her sensitivity she could get us a deal. That didn't mean going to bed with anybody, it just meant that . . . you know, use your charm rather than trying to go in there and be this man, because you're *not*.

And then my sister was introduced to this one guy who had a band. And, I don't know how she got this, but it was really cool. She ended up talking to this guy and found out everything he did, and found out that he had a demo and he was gonna take it to this woman named Danielle. And he was gonna try to get his band signed to her. So we all went together, and she said, "Can my little brother come in?" And she said sure. So we were all sitting there, and Danielle said, "Alright, put your tape on." So he put on the tape of his band. That tape was pretty terrible, and Danielle said so, and the guy started making excuses, saying, "Well, that's not the real guitar player, *or* the real singers, so don't worry about it." And she said, "Well, why did you bring a tape that doesn't have the real musicians?"

Then my sister started telling Danielle about me and finally she asked me to sing. And I said no (laughs). And she said, "Why not?" And I said, "Because I'm scared." And she said, "You don't have to be scared." And they turned the lights down, and it was really strange.

That same day I had just written "Baby," and I didn't really have it all together, but I sang the melody and she really liked my voice. She said, "I don't care what you do, just hum, because I just want to hear you sing." So that's what I did, just started singing and humming, and making up words and really stupid stuff.

MUSICIAN: *Were you singing in your upper register then?*

PRINCE: I only sang like that back then because, I don't know . . . it hurt . . . it hurt my voice to sing in the lower register. I couldn't make it, I couldn't peak songs the way I wanted to, and things like that, so I never used it.

MUSICIAN: *Oh! I would think it would hurt to sing in a falsetto.*

PRINCE: Well, not for me. I wish it was that way, but . . . .

MUSICIAN: *Did Danielle sign you to a contract?*

PRINCE: Well, she wanted to start working with me immediately. Nevertheless, this guy was pretty upset that he didn't get his band in there. He and my sister fell out right away, but she didn't care. And that's what I dug about her. So I talked with Danielle, and she told me to come over to her apartment. She was very beautiful, too, which made everything a lot easier, I remember that about her. And she made me bring all my songs, and we went through 'em all, and she didn't like any of 'em.

MUSICIAN: *None of them? Not even "Soft And Wet"?*

PRINCE: None. Except for "Baby." She wanted me to do "Baby" with a lot of orchestration, tympani, strings, and . . . .

MUSICIAN: *How'd that sound to you?*

PRINCE: I didn't care. You know. I was cool with it. All I wanted to do was play a couple of instruments on it, and let it say on the album that

I played something. And she said no, unless I could play better than the session guy, which I didn't think I could do if a guy was gonna sit there and read the chart, and I was going to get aced out right away. So that didn't materialize. Anyway . . . after I finished that, that's when me and my sister kinda had a dispute.

MUSICIAN: *About what?*

PRINCE: Mainly money. I had nothing; I was running up sort of a bill there, at her place, and she wanted me to sell my publishing for like $380 or something like that—which I thought was kinda foolish. And I kept telling her that I could get my own publishing company. I didn't care about money. I just didn't care about money. And, I don't know, I never have, because . . . the one time I did have it was when my step-dad lived there, and I know I was extremely bitter then.

MUSICIAN: *And did you have to go back to Minneapolis?*

PRINCE: I didn't *have* to, which was nice. Danielle knew this was gonna happen sooner or later. It was all really interesting to me back then, and I kind of would have liked to have seen what would have happened if she had managed me.

MUSICIAN: *What* did *happen? Why didn't she?*

PRINCE: Well, when I got back to Minneapolis, that's when I first met Owen Husney. I had been talking to him over the phone, and all he kept saying was that he thought I was really great, and that . . . .

MUSICIAN: *Was Owen big time then? Was he a big-time kind of promoter, or manager?*

PRINCE: Mmm. He had promoted some gigs, but he was working mainly in his ad company. And he wanted to manage an act. The main thing he said was that no one should produce a record of mine—*I* should do it. And, I still had a deal with Danielle if I wanted it, but something about him saying that to me made me think that was the way to go. So I told her that I was going to college.

MUSICIAN: *Was Danielle somebody that you had a relationship with?*

PRINCE: Mm-mm. It was only . . . it was only mind games. I mean, we'd look at one another and . . . play games, but it wasn't . . . we never said anything.

MUSICIAN: *Um . . . when you came back and started working with Owen, what did he do? Did he get the contract for you with Warner Bros.?*

PRINCE: Owen believed in me, he really did. First of all, nobody believed I could play all the instruments.

MUSICIAN: *How many instruments did you play?*

PRINCE: Well, on the demo tapes I didn't play too many—I played drums, keyboards, bass and guitars, percussion and vocals; but when I did my album, I did tons of things. Somebody counted and said I had played twenty-seven on the first album. Different ones, but I don't know, I never count things (laughs). Because the quantity is . . . people put so much emphasis on that. It's about the quality, and what it sounds like.

MUSICIAN: *It must have been a battle with the record company to produce and arrange.*

PRINCE: Well, I got a couple offers and the only difference between Warner Bros. and the others was that they didn't want to let me do production, they didn't want to let me plan anything on the records. Warners had a lot of problems with it at first but Owen was fighting for control for me. They made me do a demo tape. So I did it, and they said that's pretty good. Do another one, and so I did another one. Then they said, "Okay, we can produce your album." And they waited a week to call me back and they said I couldn't. I had to go through that process a few more times. Then finally they said okay. It was kind of frustrating at first but I got used to it.

To some degree in the earlier days I was listening to Owen and the company. I didn't want to create any waves because I was brand new, and stuff like that. But now I feel that I'm going to have to do exactly what's on my mind and be exactly the way I am. Otherwise sooner or later down the road I'm going to be in a corner sucking my thumb or something. I don't want to lose it. I just want to do what I'm really about.

MUSICIAN: *Did you know what you wanted to do when you started out? When you got that contract with Warner Bros., and they said to go into the studio and do it?*

PRINCE: I had an idea, but it was really vague, and I think that had to do with . . . at least, with having such a big budget. It was really big—over $100,000. You're supposed to go in and do an album for $60,000. But I went in and kept going, and kept going and kept going. I got in a lot of trouble for it.

MUSICIAN: *How much time did you spend in the studio?*

PRINCE: Hours. Hours. I was a physical wreck when I finished the record . . . it took me five months to do the first one. I'm proud of it, in the sense that it's mistake-free, and it's perfect. And it's . . . that's the problem with it, you know. But it wasn't really me, it was like a machine. You know, I walked in, and I was sleepy all the time. I didn't really feel like recording for eighty percent of the record. But I did it anyway, because, by the time I had gotten close to $100,000, it was like, you know, you were going to have to do something *great*. So, by that time, I didn't want to make any mistakes. The relationship between me and the executive producer that they assigned with me was horrifying.

MUSICIAN: *Did Warner Bros. ever look as if they were just going to wash their hands of the whole thing, or were they committed?*

PRINCE: No, I don't think so, because I owed them too much money.

MUSICIAN: *They had to stick with you, so you could pay off.*

PRINCE: Yeah. At least three albums. And I didn't want to do anything like interviews or touring. I was being real stubborn and bull-headed, and Owen didn't realize how to get it out of me, and make me stop. And, I don't know, our friendship died slowly after that. It just got strange.

MUSICIAN: *How did you get the whole act together? When did you get a band and decide to go on the road?*

PRINCE: Well, the band came right before I did the second album (*For You*).

MUSICIAN: *What happened when you went back to Minneapolis . . . first, after New York, and then, after you had actually recorded? Were you treated very differently? I mean, this was big time with Warner Bros., for sure.*

PRINCE: Yeah. The same people who told me I wasn't gonna be anything, treated me with a lot more respect now. And it made me a much better person. It took a lot of bitterness out of me. Because that's all I really wanted; I didn't want the respect so much as I wanted friendship, real friendship. That's all that counts to me. And I tell my band members the same thing now. I mean, you have to learn to deal with me on an up-front level, or else, you know, it's dead. I don't want people around me who don't do that.

MUSICIAN: *Has your music changed much since then?*

PRINCE: I think I change constantly because I can hear the music changing. The other day I put my first three albums on and listened to the difference. And I know why I don't sound like that anymore. Because things that made sense to me and things that I liked then I don't like anymore. The way I played music, just the way I was in love a lot back then when I used to make those records. And love meant more to me then—but now I realize that people don't always tell you the truth, you know? I was really gullible back then. I believed in everybody around me. I believed in Owen, I believed in Warner Bros., I believed in everybody. If someone said something good to me, I believed it.

MUSICIAN: *And it was reflected in your music?*

PRINCE: Yeah, I think so. It was . . .

MUSICIAN: *More romantic?*

PRINCE: Yeah. And I felt good when I was singing back then. The things I do now, I feel anger sometimes when I sing, and I can hear the difference. I'm screaming more now than I used to. And things like that. I think it's just me. It also has to do with the instrumentation. It has nothing to do with trying to change styles or anything. Plus, I'm in a different environment; I see New York a little bit more. In my subconscious I'm influenced by the sinisterness of it, you know, the power.

I hear sirens all the time, things like that. It's not like that in Minneapolis. If you ever go there you'll see it's real laid back, real quiet, and you have to make your own action. I think a lot of warped people come out of there. My friends. I know a lot of warped girls, okay? Warped to me means they see things differently than I would, I suppose. They talk a lot. They talk a lot about nothing. But I mean heavy. They get into it like you wouldn't believe. I mean, we could get into an hour-long conversation about my pants. You know, why they're so tight, or something, do you know what I mean?

MUSICIAN: *Well, why are they tight?*

PRINCE: I don't know (laughs). I don't know. Because I want them to be. I just like the way they look.

MUSICIAN: *Did Warner Bros. flinch when you put "Head" on the third record?*

PRINCE: They flinched at just about everything (laughs).

MUSICIAN: *I wanted to ask you about the cover of* Dirty Mind. *How was that done?*

PRINCE: We were just fooling around, and we were jamming at the time. It was summertime, and we were having fun. And that's what I had on. But my coat was closed, so the photographer didn't know. I was with some friends and . . .

MUSICIAN: *Does everyone in Minneapolis just walk around with bikini underpants?*

PRINCE: (laughs) No. But, see . . . I don't know. I mean . . . once . . . I mean, if you've got a big coat on. I mean, who knows what he has on? I mean, it was hot out. Everybody was saying, why you got that hot coat on? I'd say, I'm really not that hot. (laughs) And they'd say, you gotta be.

MUSICIAN: *I bet you flash.*

PRINCE: No. Not in . . . it depends on who it is. But, we were just jamming and stuff like that, and he didn't know that's what I had on. And so, he was taking pictures and I happened to open my coat for one, just as a joke, you know? He said, wow. Like that. And, well, see, I used to wear that onstage.

MUSICIAN: *How'd you pick that image of yourself? Where did it come from?*

PRINCE: Well, I used to wear leotards and Danskins and stuff, because our stage show is really athletic and I wanted something comfortable. And my management said, "You have to at least start wearing underwear, because . . . ."

MUSICIAN: *You weren't wearing any underwear?*

PRINCE: No. Kind of gross. So I said, okay, and started wearing underwear.

MUSICIAN: *What kind of friends were you hanging with?*

PRINCE: Prostitutes. Pimps. Drug dealers. Really bad people and preachers' daughters, you know? Which is strange, because they were the total opposite of their fathers.

MUSICIAN: *How did you meet them? At gigs?*

PRINCE: Yeah. I talk to people. and if they're real and sincere about what they're doing, and they don't really want anything out of me except to be my friends, then, you know, I go for that.

MUSICIAN: *The people who you were friendly with back then . . . that group . . . did they influence your style?*

PRINCE: Well, I think to some degree. They're really rebellious. They cut themselves off from the world, as I did. The band's attitude is, they don't listen to a lot of music and stuff like that. And the band is funny, the only time they'll go to see someone else is if they're going to talk about them or heckle. It's really sick. They're like critics.

MUSICIAN: *Are they all close friends?*

PRINCE: I don't know anymore. It's hard to say. When we first started I think we were. That's how they got in the group. Some of them I didn't find out if they could play until later.

MUSICIAN: *Are they concerned, now, about not being on the road? Do they feel that they'd like to be touring?*

PRINCE: Yeah. We all do. Once I stop, then I start writing again, or whatever, or start playing . . . fooling around, then I don't want to play out in public so much. I guess I write letters better than I talk, basically. I can write really good letters. And that's where the records come from. I can sit down and say exactly what I want. I don't have to worry about someone else next to me doing their job.

MUSICIAN: *It's funny, because you're a very imaginative guy. I would think for someone who draws on fantasies and wrote about dreams, fantasy would be important.*

PRINCE: Well, it is. But it's not so much when you're writing a letter. Do you know what I mean? If I were to write a letter to a friend, and tell them about an experience, I wouldn't say how it made me *feel*; I would say exactly what I *did*, so that they could experience it, too, rather than the intellectual point of view. If you give them a situation, maybe that you've encountered, or whatever, give them the basis of it, let them take it to the next stage, they make the picture in their own mind. I know I am happiest making records like this, making records that tell the truth and don't beat around the bush. Maybe I'm wrong for it, but I know the people at the concerts know exactly what the songs are about, sing right along, and are really into it. We have their attention. They understand, I think, and they're getting the message. I don't know. It seems real to me because . . . well, it is, because I'm saying exactly what's going around me. I say everything exactly the way it is.

MUSICIAN: *Do you think people think that you're gay?*

PRINCE: Well, there's something about me, I know, that makes people think that. It must stem from the fact that I spent a lot of time around women. Maybe they see things I don't.

MUSICIAN: *People always speak about a feminine sensibility as if it's something negative in a man. But it's usually very attractive for most women. Like a sensitiveness.*

PRINCE: I don't know. It's attractive for me. I mean, I would like to be a more loving person, and be able to deal with other people's problems a little bit better. Men are really closed and cold together, I think. They don't like to cry, in other words. And I think that's wrong, because that's not true.

MUSICIAN: *Is there anything that you want me to mention that we haven't talked about?*

PRINCE: Well, I don't know, it's . . . I don't want people to get the impression that sex is all I write about. Because it's not, and the reason why it's so abundant in my writing is mainly because of my age and the things that are around me. Until you can go to college or get a nine-to-five job, then there's going to be a bunch of free time around you. And free time can only be spent in certain ways. But if people don't dig my music, then stay away from it, that's all. It's not for everybody, I don't believe. I do know that there are a lot of people wanting to be themselves out there.

MUSICIAN: *Will you always try to be controversial?*

PRINCE: That's really a strange question, because if I'm that way, then I will be forever writing that way. I don't particularly think it's so controversial. I mean, when a girl can get birth control pills at age twelve, then I know she knows just about as much as I do, or at least will be there in a short time. I think people are pretty blind to it. Pretty blind to life, and taking for granted what really goes on.

MUSICIAN: *Do you think that older people don't give the twelve- and thirteen-year-olds enough credit for knowing as much as they know?*

PRINCE: I'm sure they don't. I'm absolutely sure they don't. I mean, when my mom had stuff in her room that I could sneak in and get. Books, vibrators, all kinds of things. I did it. I'm sure everybody else does. And if I can go in there and do all that, I don't see how she figures I won't know. And the way she figures I don't know is, she doesn't sit down and tell me exactly what's going on. I never got a rap like that, and I don't know how many kids do.

MUSICIAN: *I think that a lot of kids would like to feel that there's somebody who's capturing that experience for them. And I don't think anybody really has done it before.*

PRINCE: Yeah. At the same time, you're telling them about wanting to be loved or whatever . . . accepted. In time you can tell them about contraception and things like that, which need to be said. No one else is going to say it. I know I have definite viewpoints on a lot of different things: the school system, the way the government's run, and things like that. And I'll say them, in time. And I think they'll be accepted for what they are.

MUSICIAN: *So is that really you up there onstage?*

PRINCE: What? The way I act? Oh, yeah, without a doubt.

MUSICIAN: *In other words, when you go back to Minneapolis, and you go to parties, is that you?*

PRINCE: Oh, yeah. And when I'm with my friends, I'm more like that than anything. A lot of times, when I got out to clubs, if I go, I just go to observe, and I watch people. I like to watch people. The way they act and things like that.

MUSICIAN: *So what will be the first thing you do when you get back to Minneapolis?*

PRINCE: Probably take a long bath. I haven't had one in a long time. I'm scared of hotel bathtubs.

MUSICIAN: *What do you fear?*

PRINCE: They just . . . a maid could walk in and see me.

PRINCE TALKS

Neal Karlen | September 12, 1985 | *Rolling Stone*

For Prince, if not the public and press, *Purple Rain* was well and thankfully beyond range of his Thunderbird's rearview mirror by the time of this late June 1985 interview. The tour had ended in April after over a hundred demanding dates, he had been battered in the press for refusing to take part in USA for Africa, and his bodyguard had sold him out to the *National Enquirer*. And, by the way, he had released a new album, *Around the World in a Day*, that wasn't a carbon copy of *Purple Rain*. He was done with *Purple Rain* and more than ready to move on. And, of course, he had moved on, as he had already finished an early version of his next LP, *Parade*, and was prepping the companion film, *Under the Cherry Moon*.

At publication, this interview was best known for Prince breaking his two-year-plus press silence and his still-debated dismissal of the Beatles ("They were great for what they did, but I don't know how that would hang today."). Now, it's fascinating not only as a portrait of a man coming to terms with the unexpected stresses of stardom, but also as a blueprint for many future in-depth interviews. Here, Prince is literally in the driver's seat for much of this interview. It's conducted on his home turf and on his own terms. And, while he doesn't dictate the questions, he often shapes his answer more to what he wants to say rather than as a direct response to what is asked. To put it another way, this is where Prince takes control of his own narrative from the mamma-jammas. —Ed.

John Nelson turns sixty-nine today, and all the semiretired piano man wants for his birthday is to shoot some pool with his firstborn son. "He's real handy with a cue," says Prince, laughing, as he threads his old white

T-bird through his old black neighborhood toward his old man's house. "He's so cool. The old man knows what time it is."

Hard time is how life has traditionally been clocked in North Minneapolis; this is the place *Time* forgot twelve years ago when the magazine's cover trumpeted "The Good Life in Minnesota," alongside a picture of Governor Wendell Anderson holding up a walleye. Though tame and middle-class by Watts and Roxbury standards, the North Side offers some of the few mean streets in town.

The old sights bring out more Babbitt than Badass in Prince as he leads a leisurely tour down the main streets of his inner-city Gopher Prairie. He cruises slowly, respectfully: stopping completely at red lights, flicking on his turn signal even when no one's at an intersection. Gone is the wary Kung Fu Grasshopper voice with which Prince whispers when meeting strangers or accepting Academy Awards. Cruising peacefully with the window down, he's proof in a paisley jump suit that you can always go home again, especially if you never really left town.

Tooling through the neighborhood, Prince speaks matter-of-factly of why he toyed with early interviewers about his father and mother, their divorce and his adolescent wanderings between the homes of his parents, friends and relatives. "I used to tease a lot of journalists early on," he says, "because I wanted them to concentrate on the music and not so much on me coming from a broken home. I really didn't think that was important. What was important was what came out of my system that particular day. I don't live in the past. I don't play my old records for that reason. I make a statement, then move on to the next."

The early facts, for the neo-Freudians: John Nelson, leader of the Prince Rogers jazz trio, knew Mattie Shaw from North Side community dances. A singer sixteen years John's junior, Mattie bore traces of Billie Holiday in her pipes and more than a trace of Indian and Caucasian in her blood. She joined the Prince Rogers trio, sang for a few years around town, married John Nelson and dropped out of the group. She nicknamed her husband after the band; the son who came in 1958 got the nickname on his birth certificate. At home and on the street, the kid was "Skipper." Mattie and John broke up ten years later, and Prince began his domestic shuttle.

"That's where my mom lives," he says nonchalantly, nodding toward a neatly trimmed house and lawn. "My parents live very close by each other, but they don't talk. My mom's the wild side of me; she's like that all the time. My dad's real serene; it takes the music to get him going. My father and me, we're one and the same." A wry laugh. "He's a little sick, just like I am."

Most of North Minneapolis has gone outside this Sunday afternoon to feel summer, that two-week season, locals joke, between winter and road construction. During this scenic tour through the neighborhood, the memories start popping faster. The T-Bird turns left at a wooden two-story church whose steps are lined with bridesmaids in bonnets and ushers in tuxedos hurling rice up at a beaming couple framed in the door. "That was the church I went to growing up," says Prince. "I wonder who's getting married." A fat little kid waves, and Prince waves back.

"Just all kinds of things here," he goes on, turning right. "There was a school right there, John Hay. That's where I went to elementary school," he says, pointing out a field of black tar sprouting a handful of bent metal basketball rims. "And that's where my cousin lives. I used to play there every day when I was twelve, on these streets, football up and down this block. That's his father out there on the lawn."

These lawns are where Prince the adolescent would also amuse his friends with expert imitations of pro wrestlers Mad Dog Vachon and the Crusher. To amuse himself, he learned how to play a couple dozen instruments. At thirteen, he formed Grand Central, his first band, with some high school friends. Grand Central often traveled to local hotels and gyms to band-battle with their black competition: Cohesion, from the derided "bourgeois" South Side, and Flyte Time, which, with the addition of Morris Day, would later evolve into the Time.

Prince is fiddling with the tape deck inside the T-Bird. On low volume comes his unreleased "Old Friends 4 Sale," an arrow-to-the-heart rock ballad about trust and loss. Unlike "Positively 4th Street"—which Bob Dylan reputedly named after a nearby Minneapolis block—the lyrics are sad, not bitter. "I don't know too much about Dylan," says Prince, "but I respect him a lot. 'All Along the Watchtower' is my favorite of his. I heard it first from Jimi Hendrix."

"Old Friends 4 Sale" ends, and on comes "Strange Relationships [sic]," an as-yet-unreleased dance tune. "Is it too much?" asks Prince about playing his own songs in his own car. "Not long ago I was driving around L.A. with [a well-known rock star], and all he did was play his own stuff over and over. If it gets too much, just tell me."

He turns onto Plymouth, the North Side's main strip. When Martin Luther King got shot, it was Plymouth Avenue that burned. "We used to go to that McDonald's there," he says. "I didn't have any money, so I'd just stand outside there and smell stuff. Poverty makes people angry, brings out their worst side. I was very bitter when I was young. I was insecure and I'd attack anybody. I couldn't keep a girlfriend for two weeks. We'd argue about anything."

Across the street from McDonald's, Prince spies a smaller landmark. He points to a vacant corner phone booth and remembers a teenage fight with a strict and unforgiving father. "That's where I called my dad and begged him to take me back after he kicked me out," he begins softly. "He said no, so I called my sister and asked her to ask him. So she did, and afterward told me that all I had to do was call him back, tell him I was sorry, and he'd take me back. So I did, and he still said no. I sat crying at that phone booth for two hours. That's the last time I cried."

In the years between that phone-booth breakdown and today's pool game came forgiveness. Says Prince, "Once I made it, got my first record contract, got my name on a piece of paper and a little money in my pocket, I was able to forgive. Once I was eating every day, I became a much nicer person." But it took many more years for the son to understand what a jazzman father needed to survive. Prince figured it out when he moved into his purple house.

"I can be upstairs at the piano, and Rande [his cook] can come in," he says. "Her footsteps will be in a different time, and it's real weird when you hear something that's a totally different rhythm than what you're playing. A lot of times that's mistaken for conceit or not having a heart. But it's not. And my dad's the same way, and that's why it was hard for him to live with anybody. I didn't realize that until recently. When he was working or thinking, he had a private pulse going constantly inside him. I don't know, your bloodstream beats differently."

Prince pulls the T-Bird into an alley behind a street of neat frame houses, stops behind a wooden one-car garage and rolls down the window. Relaxing against a tree is a man who looks like Cab Calloway. Dressed in a crisp white suit, collar and tie, a trim and smiling John Nelson adjusts his best cuff links and waves. "Happy birthday," says the son. "Thanks," says the father, laughing. Nelson says he's not even allowing himself a piece of cake on his birthday. "No, not this year," he says with a shake of the head. Pointing at his son, Nelson continues, "I'm trying to take off ten pounds I put on while visiting him in Los Angeles. He eats like I want to eat, but exercises, which I certainly don't."

Father then asks son if maybe he should drive himself to the pool game so he won't have to be hauled all the way back afterward. Prince says okay, and Nelson, chuckling, says to the stranger, "Hey, let me show you what I got for my birthday two years ago." He goes over to the garage and gives a tug on the door handle. Squeezed inside is a customized deep-purple BMW. On the rear seat is a copy of Prince's latest LP, *Around the World in a Day*. While the old man gingerly backs his car out, Prince smiles. "He never drives that thing. He's afraid it's going to get dented." Looking at his own white T-Bird, Prince goes on: "He's always been that way. My father gave me this a few years ago. He bought it new in 1966. There were only 22,000 miles on it when I got it."

An ignition turns. "Wait," calls Prince, remembering something. He grabs a tape off the T-Bird seat and yells to his father, "I got something for you to listen to. Lisa [Coleman] and Wendy [Melvoin] have been working on these in L.A." Prince throws the tape, which the two female members of his band have mixed, and his father catches it with one hand. Nelson nods okay and pulls his car behind his son's in the alley. Closely tailing Prince through North Minneapolis, he waves and smiles whenever we look back. It's impossible to believe that the gun-toting geezer in *Purple Rain* was modeled after John Nelson.

"That stuff about my dad was part of [director-cowriter] Al Magnoli's story," Prince explains. "We used parts of my past and present to make the story pop more, but it was a story. My dad wouldn't have nothing to do with guns. He never swore, still doesn't, and never drinks." Prince looks in his rearview mirror at the car tailing him. "He don't look sixty-nine, do he? He's so cool. He's got girlfriends, lots of 'em." Prince drives alongside two black kids walking their bikes. "Hey, Prince," says one casually. "Hey," says the driver with a nod, "how you doing?"

Passing by old neighbors watering their lawns and shooting hoops, the North Side's favorite son talks about his hometown. "I wouldn't move, just cuz I like it here so much. I can go out and not get jumped on. It feels good not to be hassled when I dance, which I do a lot. It's not a thing of everybody saying, 'Whoa, who's out with who here?' while photographers flash their bulbs in your face."

Nearing the turnoff that leads from Minneapolis to suburban Eden Prairie, Prince flips in another tape and peeks in the rearview mirror. John Nelson is still right behind. "It's real hard for my father to show emotion," says Prince, heading onto the highway. "He never says, 'I love you,' and when we hug or something, we bang our heads together like in some Charlie Chaplin movie. But a while ago, he was telling me how I always had to be careful. My father told me, 'If anything happens to you, I'm gone.' All I thought at first was that it was a real nice thing to say. But then I thought about it for a while and realized something. That was my father's way of saying 'I love you.'"

A few minutes later, Prince and his father pull in front of the Warehouse, a concrete barn in an Eden Prairie industrial park. Inside, the Family, a rock-funk band that Prince has been working with, is pounding out new songs and dance routines. The group is as tight as ace drummer Jellybean Johnson's pants. At the end of one hot number, Family members fall on their backs, twitching like fried eggs.

Prince and his father enter to hellos from the still-gyrating band. Prince goes over to a pool table by the soundboard, racks the balls and shimmies to the beat of the Family's next song. Taking everything in, John Nelson gives a professional nod to the band, his son's rack job and his own just-chalked cue. He hitches his shoulders, takes aim and breaks like Minnesota Fats. A few minutes later, the band is still playing and the father is still shooting. Prince, son to this father and father to this band, is smiling.

The night before, in the warehouse, Prince is about to break his three-year public silence. Wearing a jump suit, powder-blue boots and a little crucifix on a chain, he dances with the Family for a little while, plays guitar for a minute, sings lead for a second, then noodles four-handed keyboard with Susannah Melvoin, Wendy's identical-twin sister.

Seeing me at the door, Prince comes over. "Hi," he whispers, offering a hand, "want something to eat or drink?" On the table in front of the band are piles of fruit and a couple bags of Doritos. Six different kinds of tea sit on a shelf by the wall. No drugs, no booze, no coffee. Prince plays another lick or two and watches for a few more minutes, then waves goodbye to the band and heads for his car outside the concrete barn.

"I'm not used to this," mumbles Prince, staring straight ahead through the windshield of his parked car. "I really thought I'd never do interviews again." We drive for twenty minutes, talking about Minnesota's skies, air and cops. Gradually, his voice comes up, bringing with it inflections, hand gestures and laughs.

Soon after driving past a field that will house a state-of-the-art recording studio named Paisley Park, we pull down a quiet suburban street and up to the famous purple house. Prince waves to a lone, unarmed guard in front of a chain-link fence. The unremarkable split-level house, just a few yards back from the minimum security, is quiet. No fountains out front, no swimming pools in back, no black-faced icons of Yahweh or Lucifer. "We're here," says Prince, grinning. "Come on in."

One look inside tells the undramatic story. Yes, it seems the *National Enquirer*—whose Minneapolis Babylon exposé of Prince was excerpted in numerous other newspapers this spring—was exaggerating. No, the man does not live in an armed fortress with only a food taster and wall-to-wall, life-size murals of Marilyn Monroe to talk to. Indeed, if a real-estate agent led a tour through Prince's house, one would guess that the resident was, at most, a hip suburban surgeon who likes deep-pile carpeting.

"Hi," says Rande, from the kitchen, "you got a couple of messages." Prince thanks her and offers up some homemade chocolate-chip cookies. He takes a drink from a water cooler emblazoned with a Minnesota North Stars sticker and continues the tour. "This place," he says, "is not a prison. And the only things it's a shrine to are Jesus, love and peace."

Off the kitchen is a living room that holds nothing your aunt wouldn't have in her house. On the mantel are framed pictures of family and friends, including one of John Nelson playing a guitar. There's a color TV and VCR, a long coffee table supporting a dish of jellybeans, and a small silver unicorn by the mantel. Atop the large mahogany piano sits an oversize white Bible.

The only unusual thing in either of the two guest bedrooms is a two-foot statue of a smiling yellow gnome covered by a swarm of butterflies. One of the monarchs is flying out of a heart-shaped hole in the gnome's chest. "A friend gave that to me, and I put it in the living room," says Prince. "But some people said it scared them, so I took it out and put it in here."

Downstairs from the living room is a narrow little workroom with recording equipment and a table holding several notebooks. "Here's where I recorded all of *1999*," says Prince, "all right in this room." On a low table in the corner are three Grammys. "Wendy," says Prince, "has got the Academy Award."

The work space leads into the master bedroom. It's nice. And . . . normal. No torture devices or questionable appliances, not even a cigarette butt, beer tab or tea bag in sight. A four-poster bed above plush white carpeting, some framed pictures, one of Marilyn Monroe. A small lounging area off the bedroom provides a stereo, a lake-shore view and a comfortable place to stretch out on the floor and talk. And talk he did—his first interview in three years.

A few hours later, Prince is kneeling in front of the VCR, showing his "Raspberry Beret" video. He explains why he started the clip with a prolonged clearing of the throat. "I just did it to be sick, to do something no one else would do." He pauses and contemplates. "I turned on MTV to see the premiere of 'Raspberry Beret' and Mark Goodman was talking to the guy who discovered the backward message on 'Darling Nikki.' They were trying to figure out what the cough meant too, and it was sort of funny." He pauses again. "But I'm not getting down on him for trying. I like that. I've always had little hidden messages, and I always will."

He then plugs in a videocassette of "4 the Tears in Your Eyes," which he's just sent to the Live Aid folks for the big show. "I hope they like it," he said, shrugging his shoulders.

The phone rings, and Prince picks it up in the kitchen. "We'll be there in twenty minutes," he says, hanging up. Heading downstairs, Prince swivels his head and smiles. "Just gonna change clothes." He comes back a couple minutes later wearing another paisley jump suit, "the only kind of clothes I own." And the boots? "People say I'm wearing heels because I'm short," he says, laughing. "I wear heels because the women like 'em."

A few minutes later, driving toward the First Avenue club, Prince is talking about the fate of the most famous landmark in Minneapolis. "Before *Purple Rain*," he says, "all the kids who came to First Avenue knew us, and it was just like a big, fun fashion show. The kids would dress for themselves and just try to look really cool. Once you got your thing right, you'd stop looking at someone else. You'd be yourself, and you'd feel comfortable."

Then Hollywood arrived. "When the film first came out," Prince remembers, "a lot of tourists started coming. That was kind of weird, to be in the club and get a lot of 'Oh! There *he* is!' It felt a little strange. I'd be in there thinking, 'Wow, this sure is different than it used to be.'"

Now, however, the Gray Line Hip Tour swarm has slackened. According to Prince—who goes there twice a week to dance when he's not working on a big project—the old First Avenue feeling is coming back. "There were a lot of us hanging around the club in the old days," he says, "and the new army, so to speak, is getting ready to come back to Minneapolis. The Family's already here, Mazarati's back now too, and Sheila E. and her band will be coming soon. The club'll be the same thing that it was."

As we pull up in front of First Avenue, a Saturday-night crowd is milling around outside, combing their hair, smoking cigarettes, holding hands. They stare with more interest than awe as Prince gets out of the car. "You want to go to the (VIP) booth?" asks the bouncer. "Naah," says Prince. "I feel like dancing."

A few feet off the packed dance floor stands the Family, taking a night off from rehearsing. Prince joins the band and laughs, kisses, soul shakes. Prince and three other Family members wade through a floor of Teddy-and-Eleanor-Mondale-brand funkettes and start moving. Many of the kids Prince passes either don't see him or pretend they don't care. Most of the rest turn their heads slightly to see the man go by, then simply continue their own motions.

An hour later, he's on the road again, roaring out of downtown. Just as he's asked if there's anything in the world that he wants but doesn't have, two blondes driving daddy's Porsche speed past. "I don't," Prince says with a giggle, "have them."

He catches up to the girls, rolls down the window and throws a ping-pong ball that was on the floor at them. They turn their heads to see what kind of geek is heaving ping-pong balls at them on the highway at two in the morning. When they see who it is, mouths drop, hands wave, the horn blares. Prince rolls up his window, smiles silently and speeds by.

Off the main highway, Prince veers around the late-night stillness of Cedar Lake, right past the spot where Mary Tyler Moore gamboled during her TV show's credits. This town, he says, is his freedom. "The only time I feel like a prisoner," he continues, "is when I think too much and can't sleep from just having so many things on my mind. You know, stuff like, 'I could do this, I could do that. I could work with this band. When am I going to do this show or that show?' There's so many things. There's women. Do I have to eat? I wish I didn't have to eat."

A few minutes later, he drops me off at my house. Half a block ahead, he stops at a Lake Street red light. A left up Lake leads back to late-night Minneapolis; a right is the way home to the suburban purple house and solitude. Prince turns left, back toward the few still burning night lights of the city he's never left.

———————

The Interview

Why have you decided that now is the time to talk?

There have been a lot of things said about me, and a lot of them are wrong. There have been a lot of contradictions. I don't mind criticism, I just don't like lies. I feel I've been very honest in my work and my life, and it's hard to tolerate people telling such barefaced lies.

Do you read most of what's been written about you?

A little, not much. Sometimes someone will pass along a funny one. I just wrote a song called "Hello," which is going to be on the flip side of "Pop Life." It says at the end, "Life is cruel enough without cruel words." I get a lot of cruel words. A lot of people do.

I saw critics be so critical of Stevie Wonder when he made *Journey Through the Secret Life of Plants*. Stevie has done so many great songs, and for people to say, "You missed, don't do that, go back"—well, I would never say, "Stevie Wonder, you missed." [*Prince puts the Wonder album on the turntable, plays a cut, then puts on Miles Davis' new album.*] Or Miles. Critics are going to say, "Ah, Miles done went off." Why say that? Why even tell Miles he went off? You know, if you don't like it, don't talk about it. Go buy another record!

Not long ago I talked to George Clinton, a man who knows and has done so much for funk. George told me how much he liked *Around the World in a Day*. You know how much more his words meant than those from some mamma-jamma wearing glasses and an alligator shirt behind a typewriter?

Do you hate rock critics? Do you think they're afraid of you?

[*Laughs*] No, it's no big deal. Hey, I'm afraid of *them*! One time early in my career, I got into a fight with a New York writer, this real skinny cat, a real sidewinder. He said, "I'll tell you a secret, Prince. Writers write for other writers, and a lot of time it's more fun to be nasty." I just looked at him. But when I really thought about it and put myself in his shoes, I realized that's what he had to do. I could see his point. They can do whatever they want. And me, too. I can paint whatever picture I want with my albums. And I can try to instill that in every act I've ever worked with.

What picture were you painting with *Around the World in a Day*?

[*Laughs*] I've heard some people say that I'm not talking about anything on this record. And what a lot of other people get wrong about the record is that I'm not trying to be this great visionary wizard. Paisley Park is in everybody's heart. It's not just something that I have the keys to. I was trying to say something about looking inside oneself to find perfection.

Perfection is in everyone. Nobody's perfect, but they can be. We may never reach that, but it's better to strive than not.

Sounds religious.

As far as that goes, let me tell you a story about Wendy. We had to fly somewhere at the beginning of the tour, and Wendy is deathly afraid of flying. She got on the plane and really freaked. I was scared for her. I tried to calm her down with jokes, but it didn't work. I thought about it and said, "Do you believe in God?" She said yes. I said, "Do you trust him?" and she said she did. Then I asked, "So why are you afraid to fly?" She started laughing and said, "Okay, okay, okay." Flying still bothers her a bit, but she knows where it is and she doesn't get freaked.

It's just so nice to know that there is someone and someplace else. And if we're wrong, and I'm wrong, and there is nothing, then big deal! But the whole life I just spent, I at least had some reason to spend it.

When you talk about God, which God are you talking about? The Christian God? Jewish? Buddhist? Is there any God in particular you have in mind?

Yes, very much so. A while back, I had an experience that changed me and made me feel differently about how and what I wrote and how I acted toward people. I'm going to make a film about it—not the next one, but the one after that. I've wanted to make it for three years now. Don't get me wrong—I'm still as wild as I was. I'm just funneling it in a different direction. And now I analyze things so much that sometimes I can't shut off my brain and it hurts. That's what the movie will be about.

What was the experience that changed you?

I don't really want to get into it specifically. During the *Dirty Mind* period, I would go into fits of depression and get physically ill. I would have to call people to help get me out of it. I don't do that anymore.

What were you depressed about?

A lot had to do with the band's situation, the fact that I couldn't make people in the band understand how great we could all be together if we all played our part. A lot also had to do with being in love with someone and not getting any love back. And there was the fact that I didn't talk much with my father and sister. Anyway, a lot of things happened in this two-day period, but I don't want to get into it right now.

How'd you get over it?

That's what the movie's going to be about. Paisley Park is the only way I can say I got over it now. Paisley Park is the place one should find in oneself, where one can go when one is alone.

You say you've now found the place where you can go to be alone. Is it your house? Within the family you've built around you? With God?

It's a combination of things. I think when one discovers himself, he discovers God. Or maybe it's the other way around. I'm not sure. . . . It's hard to put into words. It's a feeling—someone knows when they get it. That's all I can really say.

Do you believe in heaven?

I think there is an afterworld. For some reason, I think it's going to be just like here, but that's part . . . I don't really like talking about this stuff. It's so personal.

Does it bother you when people say you're going back in time with *Around the World in a Day*?

No. What they say is that the Beatles are the influence. The influence wasn't the Beatles. They were great for what they did, but I don't know how that would hang today. The cover art came about because I thought people were tired of looking at *me*. Who wants another picture of him? I would only want so many pictures of my woman, then I would want the real thing. What would be a little more happening than just another picture [*laughs*] would be if there was some way I could materialize in people's cribs when they play the record.

How do you feel about people calling the record "psychedelic"?

I don't mind that, because that was the only period in recent history that delivered songs and colors. Led Zeppelin, for example, would make you feel differently on each song.

Does your fame affect your work?

A lot of people think it does, but it doesn't at all. I think the smartest thing I ever did was record *Around the World in a Day* right after I finished *Purple Rain*. I didn't wait to see what would happen with *Purple Rain*. That's why the two albums sound completely different. People think, "Oh, the new album isn't half as powerful as *Purple Rain* or *1999*." You know how easy it would have been to open *Around the World in a Day* with the guitar solo that's on the end of "Let's Go Crazy?" You know how easy it would have been to just put it in a different key? That would have shut everybody up who said the album wasn't half as powerful. I don't *want* to make an album like the earlier ones. Wouldn't it be cool to be able to put your albums back to back and not get bored, you dig? I don't know how many people can play all their albums back to back with each one going to different cities.

What do you think about the comparisons between you and Jimi Hendrix?

It's only because he's black. That's really the only thing we have in common. He plays different guitar than I do. If they really listened to my stuff, they'd hear more of a Santana influence than Jimi Hendrix. Hendrix played more blues; Santana played prettier. You can't compare people, you really can't, unless someone is blatantly trying to rip somebody off. And you really can't tell that unless you play the songs.

You've got to understand that there's only so much you can do on an electric guitar. I don't know what these people are thinking—they're usually non-guitar-playing mamma-jammas saying this kind of stuff. There are only so many sounds a guitar can make. Lord knows I've tried to make a guitar sound like something new to myself.

Are there any current groups you listen to a lot or learn from?

Naah. The last album I loved all the way through was [Joni Mitchell's] *The Hissing of Summer Lawns*. I respect people's success, but I don't like a lot of popular music. I never did. I like more of the things I heard when I was little. Today, people don't write songs; they're a lot of sounds, a lot of repetition. That happened when producers took over, and that's why there are no more [live] acts. There's no box office anymore. The producers took over, and now no one wants to see these bands.

People seem to think you live in an armed monastery that you've built in honor of yourself.

First off, I don't live in a prison with armed guards around me. The reason I have a guy outside is that after the movie, all kinds of people started coming over and hanging out. That wasn't so bad, but the neighbors got upset that people were driving by blasting their boxes or standing outside and singing. I happen to dig that. That's one reason I'm going to move to more land. There, if people want to come by, it will be fine. Sometimes it gets lonely here. To be perfectly honest, I wish more of my friends would come by.

Friends?

Musicians, people I know. A lot of the time they think I don't want to be bothered. When I told Susannah [Melvoin] that you were coming over, she said, "Is there something I can do? Do you want me to come by to make it seem like you have friends coming by?" I said no, that would be lying. And she just put her head down, because she knew she doesn't come by to see me as much as she wants to, or as much as she thinks I want her to. It was interesting. See, you did something good, and you didn't even know it!

Are you afraid to ask your friends to come by?

I'm kind of afraid. That's because sometimes everybody in the band comes over, and we have very long talks. They're few and far between, and I do a lot of the talking. Whenever we're done, one of them will come up to me and say, "Take care of yourself. You know I really love you." I think they love me so much, and I love them so much, that if they came over all the time I wouldn't be able to be to them what I am, and they wouldn't be able to do for me what they do. I think we all need our individual spaces, and when we come together with what we've concocted in our heads, it's cool.

Does it bother you that strangers make pilgrimages to your house?

No, not at all. But there's a time and a place for everything. A lot of people have the idea that I'm a wild sexual person. It can be two o'clock in the afternoon, and someone will make a really strange request from the call box outside. One girl just kept pressing the buzzer. She kept pressing it, and then she started crying. I had no idea why. I thought she might have fallen down. I started talking to her, and she just kept saying, "I can't believe it's you." I said, "Big deal. I'm no special person. I'm no different than anyone." She said, "Will you come out?" I said, "Nope, I don't have much on." And she said, "That's okay."

I've lectured quite a few people out there. I'll say, "Think about what you're saying. How would you react if you were me?" I ask that question a lot. "How would you react if you were me?" They say, "Okay, okay."

It's not just people outside your door who think you're a wild sexual person.

To some degree I am, but not twenty-four hours a day. Nobody can be what they are twenty-four hours a day, no matter what that is. You have to eat, you have to sleep, you have to think, and you have to work. I work a lot, and there's not too much time for anything else when I'm doing that.

Does it make you angry when people dig into your background, when they want to know about your sexuality and things like that?

Everyone thinks I have a really mean temper and I don't like people to do this or do that. I have a sense of humor. I thought that the *Saturday Night Live* skit with Billy Crystal as me was the funniest thing I ever saw. His imitation of me was hysterical! He was singing, "I am the world, I am the children!" Then Bruce Springsteen came to the mike, and the boys would push him away. It was hilarious. We put it on when we want to laugh. It was great. Of course, that's not what it is.

And I thought the Prince Spaghetti commercial was the cutest thing in the world. My lawyers and management are the ones who felt it should be stopped. I didn't even see the commercial until after someone had tried to have it stopped. A lot of things get done without my knowledge because I'm in Minneapolis and they're where they are.

It's a good and a bad thing that I live here. It's bad in the sense that I can't be a primo "rock star" and do everything absolutely right. I can't go to the parties and benefits, be at all the awards shows, get this and get that. But I like it here. It's really mellow.

How do feel when you go to New York or L.A. and see the life you could be leading?

L.A. is a good place to work. And I liked New York more when I wasn't known, when I wasn't bothered when I went out. You'd be surprised. There are guys who will literally chase you through a discotheque! I don't mind my picture being taken if it's done in a proper fashion. It's very easy to say, "Prince, may I take your picture?" I don't know why people can't be more humane about a lot of the things they do. Now when I'm visiting, I like to sneak around and try stuff. I like to sneak to people's gigs and see if I can get away without getting my picture taken. That's fun. That's like cops and robbers.

You've taken a lot of heat for your bodyguards, especially the incident in Los Angeles in which your bodyguard Chick Huntsberry reportedly beat up a reporter.

A lot of times I've been accused of sicking bodyguards on people. You know what happened in L.A.? My man the photographer tried to get in the car! I don't have any problem with somebody I *know* trying to get in the car with me and my woman in it. But someone like that? Just to get a picture?

Why isn't Chick working for you anymore?

Chick has more pride than anybody I know. I think that after the L.A. incident, he feared for his job. So if I said something, he'd say, "What are you jumping on *me* for? What's wrong? Why all of sudden are you changing?" And I'd say, "I'm not changing." Finally, he just said, "I'm tired. I've had enough." I said fine, and he went home. I waited a few weeks and called him. I told him that his job was still there and that I was alone. So he said that he'd see me when I was in New York. He didn't show up. I miss him.

Is it true that Chick is still on the payroll?

Yes.

What about the exposé he wrote about you in the *National Enquirer*?

I never believe anything in the *Enquirer*. I remember reading stories when I was ten years old, saying, "I was fucked by a flying saucer, and here's my baby to prove it." I think they just took everything he said and blew it up. It makes for a better story. They're just doing their thing. Right on for them. The only thing that bothers me is when my fans think I live in a prison. This is not a prison.

You came in for double heat over the L.A. incident because it happened on the night of the "We Are the World" recording. In retrospect, do you wish you would have shown up?

No, I think I did my part in giving my song [to the album]. I hope I did my part. I think I did the best thing I could do.

You've done food-drive concerts for poor people in various cities, given free concerts for handicapped kids and donated lots of money to the Marva Collins inner-city school in Chicago. Didn't you want to stand up after you were attacked for "We Are the World" and say, "Hey, I do my part."

Nah, I was never rich, so I have very little regard for money now. I only have respect for it inasmuch as it can feed somebody. I can give a lot of things away, a lot of presents and money. Money is best spent on somebody who needs it. That's all I'm going to say. I don't like to make a big deal about the things I do that way.

People think that you're a dictator in the studio, that you want to control everything. In L.A., however, I saw Wendy and Lisa mixing singles while you were in Paris. How do you feel about your reputation?

My first album I did completely alone. On the second I used André [Cymone], my bass player, on "Why You Wanna Treat Me So Bad?" He sang a small harmony part that you really couldn't hear. There was a typo on the record, and André didn't get any credit. That's how the whole thing started. I tried to explain that to him, but when you're on the way up, there's no explaining too much of anything. People will think what they want to.

The reason I don't use musicians a lot of the time had to do with the hours that I worked. I swear to God it's not out of boldness when I say this, but there's not a person around who can stay awake as long as I can. Music is what keeps me awake. There will be times when I've been working in the studio for twenty hours and I'll be falling asleep in the chair, but I'll still be able to tell the engineer what cut I want to make. I use engineers in shifts a lot of the time because when I start something, I like to go all the way through. There are very few musicians who will stay awake that long.

Do you feel others recognize how hard you work?

Well, no. A lot of my peers make remarks about us doing silly things onstage and on records. Morris [Day, former lead singer of the Time] was criticized a lot for that.

What kind of silliness, exactly?

Everything—the music, the dances, the lyrics. What they fail to realize is that is exactly what we want to do. It's not silliness, it's *sickness*. Sickness is just slang for doing things somebody else wouldn't do. If we are down on the floor doing a step, that's something somebody else wouldn't do. That's what I'm looking for all the time. We don't look for whether something's cool or not, that's not what time it is. It's not just wanting to be out. It's just if I do something that I think belongs to someone else or sounds like someone else, I do something else.

Why did Morris say such negative things about you after he left the band?

People who leave usually do so out of a need to express something they can't do here. It's really that simple. Morris, for example, always wanted to be a solo act, period. But when you're broke and selling shoes someplace, you don't think about asking such a thing. Now, I think Morris is trying to create his own identity. One of the ways of doing that is trying to pretend that you don't have a past.

Jesse [Johnson, former guitarist for the Time] is the only one who went away who told what happened, what really went down with the band. He said there was friction, because he was in a situation that didn't quite suit him. Jesse wanted to be in front all the time. And I just don't think God puts everybody in that particular bag. And sometimes I was blunt enough to say that to people: "I don't think you should be the frontman. I think *Morris* should."

Wendy, for example, says, "I don't want that. I want to be right where I am. I can be strongest to this band right where I am." I personally love this band more than any other group I've ever played with for that reason. Everybody knows what they have to do. I know there's something *I* have to do.

What sound do you get from different members of the Revolution?

Bobby Z was the first one to join. He's my best friend. Though he's not such a spectacular drummer, he watches me like no other drummer would. Sometimes, a real great drummer, like Morris, will be more concerned with the lick he is doing as opposed to how I am going to break it down.

Mark Brown's just the best bass player I know, period. I wouldn't have anybody else. If he didn't play with me, I'd eliminate bass from my music. Same goes for Matt [Fink, the keyboard player]. He's more or less a technician. He can read and write like a whiz, and is one of the fastest in the world. And Wendy makes me seem all right in the eyes of people watching.

How so?

She keeps a smile on her face. When I sneer, she smiles. It's not premeditated, she just does it. It's a good contrast. Lisa is like my sister. She'll play what the average person won't. She'll press two notes with one finger so the chord is a lot larger, things like that. She's more abstract. She's into Joni Mitchell, too.

What about the other bands? Apollonia, Vanity, Mazarati, the Family? What are you trying to express through them?

A lot has to do with them. They come to me with an idea, and I try to bring that forth. I don't give them anything. I don't say, "Okay, you're going to do this, and you're going to do that." I mean, it was Morris' idea to be as sick as he was. That was his personality. We both like Don King and get a lot of stuff off him.

Why?

Because he's outrageous and thinks everything's so exciting—even when it isn't.

People think you control those bands, that it's similar to Rick James' relationship with the Mary Jane Girls. A lot of people think he's turning all the knobs.

I don't know their situation. But you look at Sheila E. performing, and you can just tell she's holding her own. The same goes for the Family. You and I were playing Ping-Pong, and they were doing just fine.

After all these years, does the music give you as much of a rush as it used to?

It increases more and more. One of my friends worries that I'll short-circuit. We always say I'll make the final fade on a song one time and . . . [*Laughs, dropping his head in a dead slump*]. It just gets more and more interesting every day. More than anything else, I try not to repeat myself. It's the hardest thing in the world to do—there's only so many notes one human being can muster. I write a lot more than people think I do, and I try not to copy that.

I think that's the problem with the music industry today. When a person does get a hit, they try to do it again the same way. I don't think I've ever done that. I write all the time and cut all the time. I want to show you the archives, where all my old stuff is. There's tons of music I've recorded there. I have the follow-up album to *1999*. I could put it all together and play it for you, and you would go "Yeah!" And I could put it out, and it would probably sell what *1999* did. But I always try to do something different and conquer new ground.

In people's minds, it all boils down to "Is Prince getting too big for his breeches?" I wish people would understand that I always thought I was bad. I wouldn't have got into the business if I didn't think I was bad.

RADIO INTERVIEW

Electrifying Mojo | June 7, 1986 | WHYT 96.3 Detroit

Prince and the Revolution released the *Parade* LP in March 1986, in anticipation of the July release of the Prince-directed *Under the Cherry Moon* film. The group played a series of Hit N Run dates across the United States before a late summer European and Japanese tour that spelled the end of the Revolution.

This offhanded interview with Detroit radio legend Electrifying Mojo took place by phone on Prince's twenty-eighth birthday, after the second of two Detroit Hit N Run shows. It's Prince's first live radio appearance, enticing as an informal discussion rather than a more mannered interview Q&A. If there's a theme to this chat, it's Prince's creative process: making a song, making a movie, pulling together the songs for *Around the World in a Day*.

This would be Prince's last interview for four years and his most extensive audiovisual one-on-one until his *Emancipation* sit-down with Oprah Winfrey a decade later. —Ed.

Mojo: We interrupt the airwaves of Earth to bring you one of its brightest stars. This is the one-man hit machine from Minnesota. Ladies and gentlemen, Prince. Hello, Prince?

Prince: Hello, Detroit.

Mojo: How are you?

Prince: All right. How are you?

Mojo: Well, Prince, I heard nothing but magic flowing down from the concert. How was it?

Prince: Mmmm, a lot of fun. Should've been there.

Mojo: Look, I was there in spirit. I wanted to be here for one reason. I wanted to be here so that the moment that the concert was over, I wanted to flood the airwaves with Prince.

Prince: Well, you know what, I was drivin' home from the gig, wipin' sweat off my brow, and I heard "Automatic." And we just got through playin' it, and we don't normally play that one, but it went over pretty good, and I think it's 'cause of you and what you've done for us. My thanks. It's a good feeling. I just want to tell all my little motor babies that I'm just happy to be here and it's just a fun way to spend my birthday, for sure.

Mojo: Happy birthday to you.

Prince: Thank you.

Mojo: Prince, you've been the entertainer that has insisted on doing things one way: your way.

Prince: [*Laughs.*] Well, you know, it's like, I worked a long time under a lot of different people, and most of the time I was doing it their way. And, I mean, that was cool, but, you know, I figured if I worked hard enough and kept my head straight, one day I'd get to do it on my own. And that's what happened. So, I feel like I don't try to hurt nobody, and I, like I say, keep my head on straight. My way usually is the best way.

Mojo: Growing up in "Minnie-wood," as it has been now called, simply because that is the hot point on this planet right now.

Prince: Well, it's been called a lot of things, but it's always Uptown to me.

Mojo: Uptown?

Prince: Yes.

Mojo: What was it like growing up Uptown?

Prince: Ah, pretty different. Kind of sad, to be exact. [*Laughs.*] I mean, the radio was dead. The discos was dead. The ladies was kind of dead. Well, I felt like, you know, if we wanted to make some noise and I wanted to turn anything out, I was going to have to get something together. Which is what we did, and we put together a few bands and turned it into Uptown. That consisted of a lot of bike-riding nude, but, you know, it worked. We have fun. So that's why I wanted to come here on my birthday 'cause I wanted to give them a little taste of where we live and get a little taste of where y'all live. To me this is like my second home. If I could spend the night in somebody's crib, you know, I would. 'Cause this hotel, they're really nice to us, but this bed is hard.

Mojo: Well, look here, all our phones right now are just, have, they've gone into cardiac arrest.

Prince: Well.

Mojo: So I'm gonna hook you up.

Prince: OK. [*Laughs.*] Why not?

Mojo: I'm gonna hook you up with somebody. I'm gonna call you back.

Prince: OK.

Mojo: But look, before we leave, let's talk a little bit more about . . . you've made fantastic albums and you've made fantastic movies, and you're making another movie right now.

Prince: Yeah.

Mojo: What's the difference between making a hot movie and making a hot album?

Prince: There is no difference. There have been people that have tried to tell me contrary to that. But, like you said before, and like I said before, I strive for perfection, and sometimes I'm a little bullheaded in my ways. Hopefully, people understand that, and there's just a lot on my mind and I try to stay focused on one particular thing, and I try not to hurt nobody in the process. The movie, the movie is a little bit more complex, but to me, it's just a larger version of an album. There are scenes, and there are songs, and they all go together to make this painting. And I'm the painter. And y'all's the paintees. You know, hopefully it's something that you can get into. Jerome Benton stars in this new film with me, and he's on his way to becoming very, very big. I'm real proud of him. He takes direction well, and he gives direction well. And I expect a lot of big things from him.

Mojo: Speaking of Jerome Benton and other people who've flown under the wings of Prince, and also speaking of Detroit's own Billy Sparks, a person that you, like, took from Detroit, put him in your first movie, and you've always maintained contact with people you've always been in contact with.

Prince: Oh, yeah, without a doubt. I mean, there's people that have flown the coop, so to speak, and gone off to do their own thing, which is great, and I stand behind them and support, support 'em in whatever they do. But, contrary to rumors, we're all real tight still, and I have a strange feeling we're all gonna be together again one day. We'll have to see.

Mojo: Do you think there's a possibility that after this movie has been released that, that that is going to take place—well, I just heard rumors through the grapevine that there's a possibility that the Time was going to record again, a possibility that . . .

Prince: Well, Mojo, anything's possible.

Mojo: Yeah.

Prince: God willing and hopefully everybody's head will be in the right place, I'd like to see all that happen. They were, to be perfectly honest, the only band I was afraid of. And they were turning into, like, Godzilla. And certain things happened, different waves flowed, different winds blew, and everybody fell apart. But I still love all those guys and hope they get back together 'cause I want some competition, you know?

Mojo: [*Laughing.*] Prince, speaking of the movie, *Under the Cherry Moon*, can you tell us a little about that?

Prince: God, I hate to blow the surprise and all, you know.

Mojo: You know, without blowing it, we know it's gonna be in black and white.

Prince: Yeah, it's gonna be in black and white.

Mojo: And we know it's gonna be quote-unquote helluva.

Prince: Yeah, it's gonna be that, it's gonna be that. All I can tell you is that you'll have a good time. I'm hoping that everyone understands where I was trying to go with it. It is like an album for me, and I put my heart and soul into it, and I worked very long and very hard. Jerome did the same. And there's a message behind it all, and I'm hoping that people think about it when they leave. You know, that's the main thing. It's a lot of fun, but there's something to think about when it's over. You know, there's a reason for everything.

Mojo: Let's talk about the album *Around the World in a Day*, which I think was one of the greatest albums.

Prince: My favorite.

Mojo: It's absolutely my favorite without question. Tunes like "Around the World in a Day," "Paisley Park." What type of mood were you in when you recorded that album?

Prince: Mmm, I sort of had a F you attitude, meaning that I was making something for myself and my fans. And the people who supported me through the years, I wanted to give them something and it was like my little letter, and those people are the ones that wrote me back and told me that they felt what I was feeling, you know. Record sales and things like that, it really doesn't matter, you know. It keeps the roof over your head, and it keeps money and all in these folks' pockets that I got hangin' around here, you know, but it basically stems from the music. And I'm just hopin' that people understand that, that, you know, money's one thing, but soul is another, and that's all we're really trying to do, you know. I don't know, it's, I wouldn't mind if I just went broke, you know, 'cause as long as I could play this type of thing and come here. You know, I mean there were a lot of people there tonight, and they turned the lights on, and I looked up, and, you know, it bring tears to your eyes because, it's just, you can feel the love in the room, you know. And that means more than money, you know. I could just, I go on for hours, 'cause I don't know, I just have fun and I'm thankful to be alive, you know?

Mojo: What's a day like in the life of Prince?

Prince: Work. I work a lot. I'm trying to get a lot of things done very quickly so that I can stop working for a while. Everyone's afraid I'm gonna die. [*Laughs.*]

Mojo: You say you are afraid?

Prince: No, *I'm* not afraid. *Everyone else* is afraid. They think I work too much. I'm not afraid of anything.

Mojo: It's been said that you work, when you're working—you work when you're on the road, you carry a studio around with you, you get up in the middle of the night, you get an idea for a tune, and you get up and go do it—there's just no such thing as Prince being off from work. I mean, some people have called you the workaholic, ever-moving, one-man storm. Is that true?

Prince: I don't know. The thing is, is that when you're called, you're called, you know. And I hear things in my sleep. I walk around and I go to the bathroom and try to brush my teeth, and all of a sudden the toothbrush'll start vibrating. That's a groove, you know. And you got to go with that. That means drop the toothbrush and get down to the studio or get to a bass guitar quick, you know. And I don't know, my best things just come out like that. To me, making a song is like a new girl walking in the room. You know, you never know what's gonna happen till all the things come together, and there she stands, and she says, "Hi," you know, and "You want to take a bite of this orange?" You bite it and it's cool, and I send it to you, you know?

Mojo: I know.

Prince: Mojo.

Mojo: I know.

Prince: Dig up.

Mojo: Look here, one question.

Prince: Yes?

Mojo: What's your favorite instrument?

Prince: Mmmm . . . it's dirty.

Mojo: You play 'em all. It's dirty? [*Laughter.*]

Prince: No, listen. I don't know, it depends on the song, it depends on the color. They all sound differently. It's very strange. I tried to be original in my work, and a lot of sounds have been used now and I'm looking for new instruments and new sounds and new rhythms. I got a lot of surprises. I don't want to give them all away.

Mojo: Look, you've done everything. I mean—

Prince: Not yet.

Mojo: You've done hard rock. You've done some of the most sensuous ballads.

Prince: No, we just scratched the surface with all that stuff. I mean, there's so many sounds. It's limitless.

Mojo: Some people say you probably have in your secret vault, in the Prince music vault, about five hundred tunes that you've done that you haven't even considered using yet. That you could put out an album for the next twenty years, two albums a year.

Prince: No, not that many. Three hundred and twenty, to be exact.

Mojo: Oh, really?

Prince: There are not five hundred.

Mojo: Three hundred and twenty songs?

Prince: Yeah.

Mojo: That have never been released?

Prince: Mm-hmm.

Mojo: And it's been rumored that they all sound different. That's why probably each album that you release is just a little bit different.

Prince: Yeah. They don't *all* sound different. There's a couple of times I copied myself.

Mojo: It's all right to copy yourself.

Prince: You think you hit on something right, you try to do it again, you know. [*Laughs.*] So, I don't know. No, I try not to do that too much. If I do that, there's usually someone around, Wendy or Lisa or someone, that'll say, "Hey, man, I've heard that. Put it away," and it goes away. And we don't hear that song for a while. Mojo?

Mojo: Yeah.

Prince: Guess what?

Mojo: What is that?

Prince: We're all gonna go see *Purple Rain* tonight.

Mojo: You are?

Prince: Yep.

Mojo: Look, you know, I've seen it twelve times . . .

Prince: I've seen it too many times, but I want to watch it again.

Mojo: I've seen it twelve times, and I'll go watch it tonight. I tell you what, I'm gonna ask everybody out there to go watch *Purple Rain*. But what time will you be watching it? In about fifteen or twenty minutes, maybe?

Prince: No, no, about three minutes.

Mojo: About three minutes?

Prince: Knocking on my door now.

Mojo: OK. Everybody's getting ready to go and turn their VCRs on right now to *Purple Rain*.

Prince: I'll tell you what I'm gonna do.

Mojo: What's that?

Prince: I'll call back tomorrow and leave a little message at about 4:30, and this one is just for all the purple people, and I think they'll understand.

Mojo: You say call you back tomorrow?

Prince: I'll call you.

Mojo: You're gonna call me?

Prince: I got your number.

Mojo: You got the number?

Prince: Yep?

Mojo: 4:30?

Prince: Mm-hmm.

Mojo: All right, Prince. It's been one big, it's been one big pleasure. I mean, like, you know, words cannot describe, you know, this moment. And I don't think words can describe how Detroit feels about Prince. So, in closing, whatever you want to say to Detroit, the airwaves are yours.

Prince: [*Gives Detroit 5 kisses.*] Kiss.

[*Revolution guitarist Wendy Melvoin called the next day with the message "God loves you." —Ed.*]

PRINCE INVITES BLACK BEAT TO PAISLEY PARK!

Steven Ivory | January 1992 | *Black Beat*

After his June 1986 radio chat with Electrifying Mojo, Prince went five years between interviews with the exception of a 1990 reunion with Neal Karlen in *Rolling Stone*. During this time he hit the critical apex of his career—1987's *Sign o' the Times*—but his commercial appeal eventually leveled out to pre-*Controversy* levels. By 1990's disappointing *Graffiti Bridge* LP and film projects, he also found himself on the wrong end of rap's commercial emergence, looking up the US charts at the likes of lightweights MC Hammer and Vanilla Ice.

Part of the reason for lagging domestic record sales was Prince's reluctance to support his records through consistent touring. In an eight-year span from 1985 to 1993, he launched only one US tour, in 1988, in support of *Lovesexy*. Conversely, he played five major tours in Europe and Japan/Australia during this time. There were complaints, even within his band, that he was turning his back on American audiences, particularly his Black fans.

Issues adjacent to this latter concern surface here in this early 1992 article.

In the run-up to the October 1991 release of the don't-call-it-a-comeback comeback LP *Diamonds and Pearls*, Prince began speaking to the press again, offering up a handful of publicity-generating interviews in late summer 1991. But, as writer Steven Ivory points out here, none of these were publications that catered to "the brother in the 'hood," Prince's early fanbase. That, in part, is why Ivory initially declined this interview opportunity.

Obviously, Ivory took up the offer, which was extended because Prince was familiar with his writing. Ivory explained the pros and cons of Prince's familiarity and offered a few other thoughts about Prince in a 2021 e-mail exchange:

Editor: Prince says your writing gives a "strange slant" on him. Can you give some background on that?

Steven Ivory: Prince's "strange slant" comment was in reference to whatever I wrote about his music that he deemed unfair or an attack. And like many artists, Prince treated *any* objective assessment of his work that wasn't a straight-up gush fest to be an attack.

By the time I met Prince for this interview, I'd been writing about him since the beginning of his recording career at Warner Brothers. I was one of the first writers to review *For You*, his 1978 debut Warner album, which I dug, for a national publication (the long defunct *Soul Newspaper*). After that, he seemed to keep an eye on whatever I wrote about him.

If the acclaim wasn't absolute—for example, if I wrote that I loved a certain song of his, and wished it were longer—the latter part of that statement is all Prince would remember. And one way or another, it would get back to me.

I'd run into a band member or someone from his organization and they'd joke about the risk of losing their gig by associating with me. Or, whenever Prince played L.A., I'd call Warner Brothers, request tickets and press passes, and the label's publicist would gibe, "Well, enjoy the show, but stay out of his sight, because he specifically mentioned not wanting you there."

Editor: What feedback did you receive on the piece, either from readers or members of the press?

Ivory: The press didn't pay much attention to it. By 1991, when *Diamonds and Pearls* was released, Prince had ceased to be "mysterious" to the press. They were still interested, but periodicals no longer rushed to reprint or quote a new Prince article where he was actually interviewed. The readers loved the article, though. We received a lot of letters saying they'd never seen Prince like that.

Editor: Would you like to add anything else?

Ivory: As a longtime fan, I miss Prince immensely. While I wasn't exactly blown away by his creative output in the years prior to his passing—experiencing a couple of decades of Prince at his peak powers will do that—during a simply brilliant career, the man set a ridiculously high standard for the complete, self-contained artist.

Prince didn't just do *some* writing, play *some* piano and guitar, and wasn't merely an "adequate" vocalist who "dabbled" in record production and entertained and led a band. He was masterful at each of those occupations, not to mention being one of rock's most gifted guitarists.

And he was all these things on a level of creativity and ingenuity that modern pop stardom no longer requires. For that reason, it will be a long time before the world sees another Prince, if ever.

All the critics love u. Even if u don't always love them back. —Ed.

The invitation came through a publicist, which was fairly odd in itself, considering that the only *real* need Prince ever had for one was to say, in various ways, the word no.

Nevertheless, here one was on the phone from New York, inviting me to Paisley Park, Prince's corporate Disneyland in Minneapolis. The idea was that I'd fly into town, watch Prince rehearse for his fall U.S. tour—designed to promote his *Diamonds And Pearls* LP—and interview members of his band, the New Power Generation. And maybe, just maybe, Prince, in a fit of infinite generosity, would say hello. My answer was as peculiar as the proposition itself: no.

It wasn't like I wasn't interested. Since his debut in 1978 with his *For You* album, I'd written volumes on Prince for various publications. Heck, in 1984, the year of his triumphant *Purple Rain*, I wrote a paperback book on the man. It was just that, for most of his career, Prince has been manipulatively indifferent with the press, particularly with the Black press. The brother in the 'hood were buying Prince records long before white audiences even knew who he was, or cared, for that matter (Detroit has been a big town for Prince since his days of bikinis and knee-high boots, and ain't nothin' *but* some brothers there), yet The Kid has made a habit of largely ignoring publications these people read. The Black press never had a problem with him not doing interviews; we had a problem with him telling us no and then seeing his mug on the cover of *Rolling Stone* under the heading, "Prince Talks." It was as if the Black press didn't matter. According to Prince's camp, the consensus was that the musician didn't think Black journalists "got it"—that we didn't understand the music or the vibe. Fact is, perhaps we got too much. For instance, ain't no Black music critic worth his word processor going for that stuff about Prince being from a mixed family—the kind of muck white writers gobbled up whole; we know Black folks come in all shades.

Besides, I thought, why should I fly to Minneapolis and hope that Prince graces me with a nod when I could shoot the breeze attitude-free with someone like Eddie LeVert, Luther Vandross or the Jacksons (most of 'em, anyway)? I declined.

What ultimately turned me around was the mere idea of taking in yet another Prince performance. I never tire of watching him do his thing onstage. I figured that spectacle alone was worth the three-hour flight from L.A. to Minneapolis, whether Prince spoke or not. I accepted the invitation.

Considering that The New Power Generation is Prince's Blackest band since he headed up garage bands in Minneapolis with Andre Cymone, *Diamonds And Pearls* is a subtle album. There isn't much rock and roll, and aside from the rhythm rituals "Jughead," "Gett Off" and "Push," there isn't a lot of all-out funk, either. There is, however, an abundance of melodic material, all of it held together with juicy musical undercurrents. There's the folky "Walk Don't Walk," a song about doing things your way as opposed to what an unfair society dictates. There's "Money Don't Matter 2 Night" and "Strollin'," both so easy-going that they'd sound quite normal coming out of the radio sandwiched between songs of Anita Baker and Luther Vandross, while songs like the power pop of "Cream" and the majestic title track both adequately demonstrate why Prince remains one of the most inventive, musically agile artists in pop music.

I walked into Minneapolis' Hotel Sofitel and ran into a publicist for the musician who went right to work. "Prince wants to meet you," he said, as if I were the inside man in a spy ring. "But he's in the middle of rehearsals as we speak, so we'll have to leave right now."

In the cab on the way to Paisley Park, the PR man took a look at my tape recorder and told me I could have left it at the hotel; Prince wouldn't be speaking into it, and besides, this wouldn't be an interview, anyway, but at best a chat. I was told not to pry. "Just go with the flow," he advised. *Gee*, Guy—mind if I breathe?

When you walk into Paisley Park you feel as if you've entered Oz. There are offices, but execs are dressed casually. In the wardrobe department, a group hovered over designs and fabric. There are studios—MC Hammer was in one of them, putting the finishing touches on his new album—and on the dark soundstage with the PRIVATE SESSION sign on the door is Prince and the New Power Generation.

I'm seated not more than 15 feet from the stage, yet Prince, running through some random guitar riffs during rehearsal down time, doesn't look my way once. Finally, he takes off his guitar, jumps off the stage and starts striding my way. He's smiling. The publicist tries to make an introduction, but Prince interrupts him. "Oh I know this guy," he says, extending a firm handshake. "I read your stuff, man."

The first thing you notice about Prince is how good he smells. Really. He walks around, shrouded in a fragrance that is tantalizing and exotic. Didn't say familiar. Let's just say it wasn't Brut. Much has been made about his diminutive size, but in person Prince's presence is imposing. The guy oozes charisma. It was two in the afternoon, yet Prince is resplendent in his idea of jeans and sneakers: form-fitting fuchsia-colored pants, matching boots and a silk shirt in his color of the moment, canary yellow.

He turned to a visiting Warner Brothers record executive and said, "Did you tell him what I told you?" The exec looked sheepishly puzzled, as if he was about to be reprimanded. "Did you tell him I'm not the strange guy he thinks I am?" Prince laughed. The exec laughed. From there, Prince proceeded to be the perfect, albeit somewhat distant host. He joked about the sound ("If it's too loud for you, we can turn it down"). When I told him I'd originally thought his trademark custom guitar was built more for looks than sound, he logged the comment away in his head. When he picked up the instrument to take to the stage, he looked at me and teased, "It looks good—it's a shame it don't sound like nothin'."

Rehearsal continued on schedule, with Prince and his band ripping through new songs like "Daddy Pop" and old favorites like "Let's Work," and a rendition of "Nothing Compares 2 U," his composition made famous by Sinead O'Connor. What's remarkable is Prince's driving sense of commitment to his work. He's jammed "Purple Rain" more times than even I have cared to hear it, yet in rehearsal he serviced it as if it were a brand new song. It was also interesting to see that all those seemingly "spontaneous" moments in any Prince performance are anything but;

virtually every little onstage gesture, his playing to the audience—it's all rehearsed to the tee. Another sign of a true showman.

After running through his set for about an hour complete with lighting and smoke, the band adjourned and toweled down while making small talk. Prince has disappeared. An interview was out of the question after all, I told the publicist. "Hey, I was surprised," he countered. "You got more time with him than most people do." I was scheduled to leave for L.A. in the morning; the PR man said that after dinner we could spend some hang time downtown at Glam Slam, Prince's club. The music would be good, he said; "Wednesday is funk night at the club. Prince might even be there."

He was. He and the Warners exec sat upstairs under the watchful eye of a bodyguard in the VIP area overlooking the crowded dance floor below. Prince gauged the reaction to the then-unreleased steamy video for "Violet The Organ Grinder," which played on video monitors throughout the club. They loved it, of course. I hadn't heard the track before either; I went over and asked Prince what it was. "None of your business," he replied. He chased the line with a smile, but there was no denying the edge on it.

"You can have a copy of it, if you don't write something crazy about it." This was the Prince I was ready for at the rehearsal, but got Sir Lancelot instead. *This* Prince, however, obviously had some points to make. The Warner exec got visibly nervous all over again, poor guy.

"Let me ask you something?" Prince continued. "Why is it your stuff always has a strange slant on it when it comes to me?"

"That's not true," I replied, surprised that this guy was even paying attention to what is written about him.

"Oh yeah, man. Your stuff seems to have a strange vibe on it when it comes to me."

I told him I was one of his biggest fans, though I admitted that my biggest crime was in periodically writing that he should get back to the stuff he built a foundation on, like his landmark *1999* album. This incensed him.

"That's why I stay here in Minneapolis and do my work, and block out you critics. Let me tell you something: *1999* amounts to me being in the third grade musically. That's where I was then, and I had to grow musically from where I was before it to make it. I had to push aside *1999* to get where I am *now*. It's called growth. You wanna hear stuff like *1999* again, then listen to *1999*. I'm someplace else now."

The conversation limped uncomfortably on about music, but it was clear that Prince had heard enough. He became indifferent, asked why I wasn't out on the dance floor, and then excused himself to sit alone, a table away. I'd apparently worn out my welcome.

Nevertheless, I didn't really realize what a showman Prince was until I met him. Forget the stage; I'm talking image-building. The guy spent years orchestrating this aura of mystery and drama, when in reality he's just a cat trying to do his thing. Perhaps he doesn't grant interviews because he feels his music alone exposes him far more than anyone should have to endure. If what *I* considered my personal growth as an artist were constantly slammed by people who didn't always understand it, maybe *I'd* be a bit gun-shy, too. I decided I liked this guy.

In any case, before heading back to the hotel, I went over to Prince and thanked him for having me down. He didn't have to do it, I told him, and I appreciated the hospitality. I then reminded him of the hypnosis-inducing vamp he found earlier in the rehearsal during "Gett Off" and how that moment alone was worth the price of admission. He seemed pleased.

"Man," he said, easing a smile, "that's what I'm down here doing every day. For me, that's what it's all about."

I can believe it.

NEW GOLD DREAM

Adam Mattera | March 11, 1995 | *Echoes*

However quirky Prince interviews and articles reporting Prince interviews were during the first fifteen years of his career, they hit a whole new level of idiosyncrasy after his June 7, 1993, birthday announcement that he was changing his name to an unpronounceable glyph. In the case of this interview, not only could the reporter not address The Artist Formerly Known as Prince directly, it was unclear if he would even entertain questions. On top of that, this interview was for a European tour on which The Artist was not performing Prince hits (no "Kiss," "Purple Rain," "1999," etc.) and was promoting an album that will "never" come out, *The Gold Experience*.

The circumstances leading to Prince's name change are well documented throughout this volume and elsewhere, so there is no need to repeat them here. Instead, a 2021 correspondence with author Mattera sheds light on the process of meeting Prince in 1995:

Editor: How were you in a position to get the interview?

Adam Mattera: In 1995, I was working as a staff writer at UK Black music weekly *Echoes* (formerly *Black Echoes*), my first full-time position at a magazine, and looking back an incredibly exciting period. It's not every day you get to meet the musical heroes you had idolized as a teenager. I was blessed enough to have interviewed many: Janet, Luther, and more. But few were more thrilling than the prospect of a face-to-face encounter with Prince. The air of mystery and intrigue around him at the time was palpable—something he of course shrewdly cultivated and maintained. So of course being invited to have an audience with "The Artist" was never going to be any kind of standard PR arrangement.

When the call came through from Prince's UK publicists that he would be doing interviews that very afternoon at Wembley Arena—and to be ready to leave in 30 minutes—I was lucky enough to pick up the phone. Even more fortunately for me there was no debate on who in the office would do the interview: I was known as the massive Prince-head and the rest of the team were shockingly (but pleasingly in this instance) not particularly bothered, being variously immersed in their specialties in hip-hop, reggae, soul, and so on. It soon became clear that the five journalists that showed up for the ride to Wembley had been tactically chosen to cover all the market—tabloid, broadsheet, music monthly, rock weekly, and so on. It was a thrill to be snuck in there, as *Echoes* was small fries in circulation by comparison, but its specific demographic and reputation meant it made the cut, thankfully.

Editor: How did you prep for the interview?

Mattera: I can't really overstate how jaw-dropping it was at the time to get the call that you had been invited for a personal audience with Prince. In retrospect the let's say "idiosyncratic" setup was totally in keeping with both his myth-making approach to publicity and fabled spontaneity, but at the time I think I was pretty overwhelmed with excitement mixed with a dash of fear. Given the circumstances, there was no real time for preparation—usually you'd get the chance to at least hear a new album or handful of tracks of whatever was being promoted before an interview . . . but of course there was nothing "usual" about this. Still being a major fan, coming up with a line of questioning en route wasn't a problem . . . the bigger issue was not being able to record the interview or even take notes: this was to be purely an encounter, an experience. So the pressure to both try to steer the conversation and remember every response was pretty immense.

The previous air of camaraderie and excitement amongst the assembled journalists quickly evaporated as each writer emerged from their encounter and frantically began scribbling notes to capture their memories of the conversations as quickly as possible. It felt like an exam, with everyone remaining tight lipped and guarded about any details of their particular exchange.

Sidebar: Something I didn't mention in the piece, but I remember as we were being led through the maze of corridors behind the Wembley stage prior to the interviews: At one point a door flung open and there was Prince. He whispered some instruction to an aide and then disappeared. It was literally like seeing a unicorn. I don't know if he timed that appearance as we were ushered past to add to the mystique or not, but if he did then it certainly worked. He knew how to be a star.

Editor: Did the article turn out how you thought it would before you went through the experience?

Mattera: If I had any expectations of this being anything like a regular interview, it soon became obvious it wasn't. Prince had a very clear message he wanted to communicate at that moment and he was very focused on that, so any questions about his previous output or anything really that wasn't totally about his agenda was quickly sidestepped and redirected. But again in retrospect wasn't that so like him—rarely wanting to look back, always focused on the moment and looking ahead.

Editor: What feedback did you get on the article?

Mattera: Well this was pre-internet explosion, so way before you had masses of online comments, it really was just a readers' letter bag if anything. I seem to remember his publicists being happy, as due to our quick turnaround, the interview was out on the shelves in less than a week, so they could deliver their client results quickly. That relationship later resulted in covering the opening of the NPG Store in Camden and interviewing Mayte for her solo album. —Ed.

♀ wants to talk. This is A Big Deal. The man that used to be Prince has kept a tight-lipped silence for over a decade now—recoiling from the idea of doing TV interviews or, god forbid, press conferences for the fear of being misinterpreted or misunderstood—only last year breaking the silence to give a number of selective audiences with a few high-profile music magazines. Now, on his royal decree, he is receiving journalists by, if not the truckload, at least the car load. Five yesterday apparently, and five more today. He must have something pretty important to say.

So it's more than a little shocking when at 2pm Wednesday afternoon—two days before his *Gold Experience* tour is to premiere at Wembley—his publicist comes on the phone offering an interview with The Artist Without A Name. Out of the blue. No, it's not a joke. Drop everything and come right now—we're leaving in 30 minutes for an audience backstage at Wembley.

And so it begins. A trip straight to the intriguing heart of the ♀ experience.

It's difficult to get a handle on the scale of the operation here—the sheer number of people mobilized in order to keep, if not his name, then his ♀ in the papers and his shows on the road. Backstage at Wembley, behind levels of security that would shame Fort Knox, scores of men and women dash about with their own formerly-Princely concerns: fixing lighting rigs, staring into digital displays.

"We're about to do interviews with The Artist Formerly Known As Prince," someone squawks into a mobile with an air of deadly seriousness.

We're led back through a confusion of hanging sheets to the labyrinthine corridors hidden backstage. There are teasing glimpses of ♀'s latest fantasy playground: a huge, glitzy gold-spread double bed with a gold-plated topless angel forming the headrest, [very *Ab Fab*]; an immense organic-looking amorphous construction that can only be the much-anticipated Endorphin-machine; doors signposted "Make-Up" and, more excitingly, "Mayte" [his Asian-babe dancer/acrobat/"muse"] left teasingly ajar to review chintzy furs in pinks and white; and everywhere the overwhelming smell of incense. The smell of ♀.

We've already been informed there are to be absolutely no recorders, notepads or pens to be brought into the room. There's even a rumor going around at one point that there are to be no *questions* directed at The Perfumed One. No one dares even question these bizarre requests. We even sign agreements to the effect.

This is His domain and if we are to enter we must play by His rules.

One of the rules is that we are to wait: to wait and ponder. If his recent public appearance at the Brits is anything to go—his only utterance being the cryptic soft-spoken burst of "Prince. Best? On record—slave. Live—totally free. Come. Get Wild. Peace."—then this will be a somewhat brief—and perplexing—conversation. The atmosphere is tense and expectant; nothing is in our control, even the order of our audience is to be determined by the throw of a coin. When I'm finally signaled as "the next one" and given a body-search to rival that of a hippy returning from Amsterdam, by a solemn faced bodyguard, I feel more than a little off-kilter. Then I'm shown into his dressing room.

The room is dimly lit by candlelight and heavy with incense. It's styled with that familiar Paisley touch—garish, chintzy velvet throws everywhere, a surprisingly modest spread of fruit, honey and french bread—your 16-year-old Goth sister's bedroom.

♀ stands before me and offers a delicate hand as I am introduced—he isn't—and we are left alone.

He wears a bright blue, silk trouser suit in the familiar style of in recent months. He's short, of course, and unexpectedly more frail look-ing—certainly not the tautly muscular Prince of *Parade* days. He's also wearing an inordinate amount of slap—heavy pan make-up and mas-cara, which adds to the clownish, unreality of his presence. His eyes are shielded by wrap-a-round glasses, so his eyes are not visible at any point. SLAVE is scrawled on his cheek.

He hasn't said anything yet.

"I feel like I've been sent to see the headmaster," I offer to break the silence. I'm totally sincere: I do find the whole affair more than a little disconcerting.

"Don't be scared," he reassures me as we sit on the sofas, covered by huge chintzy throws. Then he begins muttering, more to himself than to me, very quickly and in a voice far deeper than you'd expect.

"The doctor told me I should chill . . . I gotta stop thinkin' about it . . . It's made me ill."

It's a vague and mystifying opener. Frankly I have no idea what's he's talking about, though later it becomes a little clearer. He makes a reference to someone lying in hospital, but before I can ask him, he's already changed the subject.

"Thank you for coming," he offers directly and with unnecessary modesty.

"I want you to help me. I want you to have this," he says drawing my attention to a single glittering gold CD case on the table.

Now this is exciting. Really, all for *me*. I pick it up to examine it. It's called *The Gold Experience* and bears the ♀ moniker. It's obviously been well-handled—indeed it even appears to have been *assembled* by hand. In my enthusiasm it comes apart in my hands.

Shit. I've destroyed *The Gold Experience* and as far as I know it's the only one. ♀ doesn't seem to notice. Maybe he can't see much through those glasses. By the time I've discreetly stopped fiddling, he's been talk-ing for minutes about artistic freedom and the need to release his music when he wants to. It keeps coming back to the infamous George Michael versus Sony case, with which he appears to be obsessed.

"Take the song 'Father Figure.' Who wrote that?" he inquires.

Er . . . George Michael?

"Yeah, I think so. I think George Michael wrote that. Sony didn't write that. But now they *own* that. It's not *his* anymore. But I don't want to be like George Michael. I don't want to disappear for five years and stop making music. I can't do that."

☥ is angry with Warners. That is blatantly clear. It's written all over his face—*literally*.

"*They* put this on my face," he states dramatically and without provocation. "I'm a slave to Warners until they set me free. I'm a slave to my music too. Music is my life. Music has to be free."

He talks steadily and, yes, quite *normally*. This is like having a conversation with a regular person.

"You know the song 'Letitgo'?" he continues, "Now that was a great pop song. If Warners had promoted it properly it would have been a huge hit. Now I don't have any control of that. They can stop working an album after one single if they want to. Now I would have loved to put 'Strollin'' out to chill people out in the summer, y'know?"

So signing a contract with a major label is like signing your soul away to the Devil?

That idea obviously strikes a distinct chord with my host, who slaps his thigh and rolls back on the sofa, reiterating, "That's it, man" over and over, with gleeful approval.

"That's right, man. You be signin' your soul away to Lucifer. Those dudes kinda look like Satan too!"

Hasn't he anything good to say about Warners? When he signed at 17, he fought for total control of his project—Warners initially wanted Maurice White to produce his debut *For You*—and achieved it to a level unprecedented at the time.

Prince smirks and shakes his head.

"People always say that. They think you make all this money and they *gave* it to you. They didn't give it to me. I gave them my music. Now they own it. Like *Purple Rain*—they own the masters, so they can do what they want with it. I don't have any control. Can you believe that?

"You got to remember that all that glitters ain't gold."

It's a favorite line of his—the hook of his new song "Gold."

"They say you need a manager, you need a lawyer. There are all these people around you being nice to your face and talking about you behind your back. That's why I don't have a manager now—I deal with these people directly myself. I want to speak to their faces. I want to see my enemy."

Given ♀'s commendable, but perhaps somewhat idealist, attitude—founded no doubt on his removal from the realities of the everyday—the glut of rumors of constant personnel changes in his camp come as little surprise. Either you are with him or against him.

"They said I'm gone insane. Now I'm not crazy. I *know* I'm not crazy," he rails.

"There was a time when I thought I was going mad with all this stuff happenin' and it was makin' me ill. But that was before I changed my name."

Ah—the name. Now we can change tack a little, lighten the conversation.

What, for instance, does his mother call him on the phone?

He smirks at the presumptuousness of the question. Then he becomes quite serious.

"She don't call me 'Prince.' Only my enemies call me 'Prince.' Only those that want to hurt or offend me call me 'Prince.' 'Prince' is dead."

He pauses dramatically.

"*I killed him.*"

It seems clear that the decision to change his name was, for him, a *spiritual* choice: a breaking with a past he now despises—he refuses to play Prince songs in his live shows—a move towards his own personal "dawn." He laughs at my inquiry if the name change was an attempt to free him from his contract.

"I wish it was that simple, man. O.J. would be doin' it and walkin' free, right."

Prince has a lot to say about names. It's about personal autonomy: he can call himself whatever he wants, so long as it has meaning to him. He sees this as part of the tradition of Afro-American slavery and emancipation.

"My name is Prince Rogers Nelson. But who was Nell?" he laughs incredulously.

"I don't know any Nell. Do you? It's like when we were comin' off the ships. You can be *Black*man. You be Brown. My name didn't mean anything to me. I don't know why people are so surprised I changed it. Muhammad Ali changed his name from Cassius Clay and people accepted it. Malcolm X changed his name."

I suggest that it might have had an adverse effect: all this debate about the pronunciation of his chosen sign, declarations of intent to become a dolphin—surely it's drawing attention away from his music?

He deflects the point by bringing it back to his cyclical argument.

"They talk about that 'cause there hasn't been any new music to talk about. So everyone writes about that instead. Cause I can't put out any new music. Warners won't let me."

Of course there *has* been a deluge of Prince-related music over the past 12 months—*Come*, the *1-800-New Funk* compilation, "The Most Beautiful Girl In The World."

Has he merely forgotten these or does he no longer consider them *his* work? [*Come*—the album that marked the official death of Prince— was largely old material cobbled together to satisfy his contract with Warners.]

"You know what someone said to me the other day," he says laughing. "They said I didn't have the funk anymore. Now who's to say what's good or bad? It doesn't mean anything. You may like 'Little Red Corvette.' I happen to think 'Gold' is the best song I've ever done, but you'll never hear it. If 'Letitgo' had sold as many as 'The Most Beautiful Girl' then it would be considered just as much a success."

Does he really equate commercial success with artistic merit? There is no time to ask.

———————

It is clear he has an agenda and it keeps coming back to it.

So when exactly is *The Gold Experience* coming out?

"Never!" comes the quick reply.

He is loathe to give away any new product to Warners and wants them to fulfil his contract by releasing material from as far back as the Revolution days.

"But I'd like to send it to you. I'd like to send you whatever kind of my music it is you like—the ambient jazz stuff, the rock 'n' roll stuff. You can access it whenever you want."

Oh. I get it now. The internet. His fascination with exploring new avenues of communication is apparent to anyone that accessed last year's CD-ROM experience *Interactive*. Indeed *The Gold Experience* is littered with references to "accessing new experiences" as well as pie-in-the-sky freedom songs like "Dolphin."

He sees Internet as the key to this brave new dawn where artist and fan can immediately connect. No nasty record labels. No ugly lawyers involved.

He's getting increasingly animated, miming tapping a keyboard whilst talking about music being "free, like air." But what about the practicalities of such a venture? What about fans that can't use, or rather can't *afford*, a computer.

"We can fix that. The NPG will fix that," he replies dismissively, without suggesting how.

⚥ exists in a world of metaphysical concepts, not to be tied down by inane pragmatism.

"We will all be part of an underground network, a global New Power Generation. I want you to help me spread the word."

PAISELY PARK PRESS CONFERENCE

November 12, 1996 | Original Transcript

1996 was Prince's 1776—a year to declare independence.

The year began with Prince marrying longtime companion and New Power Generation member Mayte Garcia on Valentine's Day, followed by a brief Hawaii Honeymoon tour. The balance of the year was mostly consumed recording what would become the three-disc *Emancipation*, Prince's first release after the end of his tumultuous contract with Warner Bros. Records. To celebrate the LP and his freedom, he held his first official press conference (transcribed here) and started doing traditional product-promotion (NBC's *The Today Show*) and longer-form TV interviews (Oprah Winfrey, Chris Rock). This led to a two-year period through the end of 1998 in which he toured and performed more-or-less nonstop and conducted over 170 interviews, about one-third of his interview total. As he says in this press conference, "I got a record to sell."

Recounting the initial phase of *Emancipation* publicity is always a bit unsettling. Prince and Mayte's son was born on October 16 but died the following week of complications from Pfeiffer syndrome, a genetic disease. Prince was performing live again by October 26, promoting the LP in Japan a few days later, talking with Oprah on November 4, and conducting this press conference on November 12. No mention was made of his child's death during these interactions, and it's difficult to separate Prince's obvious joy in releasing the album—talking about the recording process, the cover songs, Egyptian culture—from the anguish he must have been feeling at the time. —Ed.

MC: Hello. How's everybody doing? The Artist is about to come in, and we want to go over some type of hospitality ground rules. We want you to be able to take photo ops, and also you can film for the first two minutes maximum. Then we want you to provide The Artist the courtesy of putting the cameras and the actual, ah, all of the other kinds of recording devices to the side. If we find that you do have them, security will take them, and we don't want that kind of a story to leave Paisley Park. There any questions?

[*Loud feedback and laughter.*]

Reporter: Turn it down before he comes in.

MC: She's ready. He's not going to have a microphone, so we're all going to have to be very quiet. Here he is. All camera crews, if you wanna leave so you don't have to stay, you can leave now. If you wanna stay, you're welcome to.

[*Prince enters.*]

Prince: OK, the hard part's over. You can go first.

Reporter: What has changed for you within this hour now? Since like . . .

Prince: This has sort of been just a dream for me. I think I saw it a long time ago. I'm sort of stepping into that dream now.

Reporter: Was it well worth the fight or was it well worth the struggle all those years?

Prince: It was very definitely.

Reporter: Many artists when they became famous they leave their hometowns, yet you've kept faithful to Minneapolis after so many years. Why does the city keep you like some towns do?

Prince: I've gone to several places in the world, and it seems like when I get back over that green and all the lakes, I'm at peace before I even land. I think God puts you where he wants you to be, and I'm gonna stay here for the rest of my life.

Reporter: In the latter part of your songs you talk about being someone else. Aren't you happy the way you are, and maybe that's the reason why you changed your name because you wanted to be someone else?

Prince: That's . . . that takes an hour to explain. [*Laughter.*] I think when you hear the new music, you'll hear a great deal more clarity and a great deal more joy. I'm very happy with who I am. I'm very happy with my name now.

Reporter: So your name is The Artist, huh?

Prince: My name is this. [*Shows Prince symbol.*]

Reporter: What is the choice of the covers? Why these particular songs, what they mean to you?

Prince: "Betcha By Golly Wow" is a song I grew up with. I think it's one of the most beautiful tunes ever written. The chord changes are very interesting. It's one of the most beautifully sung songs as well. I didn't change very much for that purpose. I must say that it was very important for me to cover songs where we could get back to the artist and songwriters. Now that we have our own record company, New Power Generation, we can— soon as we get paid we can pay the artist because the artist is the president, you know. He's gonna look out for other artists and writers first. The old way of doing things is over. "One of Us." I think it's important for every songwriter to cover that song once. It's an amazing song, and every person of color should cover it as well. It's an important statement. And "La La Means I Love You" is yet another song I grew up with. And it's very beautiful. And "I Can't Make U Love Me." Bonnie's a friend of mine, and I just think that's one of her best tunes and I wanted to do a cover of it as well.

Reporter: "One of Us" you changed the lyric from "slob" to "slave." Does that—

Prince: Ah, you heard that, huh? [*Laughter.*]

Reporter: I guess if you could partially explain why. Are you worried about any of the response you might receive from that?

Prince: No. No worries. No worries anymore. I'll leave that up to your interpretation.

Reporter: What I find incredible is, I've seen loads of concerts of yours and also after-show gigs and what I love even a hundred times more than the hits and all that is the way during after-show gigs you do trans-hypnotic versions, like, of "Head" of twenty minutes, et cetera.

Prince: Right.

Reporter: And what I find incredible is that you're the live artist of blah blah blah and you've never released a live record. I can't understand. And

I admit—you can punch me in the head—I admit to owning various bootlegs—

Prince: Security! [*Laughter.*] So you're the one.

Reporter: Why? Why no live records? It seems . . .

Prince: I can't answer. I don't know. We're going to do one eventually, though. Because this record is so deep with songs, thirty-six of them, we have to take a moment and learn 'em. I know 'em, but we have to teach them to the band, the ones they didn't play on. I did a lot of the songs myself alone in the studio. There is plans to do a live record after we, you know, get done. There's also some old tunes I'd like to bring back that I haven't played in a while. Because—

Reporter: Such as?

Prince: I'd really like to do "When Doves Cry" right. I have new equipment now.

Reporter: Because it was a flop before. The first time. [*Laughter.*]

Prince: Live, I was never really pleased with the way we did it live.

Reporter: I noticed you did a couple of seconds of "Sexy MF"—well we're amongst friends, "motherfucker"—and you didn't do the rest, and I saw you grinning. Was that a private joke or something or why did you do that?

Prince: Yeah, I have a deal with MTV not to cuss on their channel. [*Laughter.*]

Reporter: So it was a three-second threat.

Prince: Yeah.

Reporter: Speaking of "When Doves Cry," have you heard Patti Smith's version?

Prince: No, sir.

Reporter: I would like to know: We heard several rumors about this concept behind the three CDs and the sixty minutes each, is that, could you tell us a little bit about why you did that?

Prince: Mayte and I are very much into the Egyptian culture, and we're studying about how the pyramids were built and we're fascinated by the notion that they used astrology to line them up so that they could let future civilizations know what year they were built. I wanted to start with a blueprint for *Emancipation* and then fill in that blueprint, and I wanted to challenge myself with three CDs timed perfectly to an hour to the frame, you know, I'm very proud of that. It took a long time, and it's like a cliff: you jump off of it and see where you're gonna land.

Reporter: Besides the new songs, you performed "Purple Rain." Why this song?

Prince: I haven't felt as good as I do today. So I'll probably be pulling out a lotta old stuff. I don't own Prince's music. I own the publishing. I don't own the masters. I don't own "Purple Rain." But, ah, I know how to play it. [*Laughter.*]

Reporter: How specifically does your relationship, did your relationship with Warner Bros. hurt you artistically?

Prince: To be honest, I have a good relationship with them now, and I invited a few of them to come down. I've yet to see who's here, but I'm gonna look for 'em. I have a good relationship with them because as much as I had trouble with them, I had trouble with myself and just getting through a little box I had put myself into. I don't regret anything that I've done; I don't regret any relationship that I've had. And especially theirs. They helped build this place when I was just starting out and I've been in it for fifteen years. And I made a lot of music, so I owe them a debt. I owe a lot of people in my career a debt. I'm just thankful to be here. That's why I don't regret anything in the past.

Reporter: What's the most special thing about this building?

Prince: The playroom and the hallways.

Reporter: Is there a special concept, or . . .

Prince: That's a little personal.

Reporter: How many hours will you actually spend here a day?

Prince: This is my job. When I wake up, I get dressed and I go to my desk and just start churning them out. It's a curse and a blessing. If you hear a song, you have to get it out of your system.

Reporter: What inspires you to keep pushing the envelope with your music?

Prince: Heaven. The heavens.

Reporter: Who else can we expect to see on your NPG label?

Prince: No one right now. I'm just, this is a mouthful with this record, and we're just going to keep going. It's a brand-new beginning for us, as far as business and art is concerned, and we're just, we're overwhelmed. There's not enough minutes in the day to keep up with this project.

Reporter: How about the band? New members are coming up here, in New Power Generation, for example, Kathleen Dyson and Rhonda Smith. How did you meet them?

Prince: Sheila E. hipped me to them.

Reporter: Yeah?

Prince: Yeah, and I'm grateful to her for that because they're very, very talented.

Reporter: And it blends well with the old members? It blends well with the other members?

Prince: Oh, yeah. This is the smallest band I've had. The interesting thing about them is that they all play computers. We didn't get a chance to do much of that tonight, but all their instruments are computerized, so they'll be playing four, five compressed parts, especially the keyboard player and the drummer. He's a keyboardist as well as a drummer. He plays more computers, more computers than he does drums, actually.

Reporter: And you wanted to have a smaller band this time?

Prince: Yeah, I wanted to play more. We could probably just shout 'em out.

Reporter: You have three major components in your music—sex, religion, and love, it seems. How do you equate them all?

Prince: I gotta be honest. I can't.

Reporter: For years you've been notoriously shy with the press, or guarded. And suddenly here we are now, international press core.

Prince: I got a record to sell. [*Laughter and applause.*] I wasn't selling them. I made them. I wasn't selling them. I'm really out pushing this product. I really do feel it's the best work I've done. I got to empty the gun this time, so to speak. I got everything out of my system. And usually when I'm recording, or when I've finished a record, I'm recording another one. And I'll be reading the reviews of an album, and I'll be in the studio working on the next. And this is the first time I felt I don't want to be at work anymore. I want to take a vacation. And the record's very personal to me, and I had a good time in Tokyo explaining to some very nice, respectful people who just really care about music. They don't get wrapped up in all the nonsense that goes with this business.

Reporter: How did not having the reviews out while you're making the record change the process of making the record?

Prince: The whole process of this record was different. I was talking to D'Angelo upstairs, and he plays a lot of instruments, too. And we were talking about how if you're in a bad mood and you go in to record, since he's gonna do the whole band's part, the whole band's in a bad mood. [*Laughter.*] So, what you end up with is kind of a pretty laidback record. And the difference with this is that I was a free man and a happy man and a married man and a clear man. So all the tracks are clear and happy and free. And the whole album—it's uplifting. It's uplifting for me when I hear it and hopefully it will be for you.

Reporter: So did you write this album as some kind of relief album where as your last album was some kind of under pressure record?

Prince: You know, we, back in 1994, I think it was, we could see this far down the line and when Mayte and I walked through the doors at the end of the "7" video, we pretty much was looking forward to this day, OK? So, I don't like to speak about the albums in between there. It's just done. It's over with. I'm just happy to be here.

Reporter: Right now, what's the theme of your life, what's the light of your life?

Prince: Oh, there's so many things. Children. My wife. Most of all, God.

Reporter: Your music?

Prince: Music's in there somewhere. [*Laughter.*] But, again, music is my best friend and it's my worst friend.

Reporter: Why is it worst?

Prince: Well, you go to sleep at night. It's three o'clock in the morning and you've been up in the studio that whole time and a song title will come to you. And off you go again.

Reporter: Is that what you meant earlier when you said it's a blessing and a curse?

Prince: Yes. There are over a thousand songs in the vault, and a lot of them are fully realized compositions because I hate to leave something undone and I'll just finish it all the way through. And some of it isn't fit to release because of the language and the subject matter. I'm not saying it's pornographic or anything like that, but there's a lot of stuff down there that it's not time to come out.

Reporter: Has it happened that you, for instance, that you write a song in, I don't know, 1988, and you think, "I better keep it five years until—"

Prince: Yes.

Reporter: The zeitgeist—I don't know the English word—decide that the feeling of the times catches up with what was already in the song?

Prince: Yes. "Kiss" was like that, when I first, even when I listen to it today, it just sounds, wrong. I, when I did that, it just sounded strange to me. But I liked the way it sounds, and we didn't put it out for a while.

Reporter: How much marriage has changed you? I ask you this because we have seen a lot of your shows, and we listen to the music, and we loved also the girls. [*Laughter.*]

Prince: I like that. I'll put that in. Well, to be honest, I haven't performed much other than in Love 4 One Another since I've been married. Maybe four or five times. So, I don't know how it's changed my performance, but my writing has changed immensely. It's kind of a lot that goes with it. You stop looking for a lot of different things. You stop listening to a lot of different things. And you will think differently, and you'll find you'll turn different shows on television. Everything sort of changes. And, more than anything, you feel complete. And she has sort of completed my soul, and it's really got me focused. I see songs fully finished now. The lyrics, everything, and they come out really quickly now. That's why there's so many songs on the record.

Reporter: How did you know she was the one?

Prince: She was the one person who never showed me malice in any way, shape, or form. On top of that, there are several coincidences, which I now believe to be fate, where our names lined up. And it was either accept it or walk away from something that could make the difference between life and death. So, I chose her, and I haven't been sad a day since.

Reporter: What does she call you?

Prince: Uh . . . [*Laughter.*] Lots of things. [*More laughter.*]

Reporter: First of all, I just want to thank you for your hospitality.

Prince: Thanks for coming.

Reporter: And I'd like to know why the scenography was all white and what did white mean to you?

Prince: To be honest, we had done the set for the video. We had gone back and forth with filling it with things, set pieces and what have you, and someone had made a suggestion that since your band's far down, you know, you feel this way, and you feel free and you're gonna feature the music more and you're gonna play more. I just wanted to have nothing up there almost, you know? We try to have as few instruments as possible. It felt pretty good. I just watched a little bit of it on television. With this outfit on, I kinda popped out of the whites. [*Laughter.*]

Reporter: I'd just like to say, I think it's wonderful that, I said, I adore your music, et cetera, now it's proven that you're a normal, intelligent guy with a sense of humor. [*Laughter.*] No, but this is important because you've kept silent for so long and if you don't say anything, there's more room for all the assholes spreading rumors and lying and building up this thing about this . . .

Prince: Yeah, but what it does, I think, it sort of separates all of us, doesn't it? And then we take our masks off and we really see who's true—

Reporter: But this is a relief. I would have hated it if, if you love someone's music and he's . . . you know what I mean.

Prince: Yeah. I appreciate it. Thank you.

Reporter: In terms of pop music, it seems like this has been a real vital time for kind of funky, blues-oriented music. Are there artists or music that has either inspired you in a competitive way or inspired you in kind of ah . . . inspiring way?

Reporter: Yeah, what are you listening to?

Prince: I kid sometimes about competition, but I really, honestly feel no competition with anybody. I think there's room for everybody, especially now with the dawn of a new day when artists can own their work, release their work, price their work, do their own artwork, you know. I like Bjork. I like some of the things she does. I like, ah, I love D'Angelo. Tony Rich, I think's a great songwriter. You know, I gotta be honest: I really listen for musicianship. I want to hear somebody play. And most musicians, you'll find, will do that. The bands I've usually had have been great musicians, and they crucify other bands when they talk about them at rehearsals. You really got to come with something or else it's, you know.

Reporter: Have you been working with computers a lot? You said your band members have been.

Prince: Well, I have for a long time. I think they said I had the first Linn machine when it first came out. I mean, I am really interested in programming.

Reporter: Can you name someone who inspired you?

Prince: Someone who inspired you? Muhammad Ali. I get inspiration from people like that more so than musicians because I, you know, I play.

Reporter: Can I ask something? You mentioned earlier that you wanted to take a vacation, but there's also some rumors about a tour. And even some rumors about you doing this with Mayte in Holland. We would really welcome that, but . . .

Prince: We're still talking about a tour, and I was just in the talking stages. I don't know where we'll go. I do want to play in Hawaii for my honeymoon. We'll probably set that up.

Reporter: Will your wife perform again with you? On stage.

Prince: To be honest, we haven't discussed that. I mean, she just, it's a long time for her, and that's all she thinks about.

Reporter: Do you enjoy being a father?

Prince: Oh, yeah, I enjoy it. That's why you do it. That's what it's all about. [*Laughter.*] I mean, I had playgrounds built before the birth. I was into it. I love it. Thank you all for coming again.

PORTRAIT OF THE ARTIST AS A NEWLY FREE MAN

Nick Krewen | November 20, 1996 | *Hamilton Spectator*

Royal analogies abound as dozens of reporters called to the Paisley Park *Emancipation* celebration in November 1996 describe the scene—like watching supplicants at the Versailles court of Louis XIV or worker drones buzzing around the hive to get to the queen. Krewen reports here as one of the attendees granted a private royal audience. Again, struggles with Warner Bros. are explored and Prince dodges questions about his son, saying "Mayte and I have decided to let the baby make its own decisions." —Ed.

The Artist Formerly Known As Prince knows how to make a lasting impression. As the door to the conference room in his palatial Paisley Park Studios swings open, the man whose legal name is the unpronounceable glyph that combines male and female signs with a trumpeted curlicue, TAFKAP is dressed head to toe in bright chartreuse, his thin, wiry frame camouflaged by a sweater. As he accepts a cup of herbal tea from an assistant with one hand, he beckons with the other, offering a brief, but firm handshake as a greeting.

"What do you think of our weather?" he asks, "Sit anywhere."

There is none of the shy reticence or uncomfortable silence that he has generously displayed throughout his 19-year career as contemporary music's pre-eminent pop funk superstar. In fact, during the 40-minute conversation that ensues he is animated, passionate and disarmingly friendly. His gaze rarely leaves his subject. Surprisingly, he seems to enjoy being interviewed, and when his assistant knocks to announce that time is up, he grants two extensions.

Six months ago, heck—even a month ago—the idea of The Artist formerly known as The Artist Formerly Known As Prince sitting down and holding court with the press was about as infrequent as the passing of Halley's Comet. As he built his career with such multi-million selling masterpieces of atomic funk as *Dirty Mind, 1999, Purple Rain, The Batman Soundtrack* and *Diamonds And Pearls*, he became increasingly reclusive and cryptic. Interviews were granted every five years or so, usually with the stipulation that the interviewer do so by memory: tape recorders and notepads were strictly verboten.

"We all know how the universe works, and that it's often built on lies," The Artist explains. "That's why I didn't want to do interviews. Words are all entrapping. Somebody switches them around for their own convenience. I wanted my music to be my truth. I wanted to let it do the talking for me."

But as the ex-Prince will tell you himself these days, he's a changed man. He married 24-year-old Mayte (pronounced Migh-ty) Garcia on Valentine's Day earlier this year, and only weeks ago she gave birth to their first child. After a long, tumultuous struggle, The Artist finally terminated his $100 million contract with Warner Bros.—an association that began when the company signed him as a teenage prodigy and granted him then-unprecedented complete artistic control.

He's celebrating his professional divorce with a new album, *Emancipation*, three hours to the minute long and 36 songs deep that will be released worldwide November 19, and has hired the EMI Music empire to distribute the album on his revived NPG Records label.

Another sign of the new Artist: Three nights prior to this interview, he hosted a lavish party to debut *Emancipation*'s first video, a family-dominated version of the Stylistics' Philly soul classic "Betcha By Golly Wow," followed by a live concert from the 20,000 square foot soundstage of his 64,000 ft. Paisley Park Studios that was broadcast worldwide over MTV and here on MuchMusic.

As The Artist performed with his revamped New Power Generation, including Montrealers Kat Dyson on guitar and Rhonda Smith on bass, something that has been scrawled upon his face for the past two years was conspicuously absent: the word "Slave."

The Artist is free at last.

A telltale indication of the new Prince: he's even allowing reporters to use a notepad in his presence.

"I feel better than I've felt in a long time," says the 38-year-old ex-Prince Rogers Nelson, who is now referred to by colleagues as simply "The Artist."

"I've just come through a time where I was unhappy, even though I was selling millions of records. Had I not gone through it, this album probably wouldn't have felt as natural as it did.

"I must be honest: this is the album I always aspired to make. Anyone familiar with my music knows I've been leading up to something. *Emancipation* is that realization."

Citing the termination of his Warner contract and his happy homelife as responsible for his sudden elation, The Artist views *Emancipation* "as the New Dawn" in his career and seems willing to pull out all the stops in order to ensure its success. With the help of other Paisley Park staffers and consultants, The Artist has released *Emancipation* complete with "a two-year marketing plan *this* thick" that outlines several promotional press and TV appearances, plus his first world tour in six years.

Emancipation is certainly the most soulful album of The Artist's impressive repertoire, concentrating less on the sexually graphic funk slaps that dominated albums as recently as *Come*, and more on the groove-oriented smooth romanticism of the '70s soul movement.

"This whole album is the first one that I've done that is cohesive from start to finish," The Artist swears. "It's the first one where nothing got in the way of the process. All sorts of things can get in the way, including your record company, although my relationship with Warner was just one aspect of that. Sometimes you can become a slave to that process."

Asked if he ever feels a slave to music itself, The Artist visibly shudders.

"I'm so grateful to God for giving me this gift, that I can never say I'm a slave to it," says The Artist, who says he has never suffered writer's block.

"I'd be ungrateful, sour, I'd be ashamed. If I ever lost the gift, it'd be like blinding me."

Although some might feel that the fact Prince owns the publishing but none of the masters of the 19 albums he's recorded as the main reason for his disgruntled feelings for Warner, TAFKAP says it was his prolific nature that was central to his difficulties with the label.

"Sometimes I work really hard, and I found that too many ideas flooded me at once," says The Artist, who estimates his studio vault still houses over 1000 completed songs that haven't been heard by the public. "That's what I needed Warner to understand about me: That's who I am."

The Artist doesn't mention if the automatic guaranteed $10 million per album advance was part of the motive for Warner's dissuading tactics, he just knows he wasn't happy.

"We ought to have an alternative means in the music business to deal with artists like me," he says, rhyming off such names as Me'Shell Ndegeocello, D'Angelo and Ani DiFranco.

"You know, once I wanted to give ballet music to Arthur Mitchell for the Harlem Dance Theatre. I just wanted to hand them the music. I told Warner, 'You won't have to worry about a thing. I'll pay for the manufacturing and distribution, and they can keep the proceeds.' Warner said no. I said, 'Why not?' They said, 'We'd rather just give them the money, and make a donation.' I said, 'That's not the point. It's about free music. Just give them the music.'

"It was occasions like those where we were at odds. Now, I'm doing it all on my own terms."

Also prompting his desire to part ways with the major was his successful experiment with the 1994 smash hit "The Most Beautiful Girl In The World."

In an unusual deal, Warner allowed the single to be cut and promoted exclusively by Bellmark, an independent U.S. label.

"It was such a joyful experience!" The Artist exclaims. "It went to #1 even in countries where I didn't have any prior number one hits! It was my biggest hit ever, and that's including all the ones I had on Warner up to that point. It proved my point that a career is only as good as the people who are working it."

He's further pumped by the initial radio success of "Betcha By Golly Wow."

"We're all blown up with 'Betcha By Golly Wow,'" The Artist enthuses. "It's doing exactly what we'd hope for."

Encouraged by the indie success of radical Buffalo folksinger Ani DiFranco, whose royalty rate is $2 per album higher than the average assigned by majors, The Artist says it's time for his career to get back to its roots and build some important relationships.

"I've talked to DJs where they've said, 'You the man.'" The Artist states. "And I say, No, 'You the man! You're the one who has to get my music out to my friends.' It's the relationship that's the important thing.

"Heck, one of my albums once got pulled because I didn't go to dinner with somebody."

The Artist feels that self education is the best preventative medicine.

"Nothing is explained to you when you're first starting out," The Artist snorts. "You're dealing with group of attorneys who deal strictly with the label in a conventional manner, not an alternative body where you can own your own masters, or at least where the masters are yours where you can initially sell the rights. It's ironic that the music business is not designed for those who don't write and produce their own music."

As accessible as TAFKAP seems to be becoming, there are certain topics that will remain taboo. For instance, although he confirms the birth of his recent child, he is unwilling to provide any information, even its sex.

"Mayte and I have decided to let the baby make its own decisions," he explains. "Once it becomes public, its personality will become shaped by all the attention, and that's too much to wish upon it. So we're not going to relinquish its privacy. That means no clues to its skin color, or its weight or its height."

When pressed about the baby's sex, The Artist remains adamant.

"I have to think about my family's security. You know, I have weirdos who try to follow me home, too!"

And as for his unpronounceable name, initially considered a ruse to trigger an escape clause in his Warner contract, will the man formerly known as Prince revert back to his given birth name?

Not likely.

"I listen to my inner voice, which is the root of my inspiration," he says. "One day, I was told to change my name. I didn't hear anything, but discovered the symbol while doodling, and realized it has been following me around since the beginning. I was told by my inner voice that if I accept it, I'd see other things. So I accept to me what is inevitable."

PORTRAIT OF THE ARTIST: THE SOUND OF EMANCIPATION

Robert L. Doerschuk | April 1997 | _Musician_

This interview was conducted in person at Paisley Park and augmented with Prince's responses to faxed follow-up questions. The latter would soon become his preferred means of communication with the media, a method eventually replaced by e-mail.

Among the many _Emancipation_ interviews, this one stands out for the specificity of Prince's discussion about how individual songs developed as well as his appreciation of the simple beauty of Miles Davis. As befitting an article in _Musician_ magazine, the interview is primarily about the music and not about the name change or Warner Bros. or any of his other personal baggage.

Who knew Prince could play the harp or thought that an analog kick drum "sounds like a fat dude getting stomped in the back with a timbaland?" —Ed.

The weird complex, anchored on the Minnesota tundra like a space probe on the moon. The paranoia over tape recorders. Those gaudy evocations of martyrdom on his last Warner Bros. albums. Twenty years of provocative imagery and sullen seclusion. And now, that business with his name.

Nothing about the artist once known as Prince is easy to explain. The surreal vibe at Paisley Park doesn't clear things up either; here his employees and intimates call him "Boss" and pass beneath Orwellian reproductions of the unpronounceable glyph that has become his signature.

Real or illusory, all of this is distraction. Though all the hype made good copy, none of it is as impressive as hearing the Artist actually play.

Which is why we're in Studio C, the smallest recording room at Paisley Park, the former Prince's *sanctorum*, on the evening of the first serious blizzard of the year. As it is, there's plenty of room for the band, which is spread out against one wall. In sweater and black beret, keyboardist Mr. Hayes is on a riser in the far corner, surrounded by synths, a bag of popcorn perched atop the customized Plexiglas frame of a Hammond B-3. Guitarist Mike Scott, the latest addition to the band, is trying out a few funky licks on his Gibson 335, while Kat Dyson uses her Tele to shower the room with samples from her Rocktron Chameleon. Bassist Rhonda Smith is next to Dyson, and to her left Kirk A. Johnson, the Artist's drummer and co-producer, sits behind a pile of electronic and acoustic drums.

"Okay, here we go," Johnson announces. Four stick clicks, and the band begins jamming through a selection of titles from the Artist's recently released triple CD, *Emancipation*. Listening to them is something like shifting through a transmission and feeling each gear sliding into place. Johnson's beat, locked to a rock-hard kick drum, drives this machine; they hit the changes perfectly, leaving no skid marks.

The doors open, and the Artist walks in. The band doesn't acknowledge the entrance, but there's a change in the air. He's short, even in his high-heeled white boots, but there's nothing fragile about him. He's wiry rather than delicate, with a businesslike, confident charisma; you might say he acts like he owns the place.

On the far side of the room is what looks like a violet concert grand piano, with the word "beautiful" scripted in white on one side. It's actually a Roland A-90 built into an artificial frame. The Artist plants himself here, rocking back on the heel of his left boot and tapping fast eighth-notes with the toe of his right foot as he comps furiously with the group. His licks are nimble, with quick cross-hand runs threading through jazzy voicings. After a minute, he spins away from the keys, strides toward the band, and straps on one of his custom-built guitars. Here, too, he plays with blazing intensity, wailing through bluesy lines that end with emphatic cadences and a defiant foot stomp.

Later, when Smith excuses herself to run an errand, the Artist picks up his Washburn bass and winds up killing on it too. But by then he's made his point: This guy is, if anything, underrated as a player. If he were starting out today, unburdened of his reputation, freed from all the excess baggage and left with only his music, he would still blow us all away.

The problem is that he doesn't have that option anymore. When he goes on the *Today* show, the first thing Bryant Gumbel tells his viewers is that the Artist was known to his high school friends as Skippy. One cringed with sympathy for the Ex-Prince, who seems fated to be called to the carpet again and again for the sins of eccentricity. Of course, it's also true that he is the architect of his image. If he got burned by the press, the match was lit in his hands.

So it is with his two most recent trials, the name change and the long dispute with Warner Bros. On his 35th birthday, June 7, 1993—only a month after announcing his decision to retire from recording—Prince declared that he was changing his name to a morphed male/female symbol. Warners wasn't thrilled with this development, which in retrospect was a portent for the semi-public struggle to follow. The issue was control—specifically, ownership of his masters. Though he insisted in various interviews that he bore no grudges, the Artist had no problem adorning his final Warner releases with images of oppression that skirted the line of self-pity: The only mystery was why the Artist felt the need to publicly bash his label of eighteen years.

Whatever the reason, the end of his Warners contract last November began what the Artist considers to be his liberation. Thus, when *Musician* sat down with him behind the API console in Studio A, the Artist seemed almost elated at the prospect of actually talking about his music. He folded himself into a chair, swung his legs over the edge, gestured expressively, broke into frame-shaking explosions of laughter. The man was obviously having a good time, as was the interviewer, except for one problem: The Artist's interrogator would not be allowed to use a tape recorder. (In what Paisley Park officials apparently considered a sign of the Boss' good will, we were permitted to take notes.) While *Musician* wasn't singled out—this restriction has applied to all print interviews for years—it was nonetheless an annoyance, especially given our obligation to turn an hour's worth of hurried scrawl into accurate information. For this reason, we suggested that, in the interest of getting it right, he might reply to a series of follow-up questions via fax once we got back to New York and deciphered our notes. Delighted with the idea, he agreed.

What follows is a two-part encounter with the Artist. The first was real, there in Studio A. The second was virtual. From start to finish, the subject was music.

You've said that Emancipation *was created in a freer climate than that under which you recorded for Warner Bros. Yet there doesn't seem to my ears to be a significantly "freer" sound on the new album than in your earlier work.*

Well, when you're in the creative process, the first thing you naturally think about is the "bombs," the great ones that you've done before. You want to fill in the slots on your album with the songs that will make everyone the happiest: fans, musicians, writers, and so on. I used to try to fill those gaps first whenever I was doing something new, or wait to challenge myself to do another great one.

This means that you think about singles: time constraints, for example, and the subject matter. [For that reason] my original draft of "Let's Go Crazy" was much different from the version that wound up being released. As I wrote it, "Let's Go Crazy" was about God and the de-elevation of sin. But the problem was that religion as a subject is taboo in pop music. People think that the records they release have got to be hip, but what *I* need to do is to tell the truth.

So one element of creativity missing for you in the Warner years was that freedom to say what you wanted to say in your lyrics.

Right. I had to take some other songs, like "A Thousand Hugs and Kisses" and "She Gave Her Angels," off the Warner albums because they were all about the same subject. But now I can write a song that says, "If u ask God 2 love u longer, every breath u take will make u stronger, keepin' u happy and proud 2 call His name: Jesus" [from "The Holy River," on *Emancipation*], and not have to worry about what *Billboard* magazine will say. Plus I'm not splitting the earnings up with anyone else except the people who deserve to have them. The people here in my studio will reap the benefits of how *Emancipation* does, not people in some office somewhere who didn't contribute anything to the music.

Now, the record industry can be a wonderful system . . . if you want to go that route. After all, some people don't want the hassle of getting on the phone and talking to retailers about their own records; they want someone to do it for them. I'm just not one of those people.

So lyrically you've got more freedom than before. What about the music itself?

If you're working in a happier atmosphere, you'll hear things differently and play them differently. "Courtin' Time" [from *Emancipation*] is different from "Had U," from *Chaos & Disorder*. That whole album is loud and raucous, but it's also dark and unhappy. Same with *The Black Album*.

Your drummer, Kirk A. Johnson, co-produced much of Emancipation.

That stems from his being a drum programmer. He's good at using the computer to put a rhythm track together. I don't like setting that kind of stuff up, because a lot of times the song will leave me while I'm doing it. But when Kirk and I work together, we can keep each other excited. I *can* do all the programming myself. *1999* is nothing but me running all the computers myself, which is why that album isn't as varied as this one. Technology used to play a big part in my music; it only plays a very little part now.

Why?

The problem was that regardless of what I heard in my head, I'd work with the sounds I had in front of me. Actually, I very seldom wrote at any instruments. But I'm definitely into letting sounds dictate . . . not the way I write a song, but the way I develop my ideas. "In This Bed" [from *Emancipation*] is experimental; as we were working on it, I put a guitar on the ground and just let it start feeding back. After a while I hit this button and let the feedback pattern repeat. Does this mean that instruments have a soul or a life of their own? Will *they* end up writing the song?

It's like how after Mayte and I got married, I took her to see the neighborhood where I was raised as a baby. When we got there, everything was gone: The house where I grew up, all the buildings, everything had been torn down, except this one tree that I used to climb on when I was a kid. That's all that was left. So I went over to this tree, put my hand on it, and let the memory of that time flow back into me. If that's what energy is all about, if this tree could remind me of something, even if it looks raggedy and old, that's the most beautiful thing. The sounds in my music are chosen with a lot of love too, and always with the idea of which color goes with which other color.

How do you know whether to do the bass part in a song on synth or bass guitar?

I'll listen to the kick drum. The bass guitar won't go as deep as the synth, and the kick drum tells me how deep I have to go. My original drum machine, the Linn, had only one type of kick. I think I had *the* first Linn. I did "Private Joy" [from *Controversy*] with a prototype of that Linn.

Do you use the Roland TR-808, the rapper's choice, for bass drum sounds?

Sure. I used that on "Da, Da, Da" [from *Emancipation*]. But I need to remind you that I'm not a rapper. I'll do rhythmic speaking. "Style" [from *Emancipation*] calls for words to be spoken, but you can't [vocally] riff on it. It's like James Brown: He'll talk his whole song, but he's not a rapper either. There's music behind my groove; it's not just loops and sample.

On "Courtin' Time" you drew a lot of big-band phrasing for your vocal parts; the whole thing comes from swing jazz. So why did you stick with a backbeat rhythm track, instead of loosen it up into more of a swing feel?

I wanted it to be a dance record. [Saxophonist] Eric Leeds played me this record, *Duke Ellington Live at Newport*, with that long saxophone solo [by Paul Gonsalves, on "Diminuendo and Crescendo in Blue"]. He was telling me that one reason the solo went as long as it did was that this lady jumped up on a table and started dancing to the rhythm, so naturally nobody wanted to quit. That's the vibe I'm trying to capture. I played "Courtin' Time" with Eric once for twenty minutes, and he was wailin' that whole time. That's why even people who are into hip-hop still get "Courtin' Time."

Like "Courtin' Time," "The Holy River" stands out on Emancipation *as a departure for you in terms of the rhythm.*

Well, the melody came first on that one. Sometimes I'll be walking around and I'll hear the melody as if it were the first color in the painting. If you believe in the first color and trust it, you can build your song from there. Music is like the universe: Just look at how the planets, the air, and the light fit together. That's one reason why *Emancipation* is so long—because of the sense of harmony that keeps it all together.

"Soul Sanctuary" is more of an orchestral experiment, with a mixture of what sounds like Mellotron string lines, harp, and marimba.

I'll start a track like that piece by piece. I'll have a color or a line in mind, and I'll keep switching things around until I get what I'm hearing in my head. Then I'll try to bring to Earth the color that wants to be with that first color. It's like having a baby, knowing that this baby wants to be with you. You're giving birth to the song.

Was that a real or a sampled harp on "Soul Sanctuary"?

That was a sampled harp. I wanted to be able to play it perfectly, and while I can play a few simple things on a real harp, the sample helped me get it the way I wanted it. Samples are good for music; you almost can't compare "It's Gonna Be a Beautiful Night," the uptempo song from *Sign o' the Times*, with "The Human Body" [from *Emancipation*] because of the difference that samples make.

Yet your songs don't rely on samples in a structural sense. Unlike a lot of dance-oriented musicians, you use samples to adorn rather than to support a tune.

I am *so* glad you said that! I've heard a whole lot of musicians who have had a hit record and then come to Paisley Park to set up and jam with the New Power Generation. Now, I'm not a judge, but I know when I see someone jamming and when I see someone *drownin'* [*laughs*]! I have to pull their plug and save some of their asses. Man, *learn your instrument!* Be a musician! You can't call yourself a musician if you just take a sample and loop it. You can call yourself a thief, because all you're doing is stealing somebody's groove. Just don't call it music.

How can you tell when the song you're working on has potential?

Well, see, I can't say anything about that, because I hate criticizing music. If you judge something, maybe that means you get judged back someday. I wouldn't tell you that some song you wrote isn't any good. I wrote this song called "Make Your Mama Happy" that would probably really frighten you. And this other song I wrote, "Sexual Suicide," has this horn section that's nothing but baritone saxes; it sounds like a truck coming at you. So who can say?

You don't rate any of your songs as more noteworthy than others?

The thing is, everybody has an inner voice. Mayte and I are into this thing now of wondering whether we're supposed to get up out of bed when we wake up. If you sleep past this point when you're supposed to get up, then you're groggy for the rest of the day. It's the same thing with songs: Each song writes itself. It's already perfect.

I remember when Miles Davis came to my house. As he was passing by my piano, he stopped and put his hands down on the keys and played these eight chords, one after the other. It was so beautiful; he sounded like Bill Evans or Lisa [Coleman], who also had this way of playing chords that were so perfect. I was wondering whether he was playing games with me, because he wasn't supposed to be a keyboard player. And when he was finished, I couldn't decide whether it was him or an angel putting his hands on the keys.

The point is that you recognized something in what Miles was doing, a kind of excellence that you might not hear in the work of other musicians.

For me, excellence comes from the fact that God loves me. But what is excellence? You've heard about these people who will bomb a building and kill all these people in God's name. You could say that they did an *excellent* job at what they were trying to do, right? Now, when I look at my band, Dyson is a different kind of guitar player than Mike. She looks cool, she has that kind of punk attitude. But that's her; that's not Mike. Lisa was never an explosive keyboard player, but she was a master of color in her harmonies; I could sing off of what she had with straight soul. I don't know if the people in the band I'm with now will go on to greatness on their own, but everything they do gives me something that I need right now.

You don't differentiate between musicians either? You don't point to this person as a better player than that person?

God gave us all gifts. If we accept that, we'll all do the best that we can do. Miles took some soul-type players and put Keith Jarrett on top of that; it was magic. And Fishbone—are they good or not? The last time I saw Fishbone, the drummer played the whole gig facing the wall. But in that kind of craziness there was a certain kind of excellence too.

Still, you presumably audition musicians for your bands. That means you have to put them on some kind of scale to rate one as being better, or at least more appropriate to your needs, than another.

Well, "auditions" . . . The idea of a judge is in there somewhere, and I don't want to be a judge anymore. A lot of people criticized the last band that Jimi [Hendrix] had, but they were able to start and stop at his will; they were right for him at the time. I've even hired dancers whose only job was to be there and make me feel good. See, *anybody* can play with me. I can play with any musician and make them sound good, and they can bring something to me. This hit me when I married Mayte and accepted my name for what it is.

With that, the Artist suddenly stood and stretched. "My band will kill me if I don't get in there with them," he announced, bringing the interview to an end. Within a week or two I had translated and transcribed my notes, then called Paisley Park to arrange for the follow-up Q-and-A. The Artist picked up the phone—"You're not taping this, are you?" were his first words—and asked me to send the questions his way via fax. Within a day he had them, and a couple of days later his replies were in my hands. Here, as written, is the final round:

What are the positive sides of music software? Could you cite examples of where running a certain program yielded results that you might not have obtained otherwise?

The body of a human (when healthy) runs like a sequencer. It was obviously programmed a long time ago by an absolute genius. This was the notion behind the groove "Human Body" on *Emancipation*. Every track of the song is its own "cell," so 2 speak, running in harmony with its "cellmates." A living being of sorts is created every time computers are put 2 use this way. No other way yet discovered would be as rewarding.

You noted that one element of using music technology is that the instruments themselves might end up "writing the song." While some artists seem to consider this a reason not to pursue sequencing and sampling, as if the products somehow shift control of the creative process away from the person, you take a more intriguing view, as if you have an almost organic partnership with the tools of your trade. How, then, do you get to know a new instrument?

Something very soul-like attracts me 2 some instruments moreso than others. It starts with the sound and then the shape. I dig instruments that appear as if the makers were in love with them.

Some of your most memorable songs have been structurally pretty simple; if you write a lead sheet of, say, "We Gets Up" [from Emancipation*], what you see is pretty much rooted on the I chord, with minimal melody. What, then, distinguishes a song that doesn't rely on unusual chord changes or an extended melody?*

One-key songs designed 2 put the participant in a trace are best filled up with sound provoked by the spirit more than, say, a structural melody that's best complemented by color. This 2 me is the root of funk: the choices one makes.

You've had a number of customized guitar designs over the years, including the "white guitar" from Purple Rain; *to what extent does playability factor into your design for these instruments?*

I have compromised playability 4 the look of an instrument in many instances. Keyboards, though, have 2 have "the touch." Everything is sort of patterned after the 1st violet piano I received as a gift in 1986.

Chords sound and feel the prettiest on that instrument. Chords are important. Every note in a chord is a singer 2 me. This approach gives my music its life. 2 look at music this way is a reason 4 living, as far as I'm concerned.

You're set up at Paisley Park for analog as well as digital recording. What are the pluses and minuses of the two technologies?

Warmth. Digital is faster. Analog . . . well, the kick drum on analog sounds like a fat dude getting stomped in the back with a timbaland! It's all personal preference.

What approach do you take in rehearsing a new band?

Again, let everybody play their strengths. Because Rhonda's so smart, 4 example, I tend 2 lean toward bassier grooves moreso than with my other bands. She has a nuclear future sure!

What are your thoughts about the state of songwriting today?

I will always respect people like Duke Ellington—someone who has their own style and just watches music change around them. Carlos Santana has more fans now than when he played Woodstock!

You're preparing to tour. Do you find that you compete with the high standards you've set for yourself in past tours? What insights about performing can you share with artists who are working with limited budgets in relatively funky venues?

My own competition is myself in the past. "At war with himself." Y'all said it 1st. 2 the new artists: Be wild and all else follows.

18 QUESTIONS FOR THE ARTIST (STILL GENERALLY KNOWN AS PRINCE)

Ben Edmonds | August 1998 | *MOJO*

On top of a consistent slate of live gigs, 1998 found Prince deeply involved in business and management aspects of his music empire.

January saw the NPG Records release of the three-CD alternates and outtakes collection *Crystal Ball*. Originally mentioned in the *Emancipation* (1996) liner notes, Prince began selling the LP by phone in the first half of 1997, with sporadic Internet updates throughout the year. Confusion ruled. Some customers received the collection by mail in January 1998, while many didn't receive it until after the March retail release, albeit with the inclusion of both the retail bonus LP *The Truth* and the direct-order-only *Kamasutra Orchestra* album by the NPG Orchestra. Still others never received *Crystal Ball*, but in August found an unexpected copy of "The War" cassette in their mailbox (my hand is raised). This is context for author Edmonds's observation that Prince responds "slightly defensively" when asked about how online sales went.

This time also saw Prince assemble a tight label roster composed of his early 1970s musical inspirations, singer Chaka Khan and bassist Larry Graham. He discusses working with the duo, who would each release Prince coproduced material over the next year. This interview was conducted to support the brief summer 1998 European New Power Soul tour, which featured Graham both opening and performing with Prince, with an occasional appearance by Khan. —Ed.

How did you spend your 40th birthday?

Making a video for "The One" (from *Newpower Soul*). Maybe we went bowling; I don't really remember. I stopped celebrating those things a while back. It's the idea of age that causes you to get old and die, so I won't even think about it on those terms, thank you.

As any performer—artist or athletic—matures, there's a constant rebalancing: you lose things, you gain things. Where do you stand?

What have I gained? Everything. What have I lost? Nothing. I can't think of a single thing I'm not better at now. An artist like Larry Graham or Chaka Khan doesn't lose anything. I saw Gladys Knight in New York last week, backed by Maceo Parker's band. Don't try and tell Gladys she's lost anything, or that Midnight Train will roll right over you.

You're making albums with Larry Graham and Chaka Khan. Are they signed to Paisley Park Enterprises?

They ain't signed to nothing and that's the way we like it.

There's no contract between you?

We don't need a piece of paper telling us who we are to each other. Like Larry commented, "What could it possibly say?" (laughs). That we love and respect each other and promise to be creative? We know what's between us. As soon as it's written down, that piece of paper becomes something else, the words on that piece of paper.

So how do you recoup your costs?

What costs? I own this studio, all I have to pay for is the electricity. I play music with Larry. I don't need to play electric company and send him the bill. All I'm doing is offering my time and friendship, and some of the tools I'm blessed to have at my disposal. Which I give freely and with love. This man's music with Sly and Graham Central Station has given me so much over the years—hey, I named one of my earliest bands after him. But forget about me. How does he recoup all he's given? Find me an accountant who can calculate that . . .

Are you producing these Graham and Khan albums?

I don't know what that means. We're trying to get beyond those des-ignations. I couldn't presume to produce a Larry Graham or a Chaka Khan. If anything, these people have produced me, you know (chuckles)? So I'm grateful for the opportunity to offer them my creative support. Each of them is the creator of their own work. We've come up with a saying: "Ask the creator." It really simplifies things. If there's a question that arises out of the art, don't ask an attorney or a manager or a record company VP. Ask the creator.

I gather that there were times when all three of you were working on your projects simultaneously in the Paisley Park complex. What was that like?

I don't think I've ever heard the words to describe it. It was incredibly intense, but easy at the same time. Larry says he has a mental picture of me dancing between the studios, literally off the ground. That's what it felt like. You know good dreams, how they have that kind of flow? Like that. And when I flowed in another direction, something moved into the space where I had been. Example: one night Larry and I had recorded a vocal on him that we were happy with. When Chaka came in the next day she said, "What's Larry doing singing that part in falsetto? If he sings it lower, you'll hear something you ain't hearing now." We didn't see it, but why not? Because there was no clock there was no fear. And damn—the girl was right! It brought out something we didn't even know was there. But does that make her the producer? No, we were just three free people sharing our creativity with one another. And it was one of the most beautiful experiences I have ever had in music.

What prompted you to become actively involved in resurrecting their careers?

This is not a rescue mission. These are not salvage projects. Here you have two strong, talented, creative people who have won their freedom. Like me, they won it the hard way. They've had plenty of bad advice, and bad decisions forced on them. With artists of their stature, you can always tell when it isn't organic. With certain records they've made, you can hear the people behind the glass, you can see the machine at work. Here (gesturing at the Paisley Park complex around him) they can exercise the complete freedom that is theirs.

But the Paisley Park studios are no longer open to the public.

No, renting the studios turned out to be an unproductive arrangement for me and my friends. Like, Lenny Kravitz . . . will come by, and we'll be upstairs shooting pool and hanging out. Lenny's a creative guy, and we spark off each other. If he says, "Hey, I wonder what a backwards oboe would sound like doubled with a 12-string guitar," we'll run down to the studio and do it. There's not much wasted space here. Contrary to what you may have heard, I have quite a few friends.

Artists like Frank Zappa and George Clinton amassed such a backlog of work that producing an album became a matter of pulling stuff off the shelves. Sometimes the art suffered. You're a prolific as either of them. How do you avoid this trap?

Crystal Ball was that kind of an album by design. So were other compilations that we agreed to. Except for that I don't have much interest in the old stuff. It was recorded by somebody else. When I put a record out, I want it to tell me something about myself when I made it. Look at Miles Davis or John Coltrane and you'll hear distinct periods. It's because they were free to follow their muse and capture those changes. That's important to me, too. Look, everybody thinks the breakdown with Warner Bros was over some flood of "product" I wanted to bury the world under. But it started over a single. One song, I had "Let's Work," which was then called "Let's Rock," and I wanted to get it right out on the street. Warners said no, and it escalated from there. Now we've got the process simplified.

From the outside that process can look dauntingly complicated.

Well, that's what they'd have you believe. I was always told there had to be a six-week delay for manufacturing and distribution. When I finally went to the plant to see for myself I discovered they can press 250,000 discs in a day. So it takes the other five weeks and six days to get from the plant to the store? You've got to find out about these things yourself, so you know what's real.

What about the nuts and bolts dirty work of promoting the record?

Once again, you find it doesn't take a degree in rocket science. I get the music to radio and they play it. I get the video to TV and they show it. I go on Vibe. I go on Oprah Winfrey. I talk to you. Isn't that promotion? What else is there? When you break it down, it isn't really that hard.

You've used the internet to sell your music. How's that worked out?

(*Slightly defensively*) Fine. Perfect, in fact. It's done everything we wanted it to do. If people don't think it's successful, maybe they need to change their perception of success. I may have sold a few less records doing it myself, but I make seven dollars on every one as opposed to a buck. Figure it out.

Beyond Larry and Chaka, can you see yourself working with any new artists?

I have no plans to do that. I have no plans not to do it either. I let the spirit guide me, where I am in my life, though it has to be more than music. I'll only work with people I like, nice people who are comfortable to be around. I'm not the president of a record company. I don't want to be the CEO of anything. No titles. The minute you've accepted a title you're a slave to it. You're no longer free.

Does that relate to why you changed your name to an unpronounceable symbol—the ultimate non-title?

That's a lot of it. Black people understand the yearning to find a name that's your own. Show business people understand about reinventing yourself. So what's the fuss? Mostly it's about breaking down any barriers between you and the music. That's all that counts.

Calling yourself by a symbol might be weird. But I imagine nothing could have been weirder to a child than to be called the name you were Formerly Known As.

Yes, I suppose it was. At that age you don't understand the things that make you special—you can only feel it as being different. Children, as we know, can be quick to point those things out. That was when I began to find other people in myself. At first, it may be an escape, but at least it forces you to open up those other doors within yourself. Later, when you understand this, you can see it as strength, though it doesn't erase the pain. But that was a long time ago.

What advice can you give to children who find themselves fascinated by the musical path you've gone down?

It's quite simple. I've said it before. I'll say it again using the exact same words. If you don't own your masters, your masters own you. Underline that. The more people you allow to come between you and your music, the further it moves away from you. This isn't your business, it's your life.

Any final words of wisdom?

Exhale.

THE ARTIST FORMERLY KNOWN AS PRINCE . . . AN EXCLUSIVE INTERVIEW

Jesse Nash | October/November 1999 | *OCA Magazine*

In February 1999 Prince released the re-recorded "1999: The New Master," a low point of his recording career. Out of sight through August, the final four months of 1999 saw Prince engage in a flurry of public activity, mainly media interviews and TV appearances. This press full-court press was in support of his first stand-alone LP of Prince/The Artist new material in three years, *Rave Un2 the Joy Fantastic*, and his year-ending pay-per-view special *Rave Un2 the Year 2000*. Foregoing total independence, *Rave Un2 the Joy Fantastic* album is notable not only because it marks his first collaboration with outside artists (such as Eve and Chuck D), but also because Prince retained possession of the song master recordings even though the album was released through a major label, Clive Davis's Arista Records. This is a market-aware, needing-a-distribution-win version of the freedom he fought so long to achieve.

This exclusive interview was conducted on September 16, 1999, during a New York press junket. It's a fun interview in which Prince's playfulness and sense of humor come to the fore. In addition to discussing the masters and circumstances surrounding the Arista deal (an agreement that ended quickly and not well), Prince holds forth on his ideas about the "Truth" and the existence of time, marking a pivot from his previous Mayte/Egypt spiritual outlook to a Larry Graham/Jehovah's Witness–influenced belief system (although he still swears here). More on this in the next chapter and others to follow. —Ed.

When I arrived at the New York Palace Hotel for my exclusive interview with The Artist we all used to know as Prince, whom we still think of as Prince, and who even uses his real moniker as "his favorite producer" on his first major label release in three years, *Rave Un2 The Joy Fantastic*, through an arrangement with Arista Records, I found a horde of journalists gathered in the hotel lobby.

"Could all these journalists be here to talk to Prince?" I thought. This is NOT the norm for this artist . . . ahem . . . I mean, The Artist, as he likes to be addressed. This is a guy who used to NEVER talk the media . . . especially en masse. But it seems after his much-publicized, close to a decade long, excruciating public battle with Warner Brothers Records, Prince Rogers Nelson [The Artist's real name] seems a bit humbled. Not so much in the interview process—he insisted he not be tape recorded, photographed or videotaped by ANYONE during interviews—but just by the fact that he is now so willing to talk to those in the media who are willing to listen and, of course, publicize his new disc.

The insider's perception of The Artist, now 41, is a bit skeptical. Most of my friends, peers and the like, all have expressed a similar opinion on him—"passe" was one word used quite often. "Has-been" came up even more during our many conversations. But yesterday's opinions and perceptions might be long forgotten if Mr. Clive Davis, the founder of The Artist's new label and the man who lured him in, works his hit-making magic.

The day before the interview took place, a group of about one hundred journalists and record company people spent the afternoon at New York's Equitable Center Auditorium for a very private listening session to embrace The Artist's new album. Hurricane Floyd was creating havoc outside so it was the perfect alternative to an otherwise dreary day. We spent about two hours listening to about seven or eight tracks [out of a reported fifteen to sixteen] with Mr. Davis the ever enthusiastic pitch man. And despite some sound system problems, the experience was a good one. In my opinion, *Rave Un2 The Joy Fantastic* [due out November 2nd], is a well-written album—not ground-breaking [this is NO *Purple Rain* or close to the level of any of his other classics] but memorable. Guest performances with No Doubt's Gwen Stefani and Sheryl Crow stand out. And the first single [to be released September 28th] "The Greatest Romance Ever Sold," is a pleasant track. But success is not always determined by how ground-breaking something is or isn't. And if Mr. Davis's determination to make us walk away loving "The Greatest Romance Ever Sold" [he played it for us three times!], The Artist is in good hands. Right now, Davis is hot having just given another label act—Carlos Santana—his most successful charted album [*Supernatural*] of his long career.

And, of course, lest we not forget the consistent success he has bought to Whitney Houston: Yes, Clive Davis is the consummate hit-maker and that's exactly what Prince Rogers Nelson needs right now—hits.

A surprise one hour concert that took place afterwards revealed one thing about The Artist—his greatest love is playing music, being on that stage and rocking the house. Yes, he may like to show off the same old defiant attitude but, one thing is for sure, these days he is defiant—with an agenda—hoping to recapture some of his former glory.

The following is an exclusive with The Artist Formerly Known As Prince, the producer who IS known as Prince, and Prince Rogers Nelson—one and all—in a rare interview that is one of his most profound. He opens the door for the first time and gives us a look-see at his family relationships, his childhood, his views on freedom and politics, his look at his life, his strong faith in the Bible and what he calls "The Truth"—and reveals that underneath that old defiant attitude and his current agenda, he may be just as human as you and me after all.

OCA: WHEN WE WERE INTRODUCED EARLIER, YOU SAID TO ME THAT YOU HAVE YOUR FREEDOM FOR YOUR NEW ALBUM, *RAVE UN2 THE JOY FANTASTIC*, AND THAT FREEDOM COMES FROM THE SIMPLE FACT THAT YOU OWN YOUR MASTERS FOR THIS RECORD.

Prince: Yes?

OCA: AS AN ARTIST, I CAN UNDERSTAND THAT KEEPING THE OWNERSHIP TO YOUR CREATIONS IS ONE OF THE MOST IMPORTANT ELEMENTS IN BEING A FREE ARTIST.

Prince: Freedom. Mr. Clive Davis has allowed me to keep my freedom for this record. And yes I own all the masters. This freedom is key.

OCA: WHAT IS THIS FREEDOM ABOUT FOR YOU?

Prince: Larry Graham [of Sly and The Family Stone] taught me about freedom by helping me to read the Bible. And the Bible taught me The Truth. Once I understood that I couldn't go against The Truth in life, once I learned to give of myself, then I learned about the real meaning of freedom. When you achieve that, it opens you up, your senses, your creativity. For example, God got Adam. Adam ate the apple and once Adam ate the apple he discovered free will and—literally—all hell broke loose. [Laughs.] Hell came into existence. And that's it. We all have free will. We all have to make choices. But in those choices we must stick to the truth. It's like the stock market. It goes up and down and up and down but it doesn't tell you what's really happening out there. The bible tells the truth. Jimi Hendrix gave up his masters and the truth is out—his music's doing better than ever now. The truth is in the greatness of his music. All I have is this [points to his new CD]. If I give this up, what's left? This is all I have. This is my soul, my identity. If I don't own the thing I created, if I can't do what I want with it, then I'm lost.

OCA: YOU SEEM LIKE YOU'VE BECOME A VERY RELIGIOUS MAN SPEAKING ABOUT THE BIBLE THE WAY YOU DO . . .

Prince: This is NOT about religion. I am NOT religious. This is about The Truth. Most people just don't get a chance to hear The Truth. And most people don't know it when they hear it. After they [might] know it when they hear it but they just don't want to respond to it. Remember The Truth and stick to it!

OCA: AGEING. YOU'RE 41 MAN.

Prince: I am?

OCA: THAT'S WHAT I'VE BEEN READING.

Prince: I'm 400! [Laughs.]

OCA: HOW DO YOU FEEL ABOUT THE AGEING PROCESS. MOST PEOPLE WHEN THEY START TO REACH THEIR FORTIES, THEIR CREATIVE PROCESS DIMS. YOU'RE EXPLODING.

Prince: I'm gonna tell you the truth about this. And if you don't get this right, I'm on the internet and I'll find ya and I'll write, "You didn't get this right!"

OCA: I'LL GET IT RIGHT. JUST TELL ME.

Prince: My mother was sick. She was really sick. She thought she was going to die. And I asked her, "If you could have anything that you want, what would it be?" "More time," she said. "I want more time." I said, "What?!" She said, "I want more time to do the things I've always wanted to do." So ultimately what she really wanted was more days. You want more days. You gotta break it down. If there were only four months to a year instead of twelve, what do you have? You have more days. You'd think in terms of days. You see, what we really have here is like a mind prison. For example. if you could live to be a thousand, would you count birthdays?

OCA: MAYBE. I DON'T KNOW. MAYBE NOT. BUT I'M NOT A GOOD PERSON TO ASK THAT QUESTION TO BECAUSE I DON'T THINK THE AMOUNT OF TIME I WILL HAVE ON THE PLANET WILL EVER REALLY BE ENOUGH.

Prince: Do I . . . would I wanna live to be a thousand—AND look like I do? YES!

OCA: IF YOU COULD KEEP YOUR GOOD LOOKS . . .

Prince: But I can. If I control time and don't let Time control me.

OCA: EASIER SAID THAN DONE.

Prince: No there are ways.

OCA: YOU LOOK BASICALLY THE SAME AS YOU DID TEN YEARS AGO. YOU'RE AGEING VERY NICELY.

Prince: Because I've learned about . . . one thing I've learned is to be stress free. And there have been many times in my life in the past when I've had a lot of stress.

OCA: VERY IMPORTANT THING YOU JUST SAID. STRESS MANAGEMENT.

Prince: But the main thing I'm concerned with now ... time is a joke, you see. It's a trick. For example, the month of August was created because Augustus [during Greek times], he created it. So they added it to the calendar year. And where do you think they got July from? Julius. July. Julius Caesar. They made it up. Why? Because of their ego. They wanted a whole month to he devoted ... all that time devoted to them. So now, they're like, I'm gonna make a whole month out of it. We [as human beings], we are always counting. But Larry [Graham]? Larry doesn't celebrate birthdays. He wouldn't tell me why but he just doesn't celebrate them. Knowing what I know and how I feel about age, I think I understand why.

OCA: IF YOU COULD LOOK LIKE YOU DO NOW, WOULD YOU REALLY WANT TO LIVE TO 1000?

Prince: Yes. Think of how much more I'll know. How much more I'll burst the process. Creation ... Masters ... Slavery ... Husband and wife. THE CONTRACT. Whew! That's a big one! Mayte and I dissolved our marriage contract. Too many weird things are said in there. Meanwhile, so many people are in prison. Their minds are in prison, their bodies are in prison ... everybody's getting divorced. The divorce rate is sky high! Maybe it's got to do with the fact that there's just so many more people but I think it's much more than that—and you can tell me what you think—but I think it has all to do with that contract. There's a contract and a license to be married. You have to have it. And then there are also some vows that are very weird. Too weird for me, man.

OCA: LIKE THE PART WHERE IT SAYS THE WOMAN'S SUPPOSED "TO OBEY" HER MAN?

Prince: Yes!

OCA: *THAT* I HAVE A PROBLEM WITH.

Prince: You wanna get into that?! I could go on and on!

OCA: YEAH, YEAH, YEAH! BRING IT ON HOME!

Prince: I mean, look, between a man and woman you must ask this question: What could you do that I can't do? The answer? Have a baby. I couldn't do that. I'd fall out and faint if I had to do that! You have something I can't do and I as a man have something you can't do—I can protect you. Cause most men are simply physically stronger. Larry Graham and my friend Ananda . . . she challenged him to an arm wrestle. He won every time. Men, for the most part, are physically stronger than woman.

OCA: LET'S FACE IT, MEN AND WOMEN HAVE MENTAL DIFFERENCES. AND THE ISSUE OF SEGREGATING WOMEN BECAUSE SHE'S TOO GOOD FOR THE JOB . . . WE'RE SIMPLY DIFFERENT AND WE SHOULD UNDERSTAND THAT. AND YET WE SHOULD GIVE EACH OTHER THE RESPECT THAT GOES ALONG WITH THAT.

Prince: But society is NOT based on the democratic oath. If society was based that way, you wouldn't have bad trust. You didn't have that trouble a long time ago.

OCA: BUT WE NEED MORE IN LIFE THAN JUST BEING A MAN AND A WOMAN? DON'T WE ALSO NEED A SENSE OF PURPOSE?

Prince: And where do you get that from?

OCA: ME PERSONALLY?

Prince: Yeah.

OCA: OKAY I'LL GO THERE . . . MY SENSE OF PURPOSE COMES FROM INSIDE.

Prince: Exactly.

OCA: AND THAT PURPOSE, THAT STRENGTH IS SOMETHING I BELIEVE GETS DEVELOPED FROM CHILDHOOD THROUGH ADULTHOOD. I BELIEVE EVERYTHING THAT HAPPENS TO YOU AS A CHILD AFFECTS WHO YOU BECOME, WHAT KIND OF PERSON YOU END UP BEING AND HOW STRONG YOU ARE AS AN ADULT.

Prince: That's exactly right. Yeah. So when you're a child and somebody's telling you, "You are strong. You are intelligent. You are a prince . . . ."

Yeah . . . That's what they told me when I was little. They told me, "YOU'RE A PRINCE." Your name is Prince. That's your name.

OCA: SO THAT'S WHERE IT ALL STARTED?

Prince: Yeah man. My sister named her son President! I said, "What did you call him?!"

OCA: WHAT?! [LAUGHS.]

Prince: Wait, wait . . . she named her other son Sir. That's right, Sir. So people have to say "Sir" to him. You know, because he's a black child. You understand? So he's got to come in a society where they will he . . . I don't know if it's right or wrong what my sister did. But I do see what her purpose is.

OCA: DO YOU THINK THE KIDS WILL UNDERSTAND?

Prince: They'll understand this entirely. This is what Arab children hear all the time when they're growing up when they're in Saudi Arabia. "You are a King." They call you that. "Here's my little King." "Here comes my little Prince."

OCA: I SEE.

Prince: And that's why what you see and hear as a child is so important. These are the foundations for a child. And that's why television is scaring me to death. When I watch certain stuff, I'm like, "Oh no, no . . . you just didn't go there on me!?!"

OCA: DID YOU EVER NOT UNDERSTAND? DID YOU EVER ASK YOUR FATHER . . .

Prince: Why he named me that? My father wanted to be a great musician. He played piano. He was very good but he wasn't great . . .

OCA: YOU PORTRAYED HIM LOOSELY IN *PURPLE RAIN*, YES?

Prince: Very loosely. [Laughs.] Anyway, I remember being small and my mother showing me how to write it. That's different than when you go to school and they ask you, "What's your name?" I had a teacher who refused to call me that. Because it's like they're saying King or something. He was like, "We're not going to call you that." He just wouldn't say it.

It was like, "Eh, ah, uh, ug . . . [makes all these sound effects noises]." He wouldn't say it. Uh-uh. [Laughs.] He'd call me everything BUT that, you know. One teacher, you know . . . one teacher once tried to tell me, "You know, that's not your name. That's just made up!" Of course it's made up—my mother and father made it up . . . for me!

OCA: THE SONG OFF THE NEW RECORD CALLED "I LOVE YOU BUT I DON'T TRUST YOU ANY MORE." THAT SEEMS TO BE A BIG PROBLEM GOING ON TODAY. NO TRUST BETWEEN PEOPLE. AND YET, WITH SUCH A SERIOUS SUBJECT MATTER YOU WRITE THIS BEAUTIFUL MELODY.

Prince: Because love ultimately conquers all. I mean, you don't want to base it. . . . I mean, imagine that thing [song] in all minor chords. I could play it for you and the melody would work, the lyric would work but the feeling would be sooo different that you'd think instead he was going to shoot her. The melodic line is the way it is because you gotta get home one way or another. Mistrust just doesn't work. It just doesn't work.

OCA: YOU HAVEN'T DONE INTERVIEWS LIKE THIS IN A LONG TIME. DO YOU ENJOY IT?

Prince: This is the best kind of day for me. This is better than gigging. Because I get a chance to see light come up. We all know it. We all know it but we just don't have anybody to share it with.

OCA: INTERACTION WITH PEOPLE IS VERY IMPORTANT. WITH-OUT THAT, YOU'RE REALLY IN THE DARK. AND ISOLATED.

Prince: Right. I asked my friend Ananda Lewis [from MTV], "Do you find it hard to talk to people?" And she said "Yeah." She said something interesting about the spraying of New York for those deadly mosquitos. On the news it said we're going to spray all up and down Manhattan to kill those deadly mosquitos that are killing people.

OCA: I GOT SICK I THINK FROM THAT BUG SPRAY.

Prince: You see! That's right. All up and down Manhattan. Except at a certain point, a certain street, we're gonna stop. You all know what street that was. We ain't gonna spray up there. What's up with that?

Now, of course, Ananda wanted to say it on MTV. They're not going to let her say that on MTV. Excuse me, you all, but I'll take my chances with a mosquito biting me before I'd take a chance with you spraying with all the children and the pets. That's a whole lot worse! Ananda saw the trucks go by. And she called up instantly and told them, "Are you outta your fucking minds?! This is crazy!" And then the hurricane was coming and what they want us to do is freeze. We want to know the real truth about these things.

OCA: THE TRUTH IS YOUR BEST DEFENSE.

Prince: Oh boy!

OCA: WHEN DID YOU FIND THE TRUTH? WHEN DID YOU START TO READ THE BIBLE? HOW LONG AGO?

Prince: I started to read the Bible when I ran out of answers. When you can't come up with the answers. It's like you're asking and asking but you just don't know. When you know the truth, people can't lie to you any more. They can't steal from you. Strange people don't even want to be around you. If they're weird, they don't want to be around you because this is all you're gonna talk about and they don't want to talk about this.

OCA: IS THAT WHEN YOU STARTED TO CONTEMPLATE THE LETTER YOU USE TO IDENTIFY YOURSELF? AND WERE YOU ABLE TO FIND THE ANSWERS WHEN YOU WERE FIGHTING WITH WARNER BROTHERS TO GET FREE FROM THAT CON-TRACT?

Prince: Yes. I couldn't find the answer how to get out of it. And Londell [McMillan] said something that really stuck with me, "You have to get them to agree." What it is, is that you all are disagreeing now. And it's based in that contract. The contract has stuff in there that you didn't agree with when you signed it. You see? And if you don't agree with it, it's not an agreement [laughs]. You know? I don't agree with the idea that I can't go record with Sheryl Crow when I want to. I don't agree with that.

OCA: THAT TAKES THE FUN OUT OF BEING A CREATIVE MUSI-CIAN. TO BE ABLE TO GET TOGETHER WHEN THE INSPIRATION HITS YOU AND JUST DO IT.

Prince: Right! For the music's sake.

OCA: DO YOU HAVE A CONTRACT WITH ARISTA TO DO A SECOND ALBUM?

Prince: I don't have a contract with Arista.

OCA: SO YOU'RE NOT SIGNED FOR A SECOND ALBUM?

Prince: No. I have an agreement with Arista. Not a contract.

OCA: RECORD COMPANIES . . . HMMM . . .

Prince: I had an argument with a record label many years ago on my second record. Earth, Wind & Fire was rolling at the time and they said, "We gotta put some percussion on your disc." And Maurice . . . Maurice White is just the guy I want you to sit down and talk with. Well, I was like, "Well, I don't want to put percussion on my album." Everybody had it. Everybody had percussion with cow bells and all kinds of stuff. I said, "I don't want that." I want it to sound different. Standing up for something . . .

OCA: I LOVE MAVIS STAPLES. I LOVE THE RECORD YOU DID WITH HER IN 1988.

Prince: I put out a few albums with her but nobody will play them . . . She's just such a reason . . . the point of making things out there that are about something successful. That's what you pump up on TV. But Radio was like, "Nah, that's not our format." You just want to . . . excuse me [stands up and mockingly starts strangling the pillow the chair next to him as though it was a person's head] UGHHH!!!!!!!! [Screams.] Mavis Staples can still sing.

OCA: YOU MUST HAVE AN AMAZING GUITAR COLLECTION. I NOTICED YOU PLAYING A GUITAR IN THE SHAPE OF YOUR SYMBOL. DO YOU DESIGN YOUR OWN GUITARS?

Prince: I tell them what I want it to sound like. I'll play for them and tell them to make it sound like this. Give me more gut. I don't get into pick up positions or wiring . . . I don't know technical terms.

OCA: IN TERMS OF COLOR?

Prince: That I tell them. Purple. Stuff like that.

OCA: HOW MANY DO YOU THINK YOU HAVE?

Prince: Guitars? Uhm . . . probably about 30 . . . no 40.

OCA: AND YOU USE THEM ALL?

Prince: At one time or another. I get a lot of gifts too. Guitar players will just give me stuff. ZZ Top just gave me a gift.

OCA: BILLY GIBBONS?

Prince: Yeah. He gave me a guitar shaped like Texas! [Laughs.]

♀: PORTRAIT OF THE ARTIST AS A FREE MAN

Dimitri Ehrlich | December 1999 | *Notorious*

This interview was conducted for P. Diddy's *Notorious* magazine in the fall 1999 during the *Rave Un2 the Joy Fantastic* media blitz. While some of the same topics (masters, reality, age, etc.) as in the previous chapter are covered with similar good humor, there's more gravitas as Prince here professes his issues with profanity and digs a bit deeper into the current status of his marital relationship. And, overall, beyond the interview, it offers a compact and pointed Prince biography as the calendar turns to the year 2000. —Ed.

"Are movies real?" The man sitting across from me in the multi-million dollar recording studio asks the question patiently the first time. "Are-they-real?" he asks again, enunciating each word as he grows more animated. I stammer. He continues. "Just tell me your first thought: are they real or not?"

"Umm, I guess not," I say, unsure of his line of questioning and of why he seems to be interviewing me, rather than the other way around.

"Okay then. Just stay with me, brother. What's the scariest movie you ever saw?"

"Umm, *Silence of the Lambs*, I would have to say."

"Ok, good, that was scary. Now did that movie have an effect on you? Do you still remember it? How long did it take for you to get over being scared by it?" He is almost bursting with glee as he builds the logic of his argument.

"About a year," I admit sheepishly.

"So how can you say movies aren't real? See what I'm saying!?!"

He jumps out of his chair laughing.

"That's what I'm saying, my brother! Movies are real. Music is real. If it affects people, it's real!" He is chortling and pacing around the limited space behind the million-dollar SSL recording console, pivoting on his feet, swiveling back to face me, and stabbing his finger in the air like a preacher.

"Okay, I see your point," I say. "You're saying that whatever entertainment we expose ourselves to, it's almost like we're being brainwashed by the particular set of values in it, right?"

At this, The Artist, who used to be known as the Artist Formerly Known as Prince, who used to be known as Prince (which is what most of his staff secretly still call him behind his back) leaps into the air with a Rasputin-like blaze in his eyes.

"That's it!"

The Artist is talking about hip hop, using horror movies as a metaphor. It's not that he's a hater—after all, he did tap Eve to make a cameo on "Hot Wit U," from his new album, *Rave Un2 The Joy Fantastic*. And it's not that he finds rap's trademark four-bar loops repetitive from a musical point of view; nor is he jealous of others' gifts for flipping the script. No, the reason he's holding forth on why it isn't all good has to do with something less expected—it's the violent imagery and all the foul language in hip hop that he doesn't like.

"The other night," he says, "I went to a club and I watched the DJ control the entire room. Even politicians can't do that. I watched this DJ, Brother Jules, reach for the new album by B.I.G. and put it on, and the crowd went crazy. I asked him, 'Do you know what he's saying in those lyrics?' He said he didn't know. Then he tried to tell me he wasn't playing it for the lyrics, that for him, it's all about the beat. But it's affecting people. Everything we put out there is affecting people. The message matters, my brother!"

Wait a minute. Run that back again. Is this the same guy who wrote "Sexy Motherfucker?" The same guy who released the infamous *Black Album*, arguably the most listenable example of porn on wax ever recorded? Yes and no. That guy has been slowly disappearing for a few years.

There are several reasons for the change: one, to be sure, is his relationship with Mayte Garcia, a dancer he married in 1996. The intensity of their bond has induced him into some semblance of settling down. (He may also have simply grown up a little with the passage of time. He's now 41.) On the career tip, he's also come into his own, having managed to free himself from an onerous relationship with Warner Bros. and negotiate a conspicuously liberated agreement with Arista Records. The latter are handling the distribution and promotion of *Rave Un2 The Joy Fantastic* through an unusual agreement. An attorney for the label says The Artist's contract is "unprecedented." But perhaps the most important factor is the arrival at The Artist's NPG records of Larry Graham.

Graham, best known as bassist for Sly and the Family Stone, is now a recording artist signed to The Artist's label. And ever since Larry Graham showed up at Paisley Park, the tall, quiet, ever-smiling bassist has brought about a major transformation inside the House that Prince Built. A deeply devout Christian, he's engaged The Artist in countless hours of biblical discussion, and slowly but surely brought about some remarkable changes. For one thing, The Artist doesn't perform "Sexy Motherfucker" anymore. He's dropped it from his playlist. He no longer curses during his concerts—in fact, nobody curses inside the Paisley Park complex. Nobody smokes or drinks there, either. And nobody brings any meat or fish in the building. But those aren't the important changes. The transformation of The Artist has been immense, and if it's not been obvious to the outside world, that's because unlike changing his name, this has been an inner change, an attitude adjustment. The fact is, The Artist is more calm, clear, and relaxed than he's been in decades.

According to one staffer who asked not to be identified, he used to demand that every piece of communication be done by memo. He never used to talk to anyone. No crew members were allowed to look at him or talk to him. I literally saw him fire a guy for looking at him. He just said. "Why is that guy looking at me? Tell him to leave." But ever since Larry came around, "he's relaxed. He's just a lot happier."

On musical terms, The Artist had idolized Graham for years before meeting him, but Graham, for his part, had never even listened to any of The Artist's albums until being signed to his label and joining The Artist's band. He now refers to his boss affectionately as "Baby Brother," a term few others could get away with, and the warm synergy between the two men is remarkable.

The Artist used to be surrounded by bodyguards. Now he and Larry go out at night by themselves, rent movies, go grocery shopping—The Artist even pumps his own gas. He used to periodically fire his entire staff, and has had 46 guitar technicians, none of whom lasted more than a year. But his current guitar wrangler has been with him for three years and running, and despite occasionally making mistakes, has been graced with forgiveness. What is going on at Paisley Park?

The Paisley Park Complex is a sprawling modem building set on a couple of tightly manicured acres of lawn amid the fields of corn, soybeans, and crumbling farmhouses of Chanhassen, Minnesota. Surprisingly not purple, the building exterior is covered with huge white blocks, each about four square feet. Inside, the walls are painted sky blue with tufts of cumulus clouds; columns are purple with leaf trim. One hallway is lined with showing the evolution of The Artist from 1979 to Present. There is a marble floor with his name-symbol inlaid. There's a huge television and movie sound stage, three state-of-the-art recording studios, and a lot of crushed velvet furniture. There are statues from every imaginable award show on earth, including the Oscar he won for the soundtrack to *Purple Rain*, the movie. And for those of you who've ever wondered, "Just what does it sound like when doves cry?" at Paisley Park, you find out. It's an eerie rooster-like crowing that comes from a cage kept upstairs, where four white doves make an unearthly sound all day and night.

Nobody records at Paisley Park now, except for The Artist and his friends, but for years he ran it as a commercial and film studio (*Grumpy Old Men* was shot there, for example). The Artist is a basketball fanatic, so inside the room where his band rehearses every day, a net and backboard are mounted on the wall; he's known to take on all comers. (Once, during a concert in Montreal, the Chicago Bulls were in game three of the playoffs and he was watching the game from a TV at the side of the stage while he played guitar solos. He had his wardrobe girl draw up big cards and flash the score at him.) It is from within this airplane hangar-sized building that The Artist runs NPG records, sells CDs and merchandise, records new music, and generally emanates his purple majesty.

The Artist's home is just up the road from Paisley Park, and he often races back and forth in his purple 1999 Plymouth Prowler. These days, under Larry Graham's tutelage, as The Artist becomes ever more conscious of his actions and their effect on the world around him, he says he prefers to just ride his bike. If he does decide to put the pedal to the metal, he can pretty much do it without fear of consequences, because according to one staffer, the cops in Minneapolis don't give The Artist speeding tickets. He is, after all, a one-man tourist attraction, and he frequently plays benefits for the city. (There's that, plus the fact that what he pays in local taxes alone probably equals more than the combined value of all the speeding tickets issued statewide.)

A brief glance back at The Artist's career trajectory thus far: signed to a seven-album deal with Warner Bros. in his late teens, The Artist amazed the world by writing, singing, producing, and playing all the instruments on almost every track he released. His first massive success came with 1982's *1999*, which sold three million copies, but it was 1984's *Purple Rain* that made him a superstar. (Today, he has a total of fifteen multi-platinum albums to his credit.) The problem was, after *Purple Rain*, which sold 13 million copies, The Artist looked around and realized that his own success had caused him to lose his way. There was no place to go but down. He knew he could never satisfy his audience's need, or his own need, to match that height. "You can't be that again—everything to all people, and I knew it was gonna be rough."

But nobody knew how rough—or weird, it would get. After entering into a long legal war with Warner Bros., during which he attempted (but failed) to win back the right to own the masters of his albums, he left the label under acrimonious terms, but not before accepting a $100 million package in 1992. (Part of the reason he changed his name to a symbol was to wrangle himself free of his contract.) He felt so bitter about the deal that he wrote the word slave on his face and he is now in the process of rerecording all of his Warner Bros. albums from scratch so he can sell them and cut into the company's sales of his back catalogue. He's also about to release a 7-CD set of samples from his vintage music so that people can sample him without having to pay a licensing fee to Warner Bros. You gotta admit it, the guy knows how to hold a grudge.

After releasing one album with EMI in 1996, he began to sell his music under the auspices of his own NPG label, which sold CDs directly to stores and via the internet. He had all the freedom he wanted but his sales weren't exactly phenomenal. Although there aren't any verifiable SoundScan figures to rely on, The Artist claims to have sold 250,000 copies of his 5-CD set *Crystal Ball*, at 50 bucks a pop. Without any advertising or promotional overhead, The Artist got to keep most of that $50 ticket himself, but even so, it amounts to a fraction of the amount of records that say, *1999*, sold.

His new album, released through Arista, allows him to retain complete control over his master recordings while giving him the formidable marketing muscle of a major label. True to form, The Artist remains defiant, refusing to acknowledge the new deal as a retreat. "I don't sell the records, I record them. When I did sell them, we did just fine. The media casts a spell, talking about how many records I'm not selling. But when you count what the label charges you for packaging, video promotion, advertising, and so on, I got more money from selling 250,000 copies of *Crystal Ball* than Warner Bros. paid me for 13 million copies of *Purple Rain*."

While it's unlikely his new album, *Rave Un2 the Joy Fantastic* will even come close to the success of *Purple Rain*, it's still his most commercially viable album in years. Gone are the esoteric leanings of his last few independent releases, and the sense that he was searching for a new direction. The new album offers up simple new wave ditties and throwaway funk pop jams that sound like they were played for the fun of it. The real gem on the album is "The Greatest Romance Ever Sold" which features an inventive Arabic melody and an ultra-lush harmony in the chorus, featuring all three of The Artist's voices: the liquid tenor, the gravelly bass, and the serpentine falsetto. Most importantly, there's a new lightness about The Artist, and it comes across on the album.

The day I met him, The Artist had his hair blown out straight, cut shoulder length and held back with a purple handkerchief, slightly housewife-ish. He wore slender velvet boots with small heels, velvet bell-bottoms that hugged his thighs and ass, and a loose-fitting purple shirt, unbuttoned. On one hand, this is clearly a guy with too many yes-men around him, but on the other hand, who could sit around the house in that outfit and not be a rock star?

Another typical rock star trait that The Artist displays is his slight persecution complex. His vision of the media as a magical caster of spells ties in neatly with his stance on horror films and hip hop; we are all being duped by the Matrix, and we need to wake up. "The media is very important," he acknowledges, "but they get people entwined in a spell. And once that spell is there, that's it. For me, the media is doubly dangerous because I'm everchanging. They're always reducing things to soundbites. A few years ago, it was 'His royal badness.' But the fact is, that has very little to do with who I am."

"People want to sit around, play games, and say nothing. The writer is the spell caster. I give them the opportunity to say what I really think and believe. But they just want to cast a spell. The truth is the truth. It transcends all names and perceptions. That's what I'm studying: the truth. The truth is simple. Is it good? Is the new album by B.I.G. good? Was *The Blair Witch Project* a good movie? Was there any good in it?"

I say, "Oh, yeah, I know what you mean. I love Biggie but sometimes I feel a little guilty bobbing my head to some of the 'kick the bitch in the tummy' lyrics."

He freaks out. "Did you hear what you just said?" he demands, incredulous. Write that down. I'm not mad at you my brother, but I want you to WRITE THAT DOWN!" He is now yelling at the top of his lungs, so I start writing it down. He then patiently leads me through a didactic debate during which he frequently bursts out of his chair and shakes his finger at me, the main point of which is that if something doesn't stack up well against the ultimate truth, it's just no damn good.

"Eve cleaned her rap up to be on my record," he points out with some satisfaction. "When Larry walks in the room, we all become more aware, not only of swearing but even of what we talk about. He's gotten us to the point where nobody swears in the building anymore. In fact, I'm gonna have to start fining you and make you put a nickel in the jar every time you curse. Eve stopped cursing for my record. And I did it too. One day Larry asked me, 'Have you ever tried doing your concert without cursing?' And I was like, 'Wow, I never even thought about that.' I used to swear so much, but nobody should have to hear that. Some people might be offended by that. My crew looks to me to lead the way. They're around me a lot and what I do is gonna have a big influence."

What's remarkable is that The Artist's newfound sense of propriety did not come as part of some wholesale Bob Dylan–style born again revelation, so tiresomely common and predictably short-lived among rock stars. Instead, he seems to be undergoing a slow, reasoned process of spiritualized therapy. He talks about the "Truth" more than about Jesus, suggesting that the changes he's been going through have just as much to do with reason as with faith. Ultimately, the sense one gets is that despite having done a lot of things that might seem weird from the outside (taking on a giant multinational corporation in an extended legal battle, changing his name to an unpronounceable symbol, etc.), mostly, The Artist makes a lot of sense.

Of course, it isn't always perfectly logical sense, like when pressed on the fact that his new album is released by "The Artist," but says it's produced by "Prince." Exactly what is the relationship between the two?

"Our relationship is not contentious. It's an agreement. Prince has the final say. He's the producer. And basically he came in and took a look at that old Linn drum machine we used on our early hits, and he said, 'This is how we rolled in '92, and this is how we rollin' in '99.' And that was it."

Then there's the slightly illogical gap between the fact that he's waged massive lawsuits in the name of freedom, but also sued nine different websites for using unauthorized representations of his name and likeness. I ask him why he's been so hard on his fans, but he contends they're mercenary pirates. "Is it a fan if someone comes to you and says, 'I really love your car . . . and now I'm gonna take it?' We should define the word fan. It comes from fanatic. Look at what people do in the name of fanaticism. They steal property. So let's call it what it is: theft of property. One of these websites had an unreleased track of me and Miles Davis, stolen from here. This is my art!"

In a recent conversation with Arista Records chief Clive Davis, The Artist found out about something called the law of compulsory license, which basically means that anybody can record anyone else's song as long as they pay for it. The Artist was none too pleased to learn this law. "Ginuwine did a cover of my song, 'When Doves Cry.' I walked up to him at a party and told him I didn't appreciate it. He said it was some kind of show of respect. I said, it's cool if you like my song. Just call a brother up and say so. You don't have to cover it. That law doesn't make sense."

The fact is, The Artist likes to keep the reigns in his hand. This extends even to his relationship with his guru: the odd thing about the relationship between Prince and Graham is that the older man, so clearly in the teacher role when it comes to matters biblical, is subservient when it comes to almost everything else. This is partly because The Artist runs Graham's label, and partly just by dint of personality. There isn't even a question of anybody defying The Artist's will when it comes to being musical director at Paisley Park. When The Artist says, "Let's play piano duets," Graham happily obliges. When he calls for a guitar tech to stick a bass in Graham's arms, the radiantly smiling bassist switches instruments without a thought.

When I ask The Artist how he feels about the widely held perception of him as, shall we say, doing things on his own terms, he quickly sees through my euphemism. "You mean like being a control freak?" he asks. "It's about being free. When you're free, you can hear it on tape. It's a wonderful sound. I have a clearer understanding of myself and love now. It's harder to understand love when you're in a bad business relationship, like being an indentured servant to somebody, it shows in the music.

"When I was on Warner Bros. I never wrote songs about getting jacked on the business side. When I got free, I did. When you get clear you see that the record company isn't the enemy. I made the choice to get with them, utilize their services. It was like being in school. I had to get up at six in the morning, like it or not. Now I can play in other people's sandboxes."

He lets the lurid ring of this last sentence hang in the air for a moment before continuing on another favorite topic: his new business deal with Arista Records, which lets him own the master and call the shots.

"I got back into the industry to prove that contracts don't work, and agreements do. I had a contract with Warner Bros. That says what I can't do. But I wasn't free. Now I can make an album with Lenny [Kravitz] if I want to. But he can't 'cause he's still under a contract." The Artist now begins picking up steam, laughing between sentences and speaking with a more southern accent. "He's still on the plantation. But that's his choice, I'm not knocking Lenny. But he's down south. I'm up north.

"Now, ain't nobody gonna tell me I can't own my master tape— because I made such a big noise about it, that's me now. I'm known for that. I don't even have to bring it up. Clive Davis said, 'Of course you can own your own music. It's yours.' I didn't even have to ask, 'How many musicians own their own masters?' Not a lot. And very, very few of African American descent."

Another artist who does own her own masters is Ani DiFranco, who, along with Chuck D, Eve, Sheryl Crow, Maceo Parker, and No Doubt's Gwen Stefani, makes a cameo on *Rave Un2 The Joy Fantastic*. DiFranco happened to be playing in Minneapolis last July, and The Artist came to see her show. "When I left the stadium. there was a huge white limo waiting out back; the window rolls down and there's this most vivid sumptuous man sitting there," she recalls. "He just said, 'What's up?' And then he invited me and Maceo Parker up to the studio." She wound up playing guitar on "I Love U But I Don't Trust U Anymore" and was amazed by his prowess.

DiFranco, too, noted Larry's influence on The Artist. "If you're a growing person, as we get older we tend to think about spirituality more. With The Artist being a really dynamic, ever-deepening person, he was bound to just become more and more reflective and maybe that's helped him to deal with strife, to find his center. It seems like he's in a really good state of mind right now. And Larry is like a Buddha himself. He is so beautiful. The vibe around Paisley Park was really nice."

But a pleasant work environment cannot by itself explain why The Artist seems not to have aged in the last ten years. And it's not just his forever '80s fashion sense; he's got a Peter Pan–like youthfulness that's downright weird, considering he's a 41-year-old workaholic who sleeps two hours a night and does zero exercise. How can he be so well preserved? When pressed for his secret, he leans in and says, "Your magazine probably won't print this, but I don't believe in time. I don't count. When you count, it ages you. If they say you have to retire at 65, you get old at 65. People get hung up on numbers, they push their kids into it and everybody's walking around counting and becoming alcoholic, getting ulcers, evil tempers, and just being really mean. I said to Mayte, 'One day you'll be 35,' and she just jumped. She still needs to work on it."

This is the first time he's mentioned his wife, Mayte, who now lives in Spain where she's working on starting her own dance company. They're not technically married, because as part of The Artist's disavowal of all things contractual, he had their marriage contract dissolved. But it's obvious that he still loves her. While Graham may have been responsible for the philosophical education of The Artist, Mayte seems to have had an equally significantly impact on his emotional growth.

"One thing Mayte taught me was how powerful it is to ask someone for forgiveness. Just think about what an aphrodisiac those words are: Will you forgive me? Because deep down, what we all want most deeply is to learn to forgive. If you can't, you're already in hell."

It's also because of Mayte that he's begun to confront his intense possessiveness. It wasn't long ago that he wouldn't allow her to be interviewed without him in the room.

"I had this thing where I didn't like anyone to touch Mayte: someone would come and hug her and I would shoot her a look, and this change would happen. At first I didn't know where all the tension was coming from, but it would be like there was suddenly air in the room if I saw someone touching her. And then I realized the tension was coming from the words, 'my wife.' Before she was 'my wife' Mayte was a child of God. And if a man hugs her wrong, that's just another child of God doing wrong and he will ultimately pay a price for that." The Artist pauses for a moment and then adds, "and I'll be there to watch him as he gets kicked down the stairs."

After the interview ends, The Artist calls his recording engineer, Hans (who refers to himself as "Buff Daddy"), and instructs him to start recording. Then he looks at me and says, "Me and Larry are gonna jam. You wanna join us?"

Being invited to jam with The Artist is a little like having Roy Jones Jr. ask you to have a slap fight. To call it intimidating would be an understatement. I manage to get the word "yes" out of my mouth and he hands me an acoustic guitar, recently given to him as a gift from Ani DiFranco. "But don't play any originals," he warns, "we don't want to have to pay you any royalties!" It was a joke, of course, and a self-effacing one, poking fun at his own protracted fights for ownership of his music. But just in case he wasn't kidding, I sheepishly promise not to. "We'll follow you," he says mischievously. I protest but he says, "You lead, or come back." When The Artist says, "come back," he means, "go away," so I acquiesce and begin playing a fairly simple blues groove. But a few seconds into it he interrupts: "You gonna call out those chords?"

"Umm, I was just making it up," I offer, somewhat disbelieving that he couldn't (or more likely wouldn't) just get loose and respond to an unknown set of chord changes. But he's the boss, so I just stay on one chord, and vamp on a James Brown riff, too frightened to modulate or even vary what I'm doing. Just when it's getting good and The Artist and I start doing a call-and-response thing, shouting guitar phrases back and forth at each other, he decides the song has gone on long enough and that was it. My fifteen minutes of bliss hasn't even lasted fifteen minutes. But it was still cool, and one day I'll tell my grandchildren. They'll probably roll their eyes and say, "Who's Prince?" But fuck those little bastards.

AN INTERVIEW WITH THE PRINCE FORMERLY KNOWN AS THE ARTIST

Barney Hoskyns | March 2000 | *MOJO*

Conducted November 18 during the European portion of the *Rave Un2 the Joy Fantastic* publicity barrage, this is the third and final 1999 interview in this collection. All were conducted a few weeks apart, and understanding there is some degree of repetition, this article is essential for the interplay between The Artist and the continually perceptive and mischievous Barney Hoskyns. Prince's passive-aggressive greeting of Hoskyns recalls his interaction with Steven Ivory, an interviewer who had also written a book about Prince. Continuing his musings on what's real and what's made up, what's true and what's false, Prince calls out Hoskyns over a recent *MOJO* article. It might be news to legions of contemporary Prince fans that Prince thinks engineer Susan Rogers knows nothing about his music. —Ed.

First, a caveat. This is probably not the first piece you've ever started reading about FINALLY MEETING THE ARTIST FORMERLY KNOWN AS SHHH-YOU-KNOW-WHO. In fact, you're probably bored silly by accounts of waiting in the antechambers of Paisley Park to natter to the maverick chameleon who single-handedly bossed '80s pop.

That I happen to have scribbled more widely than many on The Artist Formerly Possessed of Indisputable Genius—and even written a book on the wee fella—doesn't mean I have any more claim to your attention than the various other notepad-wielding hacks who've been granted audiences with His Majesty over the past few years.

If it makes any difference, let me say that this piece about little Mr. Symbol—the Prince we knelt before, the Artist whose recent works have left most of us cold—was never intended to be another slice of pseudo-newjournalism, interviewer to the fore. If you must know, it was conceived as straight Q&A, an "inter-view" with one of pop's most towering talents, reaching back to the golden age of his music and looking forward, perhaps, to a millennial second wind as he climbs towards 50.

But know this, readers: if I'd written up my 40 minutes in the company of The Artist as "straight Q&A" you'd have swiftly concluded we were *both* mad.

So I'm standing in the corridor outside a suite at London's posh Four Seasons hotel—formerly the Inn on the Park—and I can hear a kind of high, whinnying cackle from inside, where The Artist is being grilled by a chap from *The Observer*. The cackle is almost certainly coming from the same throat that, back in 1983, urged us to party like it was 1999. Now, in that very year, an American representative of Arista—The Artist's new home—hovers anxiously beside me as she waits to usher me in to The Artist's august presence.

For me there's a strong sense of déjà vu about the situation. Seventeen years ago, with "1999" in the Top 30 in Britain, I stood outside the door of a dressing room in Kalamazoo, Michigan, and awaited an introduction to the then Prince. Never have I forgotten the suspicious little face that eventually poked its way through the faintest of cracks, barely grunting in acknowledgement of my presence. Until now, that was the closest I'd ever got to the man.

Another loud whoop from inside the Four Seasons suite. The Arista gal looks faintly relieved. More relieved than she looked three days ago, when hundreds of disgruntled meejah [*UK slang for "media"—Ed.*] folk were kept waiting at London's Mermaid Theatre by His Artistry, all the while being entertained by the sight of Arista supremo Clive Davis "getting down" onstage to the track-by-track playback of The Artist's tepid new offering *Rave Un2 The Joy Fantastic*—a spectacle roughly akin to watching Henry Kissinger do the Hustle at Studio 54.

Of course The Artist finally came on and blew us all away. And of course it was almost as exciting as seeing the brilliant delinquent sprite of

1982, parading his fishnet stockings before a legendarily sparse gathering at London's Lyceum. And who should show up to watch and worship but Beck, whose polymorphous pleasurefest *Midnite Vultures* positively fizzes with the influence of Prince-as-was . . .

And so it all comes around again.

Now I'm face-to-face with the black-clad elfin deity, right hand extended as I approach him, not so much nervous as disbelieving that this can really be him, the mercurial marvel I've studied and rhapsodized about for years.

And what does he go and do, contrary little bugger, but stick out his *left* hand. Is this some Indian hygiene issue, or is it The Artist fucking with my head?

The answer comes quickly enough.

Barely has the Arista senorita departed the room when the man jumps on my case. Turns out he's closely scrutinized a long *MOJO* piece I wrote back in 1997, a piece based on interviews with a clutch of people who, in various capacities, had worked with him: people like Owen Husney, his first manager, and Susan Rogers, longtime engineer at the Paisley Park studio in Minneapolis. Also turns out that he puts pieces like this up on his own website and corrects any factual errors they contain.

"You think Susan Rogers knows me?" he asks. "You think she knows *anything about my music*?"

Shocked lump in throat, I respectfully suggest that yes, she might know a thing or two.

"Susan Rogers, for the record, doesn't know anything about my music. Not one thing."

I see.

"The only person who knows anything about my music . . . is me."

Right.

"As for Owen Husney, that's a joke."

If you say so.

"Lemme ask you something. What you wrote about me, was that the truth or was it conjecture?"

"Erm . . . "

"Was it the truth or was it conjecture?"

"Some of it was conjectural, I suppose."

"And if conjecture is not the truth, then what is it? Isn't it just *lies*?"

Understand that all of this is said with a broad smile, and accompanied by occasional pattings of my knee. And that's just for starters. When I ask him about something Minneapolis writer and early Prince champion Jon Bream told me—that the boy wonder never once looked him in the eye in four years—The Artist rises to his feet, runs across the room and hurls himself headfirst into an armchair.

"Jon Bream didn't know me," he says when he's recovered from a virtual fit of squeals. "That's where the conjecture game kicks in real deep. How you gonna write about me when life is ever-evolving? The truth is that we human beings are separate, but we become even more separate by putting labels on each other. My wife knows me. She's the one who brings me tea in the morning. She's the one I call God's queen. Jon Bream didn't know me. Maybe I appeared to be shy, but 'appeared' is the key word there. If you look at it, I've only really ever given you music. I'd give cryptic little answers to questions that made no sense. I've always really been the same person."

Jeez, whadda ya say to *that*?! I'm sitting here literally dumbfounded by a man who didn't speak a word for years and is now spouting forth this heady brew of mysticism and embitteredness.

"People think they know my music," he continues. "They think they know where my songs come from. But you can't speculate on a song like 'The Ballad Of Dorothy Parker.' People pick these things up and that becomes the truth. It makes me fear for the planet. Well, not fear, because I don't believe there's any such word as 'fear,' but it makes me pity the planet.

"We forgot God's will at some point. God is ever-evolving and ever-revealing. Larry Graham [The Artist's bassist and former lynchpin of the Family Stone] goes door to door to tell people the truth about God. That's why I told myself, I need to know a man like him. He calls me his baby brother. Do you know how wonderful it would be if you and I could respect one another? We could really do something positive. Otherwise you're gonna further confuse an already confused reader."

Why do I have the distinct sense that this interview is turning into a covert exercise in torment?

"All these *non-singing, non-dancing, wish-I-had-me-some-clothes fools* who tell me my albums suck—why should I pay any attention to them?"

But worse is to come. When I rashly let slip the fact that I once wrote a whole book about him, he asks what it was called. *Imp Of The Perverse*, I inform him. Boy, does he love that.

"Imp, huh? That's what, a small person?"

"Um, not really. More a sprite, a mischievous creature . . . "

"What about perverse? That's the same thing as perverted, right?"

"I meant it more in terms of, you know, deviating from the norm . . . as you were doing in the '80s."

He's less than convinced.

"The book is a total celebration of your music," I protest feebly.

"Is it truth or is it conjecture?"

Oh shit, not back to that . . .

"Did you come to the source for the truth?"

"You think I didn't try to get an interview?!?"

"Yeah, but what gives you the right to write a book of conjecture about my life?"

Er, it's a free country?

"See, what I do is I look for the truth in things. We're talking about spirit and interaction. We've got to stop this madness. Jimi Hendrix was trying to do that at the point when he passed away. You're talking about a guy who played 'The Star-Spangled Banner,' but he played it in a way that showed exactly what it was about. He played it on TV on Dick Cavett's show and Cavett said it was 'unorthodox.' Hendrix said, 'Well, it's beautiful to me.' Dick Cavett, you just boxed him in, and you don't have that right!"

Keen to get away from the truth/conjecture issue, I ask him if he always knew that—like Hendrix—he was going to bridge the worlds of R&B and rock?

"You have to understand that those terms are just language. I have a bunch of great stars on my new album—No Doubt, Sheryl Crow, Ani DiFranco—but it's almost like you wouldn't notice. Gwen Stefani is just a cool sister to me. I put her on a track on the album I thought she'd be good on, and she blends right in. The more I think about it, the more music is all just based on colors and sounds."

What did he learn from people like Miles Davis and Sly Stone, artists who bridged different musical worlds?

"Yeah, but Miles wasn't thinking in terms of bridging. People wanted to play with him because they knew he wasn't going to bow to any rules. A strong spirit transcends rules. See, Maceo Parker and Ani DiFranco love one another and laugh about the same things. There's no categorizing in the studio. RZA of Wu Tang said to me, 'I ain't commercial, it's y'all who tell me whether I'm commercial or not.' You'd have to be blind, deaf or a music critic not to like Larry Graham's playing." (Charmed, I'm sure . . .)

So why has he signed to Arista after all that hoopla about only releasing his music through the Internet? Is it part of a change that'll bring him back into the music mainstream?

"Well, understand that Arista signed to *me*. I don't have a contract with them. Our agreement is just for *Rave Un2 The Joy Fantastic*. Clive Davis may not even *be* at Arista this time next year. As for the 'mainstream,' we have to define what that word means. It might mean something different to me than it means to you. My mainstream is the one that goes to my bank account! [*Loud explosion of laughter*] Am I getting my money straight away or is it TLC royalty? Mainstream is the way Ani DiFranco is doing it. She's taking $7 an album where some rapper is getting $1.50 and out of that he has to pay all his costs."

Does he like contemporary hip hop?

"I like positivity, I like the truth. I like the brothers who are gonna enrich and not degrade. Why would I want to listen to music about bitches and shooting people? It's just somebody's *idea* of what 'bitches' are. See, Eve [hip hop guest on *Rave Un2*] changed her groove up for me, and that says something about me and it says something about her and it says something about the record industry that will accept that. And yes, we all have to take responsibility for things we may have sung in the past. I take responsibility by changing."

Ms. Arista is hovering again, worried that The Artist will be late for a Top of the Pops taping of "The Greatest Romance Ever Sold," his new single. I ask him why he decided to bring "Prince" back on board as the producer of *Rave Un2 The Joy Fantastic.*

"It's funny, when you see a picture of yourself at ten years old, why do we call it an 'old' picture? Language is so confining. In fact, I might just stop talking again and not do interviews."

You read it here first.

NEW YORK CITY PRESS CONFERENCE

May 16, 2000 | Original Transcript

In a mostly quiet year, The Artist made headlines on May 16 with the following announcement:

"On Dec. 31, 1999, my publishing contract with Warner-Chappell expired, thus emancipating the name I was given before birth—Prince—from all long-term restrictive documents. I will now go back to using my name instead of the symbol I adopted to free myself from all undesirable relationships."

He followed the press release with this engaging and somewhat freewheeling press conference at New York's Sports Club L.A. The back-and-forth includes background on his falling out with Arista Records, more details on his spiritual direction, and a fair share of name-dropping. And laughing at the reporter who wonders if he's trying to appear "a little less weird."

He soon followed the press conference with his first Celebration, an early June event that opened up Paisley Park to the public for a week of tours, talks, and performances that culminated in a three-plus-hour show on June 13 at Minneapolis's Northrup Auditorium. He followed up with Celebration weeks in 2001 and 2002, and the gathering was reconvened in 2017 after his death.

This press conference transcription is incomplete but is based on the best available sources. Press conference cameraman Jon Wiederhorn, working at the time for Guitar.com, is unsure if the complete original footage still exists. —Ed.

Reporter: Hi, Prince. Welcome back.

Prince: That sounds great. I haven't heard that in a while.

Reporter: Well, you forgot.

Reporter: Prince, I know you say were not pleased with how the first album went, *Rave Un2 the Joy Fantastic*. Will you be at the helm of mocking up the second edition of it, and what do you plan on doing differently that was not done the first time around?

Prince: Well, Clive and I have an agreement where I was just gonna release on Internet only and he was gonna handle stores. So, really all I can do on that regard is just release the record and allow it to be downloaded or however we get it to consumers. That's why I want to bring them to Minnesota and just talk to people. Just let them tell me how they want it from now on. The interesting thing in *Vanity Fair*, and I used it before I even saw it, but, I always get journalists saying to me, "You're not selling as many records as you used to." And I say, "Well, I never sell the records. I only make, 'em, right?" So, you gotta talk to the accounting firm on that.

Reporter: Are you saying that at the end of June, when Clive's contract is up with Arista, that your contract is through with Arista, or . . . I'm just a little confused about what your relationship will be with Arista when Clive leaves.

Prince: I didn't have a contract with Arista—I had an agreement with Clive. And it was, it was very simple; it was like two pages. Contracts this thick [*He gestures about four inches*], there's no reason for them. Period. And I think it's unlawful and the moment artists get together and challenge it, it's gonna go right out the window. Their system is like this [*He flicks his index finger*], it's just ready to get knocked over. It's not even—there's nothing stable about it. I need Larry here to balance me. I'm about to get bounced.

Reporter: The Prince Celebration, there's talk of opening Paisley Park to fans for like a week. I was wondering if you could talk a little bit about what you can expect from that or get on the tour or whatever.

Prince: Well, people who supported my music through the years never really got a chance to go inside Paisley Park if they hadn't seen some sort of film of it or whatever, and a lot of changes have happened in there recently. It's a more public friendly place. All the studios are opened back up and they'll be ready for business in August, and there's just a lot to do there, and I'd like for them to see what they helped to create. You know, it's the interaction that went on with us throughout the years that actually painted the joint.

Reporter: Hi, Prince. When you say that Mayte's doing her thing and you're doing your thing, what exactly does mean? Does that mean that the two of you are no longer together?

Prince: I think that is difficult to discuss. It's always been difficult to discuss because . . . I always want to be on record for speaking the truth about it and together, we're all together here. You know, married, we're all kind of married here. Intimate. You know, words are interesting and she, she . . . that's the clearest that I could put it was she does her thing and I do my things. Sometimes we do our thing together.

Reporter: Five years from now do you think music will be a free commodity for consumers, and is that something you would hope for?

Prince: Well, money still has to be involved. It's a curse. You know. It's a long conversation, and sometimes we play a game at Paisley called "in a perfect world." You ask somebody, in a perfect world, what would you do today for the next three hours? A sister might say, "I wouldn't be cooking." All right. If you weren't cooking, you gotta feed your family. How would you do that, and then we start to talk about in a perfect world you would do that. So one thing we're gonna do is build a food facility right next to Paisley Park in the shape of an egg. So, the people in our community get food from this place for free. This means you don't—and it's meals designed for them and their family. This means you don't have to go to the grocery store, you don't have to think about—all of your food bills are taken of. And, of course, this is for people within our community, the ones who work at Paisley Park can actually help us with the gardens and what have you. If you take money out of the equation, it's interesting what happens. Chaka Khan was in our studio and was trippin' because she didn't have a budget. I said, "the studio's free. It's just electricity. I wouldn't know how to charge you anyway. When your album's finished, your album's finished. You know, you tell me." So, whether music ends up to be free or not, I think the question is about all that.

Reporter: Hi, Prince. You went on *The View*; you went and talked to Oprah a couple years ago. Are you trying to change the way that the masses perceive you? Now you're going back to Prince. Are you trying to come across as being a little less weird? [*Laughter.*]

Prince: These are my favorite questions. Can we get you on film first? No, I've never thought of myself as weird. The people who really know me don't think so, either. So, how you perceive me is how you perceive me.

Reporter: I wanted to know, knowing that the name Prince is gonna be on your next album, that it's gonna be a Prince album, does that change at all how you approach an album or how you would write your songs or gather them together?

Prince: You know, everybody has their own perception again about me and my music and things like that. I think, though, that if you really put everything back-to-back in a linear fashion, you'll see that "The Greatest Romance" is pretty much saying the same thing as "P Control," the same thing as "Sexy MF," you know. What people get out of it is what they get out of it. The same thing, like, as she was just saying, what I got out of the music business was, that if you don't own your masters, your masters own you. Some people find fame and fortune and they're cool with that. It's like, that system is going to be, what you're talking about, whether the music's going to be free or not, I would just like to see an alternate system. I mean, that would be cool. But there's no way right now for people to get seen or heard unless somebody that has nothing to do with the creation of the music gets paid. I mean, literally gets paid. That's just an absurdity.

Reporter: How would you suggest to a new artist that they reach the masses without taking a major label deal? Do they go through distribution companies? Or, if they wanted to try to remain independent, how do you suggest that they reach the masses without the machine-like power of a label?

Prince: Well, I, when I sit down to talk to Jimmy—one day, recently Jimmy Jam, Terry Lewis, Babyface, L.A. Reid—we just sat in a room and just started discussing things like this. You know, it's, I challenge all of them. I do and I will continue to. You know, when you get the money together like all of us have amassed, let's just sit down and create a new system so that we don't have to run back to distribution companies, this, that, and the other. And really talk with these program directors and DJs about opening up in every marketplace, at least four slots that artists can get heard and get their music out to the people. And that could revolve. All the music actually, it should just be constant revolving. But it's not like that. Everything's like these playlists and what have you. Like I said, it just needs to be altered 'cause right now there is none.

Reporter: Question over here for you. Over this side. Hi. Do you plan to continue to use the symbol to represent Prince now, or does the symbol go away?

Prince: Well, it's an internationally known logo now so, um [*Shakes his head*]. I really haven't given it much thought. What I did give much thought to was changing my name. Not changing my name, but using my birth name because there's still a lot to do. I thought it would be interesting though, to, if I ever do anything with a major label, to let them use the symbol. You know because something interesting happened. Everybody was saying, "Oh, he thinks, he thinks he can get out of the contract by changing his name." Well literally, that's what I did. Because when you go to the meetings you say, "Well, I have a new album." They say, "Well, it's gonna be under Symbol, right?" "No, it's gonna be under Prince." And they say, "Well, we don't want a Prince album." I said, "Well, that's who you signed." "Well, we, everybody knows you as this symbol now." "Well, you'll have to make a big deal of it." [*Laughter.*] So, me and Mo Ostin, and he knows it, arguing, big loud screaming matches. They would actually say, "Well, you're trying to trick us." "No, I ain't trying to trick you. Let's make a new deal then." "All right, what's the terms of the new deal?" "Well, I want my masters back." "Well, you can't get your masters back if you gave us a billion dollars." Now, make a statement like that to me means that I don't really have any power over them. Now, somebody I thought I was hiring to be my distribution company—I thought I was hiring. Because, I mean, it was between three companies, Sony, A&M, and Warner Bros. And after much wining and dining—I mean, it was crazy back then, you know. A&M was "OK, we'll give you a house." [*Laughter.*] I wasn't gonna live anyplace. I want to go on the road. This is what I lived for my whole life. I'm ready to work now. "OK, well, how 'bout this"—it was crazy. It's interesting like the fight between Disney and ABC, or Disney and Time Warner recently. You got grown people calling each other "deranged individuals" and "arrogant manipulators," right? No dis to the photographers. I've had trouble with y'all sometimes, but, it's like "OK, we gonna take turns and take pictures here now everybody starts hollering." I'm just in the back going, "This is vicious." It's just, we grown people now. Right? Let's act like it. All of us. You know, I ain't going to Washington to discuss no craziness. [*Laughter.*]

Reporter: Hypothetically, who would win in a fistfight, you or Michael Jackson? [*Laughter.*] You're both rather the same size, you both have the high-pitched sounds. What is your right hook like?

Prince: He's a plant, y'all. [*Laughter.*] But I plant him. Keep it light, keep it light. Michael's not a fighter, he's a lover. [*Laughter.*] Can I just say something? I've never really spoke publicly about Michael. We should all just kind of chill because it's, you know, he may know something none of us really know and just like, let's wait and see. Let's wait it out. Just wait it out. You never know, right? You just never know. Ultimately we all got to come back home, so . . . let's just make a home for every son. But I should right hook him when he gets here, right? [*Laughter.*] But, all right.

Reporter: Prince, thank you for being here today. Assuming, hopefully, all of us are assuming that you will go out on the road, if not later this year, then soon. Do you see yourself doing another kind of extended 150–200 date tour anytime soon?

Prince: I'm really concentrating on my spiritual studies now. I just want to do that for a while. This has been a . . . interesting journey. Recently we were working on a time tunnel for Paisley Park where kids get to walk up and down and see over time, in a linear fashion, which my career has gone. There was a, when we made the tunnel at first, the last picture was a picture of Mayte on it. Embraced. And I always thought that was the final picture. I didn't want the, you know, that's the way, I said, now it's over. And then I looked, and she ended up doing her thing and I ended up doing mine. And then, there's a door there, in the time tunnel, and it leads to the next room, but there's more wall, and I had never noticed it before because I always thought that was the final picture. So, there's more space for more events and I just really want to ask God, in solitude, what it is that he would like. It was interesting the other day. A friend of mine said, "So what should I call you now?" I said, "You can call me Prince." And it just felt good to say that again because I hadn't in so long. I am just, I'm really curious to see what happens next.

Reporter: You've been making music now for over two decades, and obviously you've now been in the business for close to that amount of time. For the past few years you've been focused on legally freeing yourself and trying to have an impact on contracts and all these things. Now that Prince is back, musically, do you have a conversation about where, kinda, R&B is now, and where it's going with hip-hop and R&B and all the different forms it's, we find it in now.

Prince: Like I said, I think the quality has gone down pretty much. I was . . . "Midnight Love" was playing last night on BET, but I wasn't watching it. I was getting ready to go out. I couldn't tell one scene from the next. All the beats were the same. All the subject matter was the same. I mean, I didn't grow up like that. I didn't know music like that. Marvin Gaye sounds completely different than the love songs of Curtis Mayfield, which were completely different than the love songs of Stevie Wonder. That's how I grew up. That's what I'm about. I think what . . . here's the truth about what I think's gonna happen. When Chaka Khan came to our studio, and I told her, "You can record in here as long as you want. If you want strings, we'll go get you strings. If you want orchestra and horns, we'll go get that. Whatever you want, we're going to fully realize your vision. When you say that you're done, then we're done." I think it's gotta somehow get to that where studios don't charge you. It's interesting how hip-hop came out of freedom. Where a kid gets to record on your own in your own cribs and such. You start to hear a different type of sound. The sound sounds free. And I had a discussion with a, uh, ex-staff when I was writing on my face and he says, "So, uh, what I call you now? This hip-hop, is it gonna last?" I was completely shocked. "Are Black people gonna last? That's a crazy question." He didn't know. So, what he did, he put some people in place to go [*He shakes*] fired all up, right? So, once again, they've [*Points*]. Seen that movie *Black and White*? I haven't seen it yet. I'm curious to see it, though.

Reporter: I think we all gotta be wondering what we can look forward to coming out of Paisley Park from you, and a lot of the works that you're looking forward to.

Prince: Well, every day's changing for me. I recorded a lot of stuff recently, and, you know, you can be in one frame of mind, playing rock and roll guitar and then Najee'll walk in, and—you know how plays—I sit down and start jamming with him and this whole other sound comes out and I'll be over there. What we're seriously considering is, because I play so many different styles, is maybe putting out numerous records during the year, that rather than trying to put so many different styles on one album, you know, have a jazz record, have a ballad record. Recently we had this album called *When 2 Are in Love: The Ballads of Prince*, and it had all the jams on there. I mean, it was—I was impressed. Right? And, you go to Warners, to license your own music from them, and you can't get a call back. Stuff like that, I mean, I could do so many wonderful marketing things with my own music if I had complete control over it. But that's what I've been fighting for all these years and will continue 'til the battle's won.

PRINCE: THE Y-LIFE INTERVIEW

Bilge Ebiri | June 2001 | *Yahoo! Internet Life*

Prince was long interested in different types of promotion, distribution, merchandising, and fan engagement. In the early 1990s, he opened brick-and-mortar Glam Slam night clubs and NPG stores. Around the same time he started the direct-marketing phone number 1-800-NEW-FUNK. He also gave away copies of his albums as part of a concert ticket purchase (*Musicology*) and on the cover of newspapers and magazines (*Planet Earth*, *20Ten*). But his most sustained, and contentious, channel relationship was with the Internet.

This interview takes a deep dive into Prince's thinking about the state of online music in the first half of 2001—about Napster, artists getting ripped off by the music industry (natch), and the Valentine's Day launch of his online NPG Music Club. NPGMC was at least his fifth crack at establishing a website since his first in 1996. He would battle against fan websites in 2007 and tinker online until he declared in 2010 that the Internet was "completely over." He returned in 2013, energized by 3rdeyegirl and social media. –Ed.

Back in August of 1997, well before the world was talking about music on the Internet, Prince—then known as the Artist Formerly Known as Prince—made an odd announcement. Recently released from his recording contract with Warner Bros., he declared that he was going to sell *Crystal Ball*, his upcoming five-CD set (it shrank to four CDs in stores), over the Web. At the time, it was easy to see the move as yet another eccentric twist in the career of a musical maverick. This, after all, was a man who in 1993 had changed his name to an unpronounceable symbol.

Today Prince seems like a visionary, not simply because he was the first major pop star to sell an entire album on the Web, but also because he has devoted so much of his career to fighting the recording companies' stranglehold on the distribution of music. The name change, for example, wasn't some kind of bizarre social experiment—it was an effort to outmaneuver Warner Bros., which still retained the rights to recordings made in his name, even after he'd been freed from certain of his contracts. (He also famously scrawled the word *slave* across his face.) It's possible now to see these actions for what they were: some of the first shots fired in the war against the recording industry, a war that continues to rage among fans, executives, and artists, with controversies over copyright, Napster, and CD price fixing.

Prince reverted to his original name in May 2000, after his final contract with Warner expired. Now, looking back on his time inside the record-industry juggernaut, he is by turns indignant and reflective. But more important, as the patron saint of wired artists, he continues to push the boundaries of technology and art. At the beginning of the year, he released two free downloadable songs on his site, NPG Online Ltd. In February, he launched a fee-based subscription service called the NPG Music Club, offering fans three new downloadable singles every month. And in April, he announced that he would release a new track, "The Work—Part 1," on Napster.

Naturally, it also helps to be as prolific as Prince. Rumors still circulate that he has hundreds upon hundreds of unreleased songs in his private vaults. That all adds up to an unlimited supply of content—"the fuel," as he called it during his conversation with *Y-Life* at his Paisley Park studios in the outskirts of Minneapolis. And content, as a Prince would know, is king.

Y-LIFE: You've been very outspoken against the music industry, going so far as to change your name and write slave on your face in protest.

PRINCE: I don't have any hate for these people. Ultimately, what people don't know is what they end up focusing on and misunderstanding. If I'm changing my name and writing on my face, they assume I'm crazy. And then they'll say that I'm not capable of distributing my own materials.

My first Warner Bros. contract was huge—full of terms, restrictions, that sort of thing. We need to stay out of the way of that. If it's the music business, then the musician should get the lion's share. And when artists figure that out, there'll be an uprising. Right now, if you resist their kind of thinking, what do they do? They'll kick you out to the curb.

Y-LIFE: Aren't all industries like that, to a certain extent?

PRINCE: At least in the movies, a successful actor can get $20 million. It's not like that in the music business. Destiny's Child brought in $93 million last year. How much do you think they themselves actually got? It's totally unequal.

Record executives will say, "Destiny's Child made $93 million last year." You ask them, "Why did Destiny's Child themselves only get $4 million of that money?" I mean, have you heard Beyoncé sing? Puh-leeze! She ain't even 20, and she's got a voice like that! Let's kick it up to $30 million. Is that fair? They won't answer. They'll say, "You don't understand. . . ."

When you talk to record executives, you'll hear an arrogance that's astounding. They're under the assumption that artists don't know the way the industry works. Sheryl Crow has this saying; she refers to people as having "no Midwestern common sense." So they'll say something like, "We have 85 percent failure expectations on new acts," meaning they expect the vast majority of them to fail. You've got 85 percent failure expectations, and you're signing them to long-term agreements? "Well, they might not fail." What does that mean? This system makes $40 billion a year. And it's all based on this type of logic.

Y-LIFE: Why don't more artists resist the record industry, then?

PRINCE: You saw *The Matrix*, right? The person in that predicament doesn't know where he is. It's a collective hallucination. The key is if you put people in a financial bind, and spread it around, they won't be able to resist. This whole country was based on division. All the way back in [the album] *Controversy*, I was trying to break from the hallucination. People said, "This is what's hittin' now, Prince." But I wasn't paying attention to that. Duke Ellington never changed. Miles

Davis never changed. Their work is intact. The companies are great at distributing, but they're not creators. They shouldn't be the ones to take my work into the 22nd century.

Y-LIFE: When one looks at musicians who have truly embraced the Net, it's the veterans, people who have been around for a while: you, David Bowie, Pete Townshend. What's that all about?

PRINCE: Because when you're a new, young act and start getting a buzz, you get approached by people with a pen and an agenda. They start right away taking pieces of you. All I can say to young artists is know that you're the genesis of what comes from you. You have to keep your masters [recordings]. The record executives say, "We own the masters." I ask them, "Where are they?" And I'll just look right at them. You know, the way Norm MacDonald will tell a joke and then just look at you? I love that! (*Laughs*) Steven Wright, too, does that. But imagine—this is the kind of standoff I'll have with a grown man.

It'll be interesting to see what happens with Lenny Kravitz. His deal's about up. And he's going to get a big carrot dangled in front of him any day now. They'll give you a choice: "You can own all the recordings, or you can be a star." But are you a star if you're broke? Let's watch what happens with Lenny. If I want to speak out against that collective hallucination, I'm not a part of it. I did one record on my own, and that's all it took. Let Lenny Kravitz do one record on his own, and see if he ever goes back.

Y-LIFE: Why, exactly, do you think the recording industry is so corrupt?

PRINCE: Let's look at it. I mean, really look at it. It's in the Bible, which I've started reading recently. Why does a person go against his Creator? In the beginning, we have a very simple story in the garden. God tells Adam and Eve, "You have everything you need." And they begin to think they can create as well. Examine that story. Now, there's somebody else in that garden, isn't there?

In every situation, you have one person who initiates, one who benefits, and one who resists all of it. And some people are happy being in every one of those categories.

Y-LIFE: What's your position on Napster?

PRINCE: I always ask people, "Are you pro- or anti-Napster?" Now, the record companies see Napster as troublesome. Napster is a mirror. How you see Napster says more about you than it does about Napster. The fans visiting Napster, they would want everything the artist puts out. They wouldn't want to pay for it. What's up with that?

But the same goes for the recording industry. How you see the recording industry says more about you and your priorities than it does about the recording industry. Napster was inevitable—a file-sharing program that allowed the user to be a part of the process—especially given the general arrogance of the music industry as a whole. I mean, $18 a CD. Where are they getting that? The production costs aren't going up, that's for sure. People are getting hip to that. This is a wonderful time, because everything is shifting. Everybody can be an artist—and there are good and bad consequences to that. But people who control their own work will succeed. Look at Bill Gates. The man is unstoppable. He never sold out. He never sold the rights to his software.

Y-LIFE: Have you ever used Napster?

PRINCE: No. Of course, I've had people go on to see if they've got our stuff, and they definitely did. Now, NPG Music Club is a subscription club. If the songs we put up on the club end up on Napster, is that copyright infringement?

Y-LIFE: You asked your fans that same question on the site. What do you think?

PRINCE: I'm asking you. The record industry said that Napster caused them to flat-line. Are you pro- or anti-Napster?

Y-LIFE: Personally, I'm pro.

PRINCE: Now, why is that? That's interesting.

Y-LIFE: I discovered more new music through Napster last year, and I bought the CDs. I've paid for more music last year than I've ever done, thanks to Napster. And I think people will still buy CDs; we like objects.

PRINCE: Do you think individuals who spend all day on the computer will care about CDs? I'm trying to see if I can sway your opinion. How many users does Napster have—60 million? Do you think all those people are buying their CDs?

Y-LIFE: Probably not.

PRINCE: See, there you go! Now we're coming to some kind of agreement. I'm not pro- or anti-anything. I just sit back and watch the whole thing. We've got an institution here at Paisley that cares for the artist. And that's the way it should be.

I've spoken to Shawn Fanning. He's just a kid. It's a real shame what has happened to him. He's in a lot of tough water. He's scared. When Fanning got up onstage at the MTV awards, the audience started cheering and booing. First they were booing Metallica; now they were booing him. And he's thinking, "Why did this happen to me?" If I was worried about booing, I'd think I had to change. So you sign up with one side or the other. And Napster, BMG—these people aren't musicians. Shawn knows the deal.

Y-LIFE: Can the Napster-BMG deal eventually work?

PRINCE: Probably. Why not? The recording industry works. That doesn't mean it's just, or right, or fair. But it's not up to me to damn somebody or something. It's in the nature of their actions to damn themselves. When was the last time the recording industry gave anything back to the community? It's a pity that there actually has to be such a thing as the Rhythm & Blues Foundation [a not-for-profit group dedicated to fostering recognition of and support for R&B music]. This industry makes $40 billion a year—$40 billion! Can we have $1 billion? Just $1 billion, to put back into our communities and help rebuild them?

Y-LIFE: But some would say that running a business is a lot different from making music.

PRINCE: I care for artists. I care for where Bonnie Raitt gets her heart from. You want to improve the production of tennis programs on TV? Let's ask Serena and Venus Williams what they think. I'm sure they're full of ideas. I know—I've asked them. When Kobe Bryant does a 360 and dunks it, that's creation. Let's let that dictate.

Y-LIFE: In February, you started the NPG Music Club on your site, a paid subscription service that allows fans to receive new songs from you every month. Was the club an alternative, or a response, to the Napster controversy?

PRINCE: Napster had nothing to do with the NPG Music Club. Anybody who has followed my career knows how much technology has meant to me. When it was three o'clock in the morning, and I'd try to get [Revolution drummer] Bobby Z to come out to the studio, sometimes he'd come, sometimes he wouldn't. But I've had this Roger Linn drum machine since 1981. It's one of the first drum machines ever created. It takes me five seconds to put together a beat on this thing. So from the very start, technology gave me a direct result for my efforts. I'm a very simple person. If somebody wants my music, I'll give it to them.

Y-LIFE: Don't you worry that if your music is distributed only on the NPG Music Club, you'll lose potential new listeners?

PRINCE: Why would a 13-year-old be at my concerts? There're tons of them there. One night I asked them, "How many of y'all have seen me before?" Half of them cheered. "How many have never seen me before?" The other half cheered. So I see how this is going. Somebody old brings somebody new. Things get passed down—it's like oral history, the way it's supposed to be. Like you and me talking right now. I've wanted to have a direct one-on-one with people for a long time. If you see the Net as a tool to eliminate the middleman, you define it. And that reflects your personality. You get in and say, "I want to use it to get to more people"—that says something about you as well.

NPG audio gives you something new. We've called the NPGMC "the experience for those who know better." Because right now, if you listen to the radio, all you'll hear is packaged pop stars. Sometimes I want to ask those people, "Do you even know a D-minor chord? Come here, play one. Good. Now step away, please. There's nothing to see here." (Laughs)

Y-LIFE: Earlier this year, you released two songs through your site as free downloads, calling it an "Xperiment in honor" and asking fans who profited from it to kick back some of those profits to you. How has the experiment worked?

PRINCE: (Laughs) It worked just like we thought it would. And that's all I'm saying about that! One of the reasons why we thought a club would be necessary is because we wanted to see how fast the music would replicate itself. And it's just incredible. It's ultimately a question of what music should be. Who should it benefit? It should benefit the creator. Ani DiFranco owns all her music.

My friend Larry Graham likes to say, "If you've got a cake pan that's dented, and you keep cooking cakes in it, then you're going to keep getting cakes with dents in them." When I do deals with record companies now, they're with people. And they're small. "I've got some music. You want it? You make some copies and give me my tapes back."

Y-LIFE: Will you still release albums from now on, or stay digital?

PRINCE: I'll probably release albums, but what's cool about the club is that the shows and the tracks change every month. So if you go in every month, you'll get to storehouse all these tracks, and by the end of the year you'll have enough for maybe three albums. I could probably release five to seven albums every year if I wanted to—polished stuff that I'm really happy with. But the market can't deal with that. So this seemed like a natural alternative.

Y-LIFE: How did you first get online?

PRINCE: Instantly, the thing that attracted me to the Net was the idea that I could reach a lot of people without going through a matrix. Unfortunately, the Net is a reflection of what's going on in the world. School shootings, things like that. It reflects that kind of violence. That's why I don't live there. Here in Paisley, it's a very isolated environment. You can't just see all that pornography and deceit and mendacity all the time. That's what the world has become. There are pockets of beauty out there still, though.

Y-LIFE: Where are those pockets of beauty on the Net?

PRINCE: That's a tough one. I'm not one to judge what is beautiful. I do know what isn't beautiful. Everybody's a critic. People are flaming each other without any knowledge of the effect it has on others—the kind of physical, psychological effect it has on them.

Y-LIFE: Have you been in chatrooms devoted to your work?

PRINCE: A couple of times—not much. When I first started, I tried one time to unify a group splintered by whether I was still "funky" or not. That question still goes on, obviously. But what ended up happening was that I got a webmaster out of it—Sam Jennings, who runs the NPG site out of Chicago. But I guess what I find beautiful on the Internet is wherever I find agreement. That's beautiful even to people who are full of hate.

Y-LIFE: Don't we need disagreement before we can have agreement?

PRINCE: I believe people of like mind will agree. This'll sound like a cliché, but people need to be under a creator. Clive Davis doesn't want to take any direction from me. Should he? You tell me. Is this the music industry? All the musicians, please stand up. Miles Davis and Duke Ellington went to school for music. They learned how to create; they became seasoned performers. Now they pop these kids out like it's nothing. And the record executives say, "We love music." You love music? You can't even tap your foot on the two and the four.

Y-LIFE: There was a quote on your site recently, saying "Beyoncé can sang!" Was that from you?

PRINCE: The tidbits of information on the site don't come from me. Sometimes people will ask me a question, and I'll give them a quote. My end is shipping out the music. But it's evident that Destiny's Child is an industry act. We want to keep the focus on why they're successful. And that's because of the people in the group, not because of the label and the marketing. That's why you'll see tidbits like that, about Beyoncé and other performers. The people that are here at Paisley with me—we're all like-minded. They stay free—and free means free. And that's what the club is about. It's a haven for anybody who's got their music and is free. We're all very down-to-earth. No matter what the press likes to write about me.

Y-LIFE: So what kind of Web sites do you like to visit?

PRINCE: I go to the educational ones. I like to study history—especially Egyptian history. I don't want to start endorsing any sites right now, but I like the ones that go back the furthest. 'Cause I'm interested in how we got in this predicament in the first place. You can talk about symptoms all day long. But I like to talk about solutions.

PRINCE OF PARADOX

Mick Brown | June 12, 2004 | *Daily Telegraph*

The Artist changed his name back to Prince in 2000, but for most people he didn't reclaim his royal throne until the *Musicology* LP and associated tour in 2004.

Prince distributed a considerable amount of enjoyable if often grouchy rock/funk/R&B music online in the early part of the decade, but beyond the truly dedicated, nobody heard it. Most of this material would be collected in 2004 alongside *Musicology* on *The Chocolate Invasion* and *The Slaughterhouse* albums.

The years 2002 and 2003 found Prince releasing some of his most challenging and non-commercial work, including the concept LP *The Rainbow Children* (which led to a successful theater-level tour and his first live album), the piano-centered *One Nite Alone*, and a trio of jazz albums (*Xpectation*, *C-Note*, and *N.E.W.S.*). Only the concept LP was widely distributed. It reached 109 on the Billboard 200, his lowest charting entry since his 1978 debut.

The commercial tides changed in 2004. First, Prince was inducted in the Rock & Roll Hall of Fame, cementing his place among pop music's firmament. Then, he released *Musicology*, his most accessible and successful work since 1991's *Diamonds and Pearls*. In support he embarked on Musicology Live 2004ever, filling arenas across America for ninety-plus dates on the year's top-grossing concert tour: Prince owned summer 2004 to the tune of $87.4 million.

He also engaged in his last concentrated group of interactions with the press, granting over fifty press and electronic interviews over a span of six months. This interview took place in Jacksonville, Florida, on April 27, 2004, one month into the tour. The article is heavy with well-written context and, as with many interviews at this time, a bit short on direct or lengthy quotes (the lack of light in this case curtailing the already byzantine process of Prince-interview notetaking).

While Prince isn't exactly reactionary in this interview, his more outrageous and taboo-breaking tendencies have been tamed by this time, or at least routinized within his stage show. He sounds less like "America's Freak" and more like a talk show caller from middle America as he reflects on the media after Janet Jackson's "wardrobe malfunction" at the February 2004 Super Bowl, saying, "I think people want order again. They don't want to turn on a football game and see someone with her breasts falling out. And I don't want to see that either." —Ed.

The artist formerly known as The Artist Formerly Known as Prince is now known as Prince once more. No formerly about it. But keeping people confused is still, it seems, part of the game. An extrovert and a recluse, a man who embodies the celebrity trait of loving attention but loathing scrutiny, Prince grants audiences rarely and with the greatest reluctance.

Prior to my meeting with him, I was given a list of conditions. I was told that he would not discuss his personal life or anything whatsoever to do with the past. Questions should be confined simply to "the music now, and in the future." Furthermore, he would not allow the conversation to be taped.

At the backstage holding area of the Jacksonville Arena in Jacksonville, Florida, where he is to perform, I am obliged to wait (clipboard scrutiny, excessive mobile-phone action) until an aide arrives with the appropriate passes to grant admittance and ferry me in a golf cart into the arena itself. I am parked in a holding area (soft drinks provided). I am reminded that no tape recorders are allowed.

At length, Prince's PA, an impassive black man in a business suit, leads me ceremoniously into the corridor and some 20 yards along to another door, swathed in curtains. This is Prince's dressing room. It is a large room, divided by drapes to create a feeling of intimacy. Two velvet sofas are set at right angles beside a low table, where scented candles provide the only light. I think, I tell his assistant, I might have trouble taking notes. He looks at me. "You'll manage."

Prince appears a few moments later from behind a curtain, as if stepping on to a stage. He is 5ft 3in, slightly built, and moves with tiny dancer's steps, as if his black suede high-heeled pumps are spring-stacked. He is wearing an immaculately tailored black suit (he shares his tailor with Louis Farrakhan and Michael Jackson) and a black shirt. A white knitted tam rests on the back of his processed hair like a halo. He is 46, yet he looks like a teenager, his face remarkably unlined, his complexion baby-smooth, suggestive of expensive unguents. A ghost of a moustache dusts his upper lip.

"No tape-recorder, right?" It's the very first thing that he says. What is this with the tape recorder? It has been variously explained in the past that Prince can't stand the sound of his own voice—a terrible affliction, one would think, for a singer—or that he doesn't want his words set in stone to come back and haunt him. A more likely explanation, offered *sotto voce* by an aide, is that he was angered after a recorded interview was once circulated without permission on the internet. But it's hard not to think, too, that Prince relishes this small exercise of power over media which he has always viewed with suspicion and distrust, and recognizes the psychological advantage it gives him.

Conversation is tricky enough as it is. There is something curiously coquettish, playful, almost flirtatious, in his manner: the way he evades a question by questioning the assumption behind it.

"Well, that's what you're saying . . ."; the quick-fire stream-of-consciousness, butterflying from one non sequitur to the next; the slightly arch, prissy turns of phrase ("Come now . . ." he admonishes me at one point); the way he keeps addressing me as "sir." "And . . ." he almost flutters his eyelashes as he smiles, "no questions about the past, right?"

"The audience you have is the audience you always have," Prince says. "You only get famous once." But how to hold on to them is another question. For a period in the 1980s and 1990s, Prince was one of the biggest—perhaps the biggest—and certainly the most provocative pop star in the world. Albums such as *Purple Rain, 1999* and *Sign O' the Times* melted the boundaries between soul and pop, giving him album sales in excess of 100 million around the world. Yet for the past 10 years he has been a negligible, if not quite forgotten figure. An object of bemusement, even ridicule. TAFKAP? Symbol? Sign? The Artist People Formerly Cared About, as the American "'shock jock'" Howard Stern took to calling him. But now Prince is Prince again, his apparently dormant career in the midst of an astonishing resurrection—not a word Prince himself, a Jehovah's Witness, would necessarily approve of.

In February, he made a triumphant appearance at the Grammy awards, performing a duet with Beyoncé that included two of his biggest hits, "Purple Rain" and "Let's Go Crazy." The following month he was inducted in to the Rock'n'Roll Hall of Fame. After years of lackluster and maddeningly self-indulgent recordings, he has released a new album, *Musicology*, which has been greeted by critics as a sterling return to form. Having vowed to have nothing more to do with the corporate music business, and having experimented with releasing his records only through the internet, he has signed once again with a major label, Sony. And having vowed never to perform his greatest hits, he has been touring in America doing precisely that, once again staking his claim to be the most exciting live performer in pop music.

"Really, I'm normal," Prince says, laughing softly. "A little highly-strung, maybe. But normal. But so much has been written about me and people never know what's right and what's wrong. I'd rather let them stay confused."

The son of a jazz pianist, he grew up in Minneapolis (his parents named him Prince Rogers Nelson, after a group, the Prince Rogers Trio, which his father had once played in). His parents separated when he was 10, and when his mother remarried shortly afterwards, Prince followed his father out of the family home. But they argued constantly and he later moved in with a family friend, Bernadette Anderson—like Prince's parents, a member of the local Seventh Day Adventist church. Despite having six children of her own, Anderson raised Prince as if he were her own son. This childhood would later be mythologized in the "autobiographical" film *Purple Rain*, released in 1984, depicting the rise of "the Kid" from an abused childhood to pop star glory.

A prodigiously gifted musician, he made his first recordings at the age of 18 with an English producer, Chris Moon, who had relocated to Minneapolis. Promoting him as "the new Stevie Wonder," Moon hawked around demos on which Prince played all the instruments himself, and in 1978 he signed with Warner Brothers and released his first album, *For You*.

Prince's early albums—*For You, Prince*, and *Controversy*—served thrilling notice of his eclecticism, and his ability to synthesize a variety of his earliest influences: Stevie Wonder's virtuosity and melodic strength; Sly and the Family Stone's harmonious melting pot of color, gender and styles; and, above all, the irresistible rhythmic impulse of the Godfather of modern black American music, James Brown. (Brown, in his autobiography, writes of a night in 1984 when he was joined on stage by both Prince and Michael Jackson: "Prince played some guitar but I think he was a little nervous. Michael fit into my thing a little better since he had been studying me for years. But later on Prince practiced and he got into it real good. When I was in California later, he came to a show and lay on the floor backstage and watched my feet. Afterward, he asked me if I had roller-skates on my shoes.")

It's the first question I ask him. Could he tell me about James Brown's influence on his music? He smiles, and shakes his head.

"I really want to focus on the present."

You won't talk about your influences?

"I don't really do biographies. I don't want to talk about the past."

OK, what did you feel when you first heard James Brown?

"Whoa!" He laughs. "That's a whole conversation! We haven't got time for that conversation."

Whatever you felt, was that the feeling you wanted your audience to experience when you started playing music?

"Music is everything to me. I love making music. I am making music. Music is spirit, it's therapy. It makes me feel a certain way, and if played with conviction and soul, the same thing occurs in other people."

He pauses. "So we're talking about James Brown after all . . . You're slick." He laughs. "But not that slick."

By the time he appeared on stage with Brown in 1984, Prince had become a bigger star than his hero. The release of *Purple Rain* that year affirmed his transition from the R&B (a euphemism for black) charts to the pop mainstream, going on to sell more than 14 million copies around the world; affirmed, too, his ascendancy to the peculiar role as pop music's high prophet of sexual license. The sly celebrations of lechery and seduction, the songs about incest and oral sex, had been there from the very beginning, along with the frills and furbelows, the highcamp thigh boots and posing pouches. But now Prince had become sufficiently prominent to excite the disapproval of then Senator Al Gore's wife, Tipper. "Darling Nikki," a track on *Purple Rain* about masturbation, provoked Tipper Gore to set up the Parents Music Resource Centre (PMRC), to monitor "pornographic" content in rock music and lobby the industry to classify records in the same way as films.

Prince was now presiding over his own studio complex in Minneapolis, Paisley Park, turning out music at a frenetic rate, as well as mentoring and producing other artists such as Sheila E and Apollonia 6. Buoyed by the success of *Purple Rain*, the movie, he directed two more films, *Under the Cherry Moon* and *Graffiti Bridge*. Both were expensive flops. By the early 1990s Prince's star had begun to wane, his music eclipsed by the inexorable rise of hip-hop and rap.

It was then that reason appeared to abandon him altogether. In 1993 he fell out with Warner Brothers over the ownership of his master recordings, and Warners' refusal to release what they regarded as sub-standard material. On his 35th birthday, in June 1993, he announced that for as long as Warners retained control of his material, he would no longer answer to the name Prince, and would henceforth be known by an unpronounceable glyph. To emphasize the point, he also began appearing in public with the word "slave" scrawled on his face. "This is what my record company has reduced Prince to," he announced. "So now Prince is dead. They've killed him . . . I don't own Prince's music. If you don't own your masters, your master owns you."

Prince had never before made an issue of his black heritage, stressing the multiracial basis of his music, and actually misleadingly intimating in the past that he was of mixed race—both his parents were in fact black. But the allusion to racial pride was reinforced when he likened renouncing his old identity to Muhammad Ali rejecting his "slave name" of Cassius Clay.

"I followed the advice of my spirit. I'm not the son of Nell. I don't know who that is—'Nell's son'—and that's my last name. I would wake up nights thinking, 'Who am I? What am I?'"

A lot of people asked the same question. His decision was a cause of some confusion even within his own organization. A photographer recalled turning up a few days after the announcement for an appointment at Paisley Park, when staff were still grappling with the novel problem of how to address their employer. The usual protocol, the receptionist explained, was to page him. "But right now we just wait until we see him in the halls, and we run and grab him."

Vowing to have nothing more to do with major companies, Prince instead began releasing albums on his own label, NPG (New Power Generation), and through the internet to members of his NPG Music Club—a practice he continues. But the sublime originality which had characterized his earlier work appeared to have deserted him, and the fans followed. Sales dwindled, and rumors multiplied that the years of profligacy had put his finances in a perilous state.

In light of all this, his decision to work with a major label again, to release an album crammed with songs which consciously play to his most accessible, and commercial, strengths, and to take to the road, performing what amounts to a "greatest hits" package, might, quite reasonably, be seen as a strategy to put himself back in the public eye.

But Prince, of course, does not quite see it this way. To suggest he is coming back into the limelight would mean admitting he had fallen out of it; to suggest he is courting public approval would suggest he had lost it. This is not "a comeback," he stresses, because "I've never been away." *Emancipation*, the triple album which he released in 1996 to celebrate his release from Warner Brothers, "sold oodles." *The Rainbow Children* (2001), his record celebrating his conversion to being a Jehovah's Witness (and his first not to register on the Billboard Top 100), was "an important album," because "that was me telling the truth for then. And the same thing with *NEWS* [a 56-minute instrumental improvisation, released two years ago, which received negligible attention]." Commercial success, he suggests, has always been a secondary consideration to artistic integrity. "You do it because it's right to do at that time. You don't do it because you can sell a million. But I wouldn't have stayed independent if I'd been a failure, I'd have been running back and saying, 'Sign me back up, put me back on the plantation, boss.'" He laughs bitterly. "I've been projected as this petulant person that knows nothing about business and now I've run back to Daddy. But it's not like that at all."

Under his new deal, he says, he has no binding contract with Sony. "It's all by mutual agreement." He provides the record and retains ownership of the masters; Sony undertake simply to manufacture and distribute it to shops, "like FedEx." Like all his most recent albums, *Musicology* was first available on download to NPG members; and the album is given away free to everyone who buys a ticket to his concerts. It's an arrangement which appears to set an interesting precedent at a time when the record industry is grappling with a solution for how best to deal with downloading. For Prince, it is a blow for artistic freedom against "the system" which he says has exploited musicians for years. "Musicians inherited this system, so that's how most musicians work, how we get the music to the people. But it used to be the tradition to have slaves on the plantation. Don't mean it's right!

"I don't need no producer, I don't need no record company, no A&R man or anyone telling me what to do. I produce my own records in my own studio. Why do I need someone telling me what to do, and owning what I do?

"Everything has to go back to God, to peace and to justice. There's no justice in taking somebody's intellectual copyrights from them. It's wrong for them to say they own it. They don't own it. This word ownership . . ." He gestures around him. "Who owns this candle? Who owns this telephone? Who owns the air? Nobody owns these things really. And then you think about the human genome. Who owns your DNA? And it's coming to that. You can be hooked up, slaved up . . . It will come to that."

This leap from the personal to the global—his "enslavement" by the record industry as a metaphor for mankind's enslavement by "the system"—seems characteristic. Talking of *Musicology*, he describes the album as a celebration of "spirit" in an age of technology. "That's really important for me. We need to keep that intact. If you use a computer, you're pretty much going to follow that and become a computer."

You don't use computers? "I do. But I don't let computers use me. It's more interesting to me to pick up a guitar and create a sound out of thin air. That's analogue. We're analogue creatures; we breathe air, we hear soundwaves, we react to spirit and color. A computer's binary." He pauses.

"See, spirit is everywhere around us, but there's so much to keep you from it—computers, pagers, all that stuff. You ain't gonna hear me beeping! No cellphones. I don't use a cellphone." He gives a cryptic smile. "No sir, ain't nobody going to reach me."

Spirit. The Truth. You don't go far with Prince before God joins the conversation. It is the subject where he becomes his most animated, and at the same time his most obtuse. "God draws you out," he replies when I ask exactly when and why he became a Witness. "You seek him or you don't. You'll hear his voice or you won't. You'll do what he asks you to do, or you won't."

And what does being a Jehovah's Witness mean to him?

"Words are inadequate! Now you're talking about the source of truth!" He rocks forward, eyes shining, as eager as a student in a Bible class, touching my knee to ensure he has my full attention (I'm head down, scribbling to keep up). "Feel me now . . . ," he says. "Feel me now . . . You want to talk about scripture? We can talk about scripture. But that's a lifetime right there!"

An important figure in Prince's conversion was Larry Graham, the former bass player for Sly Stone, one of Prince's musical heroes, and the leader of his own group Graham Central Station, whom Prince first met in the late 1990s, and who has served as his "spiritual mentor" ever since. Prince had always displayed a strongly moralistic streak in parallel with his image as a sexual libertine—disapproving of drink and drugs and forbidding his band from dabbling in either. But with his conversion to the Witnesses his beliefs became progressively messianic.

Shortly after meeting Graham, Prince changed the name of his song "The Cross" to "The Christ," in light of the Witnesses' teaching that Jesus died not on a cross, but on a stake. A planned reunion of his early backing group, the Revolution, was aborted after Prince reportedly demanded that his erstwhile guitarist, Wendy Melvoin, who is Jewish and a lesbian, hold a press conference renouncing her homosexuality and converting to Jehovah. (She refused.)

And there were reports that homeowners in Minneapolis had been surprised to answer the doorbell to find Prince and Graham on the doorstep, offering copies of *The Watchtower*.

When I ask whether it is true that he fulfils the obligation of proselytizing from door to door, he simply looks away, refusing to answer.

As his star rose through the 1980s, Prince was linked to a number of women. He reportedly had affairs with Madonna, Kim Basinger, Sheena Easton and innumerable female proteges. In 1996 he married one of his backing singers and dancers, Mayte Garcia, whom he had first met six years earlier when she was just 16. In the same year, Mayte gave birth to a baby boy, who died at a week old of a rare skull disorder, Pfeiffer's syndrome. The death was kept secret, and for a while Prince attempted to maintain a charade that all was well. Immediately after the death, he gave an interview in which he was asked about his new baby's gender. "Mayte and I have decided to let the baby make its own decisions. Once it becomes public, its personality will become shaped by all the attention, and that's too much to wish upon it."

A month later he shot a promotional video for the song "Betcha By Golly Wow" in which he was filmed dressed up in medical garb and visiting a smiling and noticeably pregnant Mayte in hospital. At around the same time, as rumors of the child's death were spreading through the media, he appeared on the Oprah Winfrey show, insisting that "it's all good—never mind what you hear."

This poignant catalogue of events could be read in two ways; as evidence either of a man in the grip of a terrible self-denial, or, more likely perhaps, of Prince's determination not to let his and his wife's private grief become an object of public prurience and speculation.

The marriage did not survive. In 1998, Prince began seeing Manuela Testolini, a Canadian, who worked at Paisley Park. His marriage to Mayte was annulled (she moved to a villa which Prince had provided in Marbella), and he married Testolini in 2001. At 27, she is 19 years Prince's junior. The couple purchased a house in Toronto—on the Bridle Path, an exclusive enclave of estate homes, and where their neighbors include the [Conrad] Blacks—where Prince now spends most of his time, and where *Musicology* was recorded.

Prince, of course, will say nothing about any of this. It's the past; it's "biography." He doesn't do either. He will say only that he "loves" living in Toronto. Among his idiosyncrasies is a refusal to sign autographs, reportedly because he believes the idolatry that an autograph implies is "an offence" against God (an alternative, and more likely, explanation offered by an aide is that he objects to people profiting from his signatures by selling them on e-Bay). When I mention this, he complains that people try to "shame me, to make me less than," because of his refusal. Asking for autographs is "just a part of the system that people have inherited. It's another part of the illusion. I would much rather talk to someone for two or three minutes than sign an autograph for them, but people don't understand that." For years, he says, the media have tried to portray him as crazy, eccentric.

"But this thing of personality, moving for people to see that, is just another distraction, just another illusion. It's just another way of preventing people from seeing the truth.

"The epiphany is where you see God, where you live at the level humanity is. You don't let money, fame, the illusion rule you." He pauses. "That's when you see God; you don't let money rule you."

So he won't sign an autograph for my daughter? He looks at me. "No, sir. I won't. But I will give you something for your daughter." He pauses. "Later." (Nothing materializes.)

His religious beliefs have had a more subtle effect on his music. If on one level, *Musicology* is good-time party music, crammed with the kind of snappy dance tunes and melodically winning love songs Prince used to write, darker currents seem to eddy below the surface.

"Call My Name," ostensibly a love song, contains references to the war in Iraq and government surveillance. "Cinnamon Girl," a deceptively innocent pop song, is in fact about the climate of fear and xenophobia following 9/11 and the "mass illusion" of the "war-on-terror alibi." Prince describes the song as "a snapshot of now. We live in a real xenophobic place." He sighs. "They talk about all these terrorists. But I didn't feel no terror until the media told me to feel it. Who am I supposed to be feeling terrified of?"

As a Jehovah's Witness, does he believe in the Fundamentalist concept of apocalypse—"end time"? "You calling it that now. I'm not calling it that. You see, sir, you have to be careful what you say. I go back to the Word, what is written, because that's where the truth is."

He pauses. Look at what's happening now in Iraq, he says; soldiers are murdering children. "You have to feel the pain of those children. But some people, they can kill because they've been programmed to do that. But you're talking about a metaphysical event. The earth is going through its phase, but it's all in the Scripture. But the Scripture also talks about that place when it's all over. That's the place I want to be."

The erstwhile prophet of sexual freedom has all but purged his music of sexual references, and no longer performs his more explicit songs onstage. But those, he says, were "different times, and I was different then. I pushed the envelope as far as it needed to be pushed, and now it's on the floor and people seem to want it to stay there. I think people want order again. They don't want to turn on a football game and see someone with her breasts falling out. And I don't want to see that either."

And does he want order, too? "Yes. I believe in order. What am I feeling now? Have I got peace? Yes. I've never felt this peaceful before. Can I be more peaceful? Maybe not. But I can make a song for this peaceful place? Yes sir. 'Call My Name' [a sweet ballad from the new album]—that's a song about peace." He leans forward on the sofa and half-talks, half-croons the lyrics. "*I can't stop writing songs about you, I love you so much.* You see, you're trying to speak the truth in a song like that."

It sounds, I say, like a love song to your wife Manuela. He smiles. "Is it about love, or is it about the Creator? It could be both. I don't like to talk about my songs. Let people make up their own minds. *I can't stop telling people about you . . .*" He sings it softly. "You see how lovely that is?"

So, I say, you are no longer a hedonist? He arches an eyebrow and smiles. "Hedonist? For years, I didn't even know what the word meant." And now you're satiated?

"Satiated . . ." He lingers on it. "That's a lovely word. I was satiated a long time ago."

Watching Prince perform later that evening, I am reminded of the immortal words of Little Richard, another flamboyantly hellbound rock 'n' roller—and in many ways Prince's spiritual avatar—who found God and became a minister, the Reverend Richard Penniman. "The god of Abraham is a true God. Now we gonna do 'Rip It Up' . . ."

Whatever travails, eccentricities or divine revelations have belaid him in recent years, Prince remains an utterly thrilling performer. The extravagant stage-sets, the inflatables, pyrotechnics and writhing go-go girls that characterized his performances early in his career have gone. Instead, this is Prince in the raw; the spine-jarring funk jams, the Hendrix-style guitar pyrotechnics, the gospel style, drop-to-one-knee theatrics—that moment in a song when it feels like a trapdoor is opening and your heart is falling through it. Hit after hit—one of the finest bodies of soul and pop songs of the last 30 years.

You can take Prince away from the devil, it seems: but you can't take the devil out of Prince. When he sings a song from his new album, "On the Couch"—a man's plea to his lover not to be shut out of the bedroom, and croons the line *"I wanna go down south . . ."* there is a deafening squeal, and you can smell the pheromones flooding the auditorium. He stops the music, and gives a wicked smile.

"What? I mean down south to Jacksonville . . ."

Beside me, a woman groans involuntarily. "He is sex . . . "

So, not confusing at all, then.

"WHERE'S MY INTERVIEW?"

Gary Graff | September 12, 2004 | *Gallery of Sound*

This second *Musicology* interview took place in Auburn Hills, Michigan, at the beginning of summer. As should be apparent by this point, different interviews around the same time can yield different results. This interview focuses on Prince's thoughts on his "how can I comeback if I never went anywhere?" commercial comeback. —Ed.

Prince sticks his head into the backstage production office at the Palace of Auburn Hills in suburban Detroit—just a few hours before he rocks the house with a seamless two-plus hours of hits and funky jams. There was a time, of course, when Prince looking for an interview was about as likely as Tipper Gore singing "Darling Nikki" on the US Senate floor. But these days Prince, happily married (to second wife Manuela Testolini) and comfortable in his career, is opening up.

At least a bit. He still doesn't do much talking, and he won't let the interviews be recorded. This year he delivered show-stopping performances at the Rock and Roll Hall of Fame, where he was inducted, and at the Grammy Awards, where he kicked things off with an assist from Beyoncé. His new album, *Musicology*, is a hit, thanks to a crafty plan to distribute a copy free to each ticket-holder on his current tour. And in an otherwise light year at the box office Prince has been a blockbuster, winning rave reviews for his fierce sets. He also says this will be the last time he ever trots out many of his best-known songs.

Mostly, however, Prince's celebratory mood is due to having his career in his own hands, the result of a long struggle that led to him abandoning his name and adopting that unpronounceable glyph, leaving his original label (Warner Bros.) after declaring himself a "slave" to the industry, and establishing his NPG (New Power Generation) imprint and NPG Music Club website that allows him to put out music—and a lot of it—when and however he pleases. "It's a respect thing," he tells the Auburn Hills audience, and there's more respect—and love—for Prince now than there's been in quite some time. But, he cautions as he pops open a can of mixed nuts amidst the candles and incense sticks in his dressing room, don't call it a comeback.

Your Grammy Awards performance celebrated the 20th anniversary of *Purple Rain*, and you find yourself now at possibly your greatest peak of popularity. Does it feel like déjà vu?

Not really. *Purple Rain* was more or less like a fever pitch type of feeling all the time—people at the hotel waiting, crowding. Now it's more businesslike. It doesn't seem like a madhouse. I'm running the affairs. I make a lot more money.

What do you think accounts for the increased level of interest at this point in time?

The more people talk about it, the more I've examined it. And, you know, take away the Grammys and the Rock and Roll Hall of Fame, put them aside, and I'd still be here in this building talking to you. I would still release this album. I'd still be out here. Twenty-seven million people saw the Grammys, so instantly there's a buzz. But all they saw us doing was what we always do. [Saxophonist] Maceo [Parker] had his band, if 27 million people saw them, there'd be a buzz about them, too.

So you don't consider this a comeback?

I never went anywhere! The vibe, with us, is not really that different. I've been touring for a while. I took a break to make the *Musicology* project. It hasn't really stopped.

Are the songs on *Musicology* relatively recent or have they been under development for a while?

It's been around. I record all the time. This one I did over a year's time; a couple of the songs are older, but I'm not gonna say which ones. What I try to do is put together an album; it's about what fits well together, what flows. I'm trying to get a certain vibe. What people are vibing off on this album is they're short songs again, little ditties. It's a medium people are used to and like. But I make a lot of records that don't get released, or that I just put on the website. It's just stuff that's pleasing to listen to on the weekend or stuff. I've got one [*Xpectation*], an experimental record, that's for dinner parties.

Dinner parties?

Yeah. I have dinner parties sometimes, and I wanted to have something I could play that kept things in a place I like. I'm not trying to shock the world with every record.

The ability to make music and release it as you see fit is something you fought long and hard for. Did you have that kind of vision at the beginning of your career?

Back in the '80s we started having discussions about releasing things under other names. I mean, George Clinton had Parliament, then he had Funkadelic—two different bands, two different labels. Then he had George Clinton records, the Brides of Funkenstein . . . He could get it all out of his system. You just keep doing stuff, and it gets stacked up and drives you crazy. And you don't know what to do about it. Studies show that things like regret, not being able to forgive other people, that's what causes cancer. It piles up, and you get irritable.

So the website and NPG Music Club let you manage the clutter.

The cool thing is it's interactive immediately. The temptation is to fill it up with new songs all the time. Freedom can get you into trouble—too much freedom, anyway. But it's so much more fun and there are so many more rewards to doing it on your own. You can become so much more connected to your audience this way. They don't need to see a chart first or hear it on the radio first or read a review. What they vibe off of is what they vibe off of. It's that easy.

It's not quite the same as releasing a standard CD, though. Do you have to divest yourself from the attitude of "stardom" in order to be comfortable working this way?

I think I've always been here. Go back to the *Dirty Mind* period; I was happy there, too. We had our little gang, our little clothes and little outfits and we'd go on stage and that's what we were there for. That's what we lived for. We didn't know what was going to happen or what this was gonna become. We loved it.

So is this tour really the last time you're going to play some of these songs, or are you just hyping us like Bowie and Elton?

I've been playing "Purple Rain" and "Little Red Corvette" a long time. I'm writing all the time—those are the songs I want to be playing. It's hard to stay away from that and rest on my laurels. I can't do that.

MY NIGHT WITH PRINCE

Ann Powers | January 11, 2009 | *Los Angeles Times*

After the epic *Musicology* jaunt, Prince avoided large-scale touring for the balance of the decade. In 2006 he backed protégé Támar (Davis) on a brief tour featuring her never-released album *Milk & Honey*, and later took up residency in Las Vegas for a few dozen Per4ming Live *3121* shows and aftershows. Likewise, he anchored himself at the 02 Arena in August 2007 for 21 Nights in London: The Earth Tour in support of *Planet Earth*.

And with less touring came less talking. Prince the interviewee returned to covert mode for the second half of the 2000s, granting a handful of interviews between the 2004 and 2009. But one of these interviews required spin control in this article.

In a brief *New Yorker* article in fall 2008, writer Claire Hoffman asked Prince about "his perspective on social issues—gay marriage, abortion." Prince responded with his fingers on his Bible, saying, "God came to earth and saw people sticking it wherever and doing it with whatever, and just cleared it all out. He was, like, 'Enough.'"

This was taken in many quarters, especially among gay and lesbian fans, as Prince dismissing freedoms and liberties he had once seemingly endorsed. In this *Los Angeles Times* article, Prince brings up the previous interview and protests that the quote was taken out of context. After reading hundreds of Prince interviews and understanding both the difficulties of accurately describing a Prince interview and Prince's habit of presenting complex beliefs as essential and unencumbered truth, it's entirely possible that it was taken out of context. Which doesn't necessarily indicate that he didn't mean what he said.

But this article explores more than just his beliefs about women's freedom to choose and homosexuality. And more than his embracing Pro Tools. As Powers notes at the end of this piece,

212

this is much more than just an interview: it's a curated, tripartite, stylized experience meant to highlight both his latest work, the *MPLSound*, *Lotusflow3r*, and *Elixir* (from protégé Bria Valente) albums, and his greatest creation, himself. —Ed.

It was 11 p.m. on the night before New Year's Eve, and I was doing something I hadn't expected would crown my 2008: sitting in Prince's limousine as the legend lounged beside me, playing unreleased tracks on the stereo. "This is my car for Minneapolis," he said before excusing himself to let me judge a few songs in private. "It's great for listening to music." He laughed. "I don't do drugs or I'd give you a joint. That's what this record is."

That morning I'd received an e-mail inviting me to preview new music at Prince's mansion in the celebrity-infested estate community of Beverly Park, where he's currently keeping his shoe rack. The summons wasn't entirely unexpected. Prince, who's less reclusive than his reputation would indicate, has spent a year and a half consulting with culture industry leaders and occasionally entertaining media types, with an eye toward taking complete control of his own musical output.

His new mantra is "The gatekeepers must change," and he's refashioned his career to become one of them.

Since beginning his gradual relocation from the Midwest to the Left Coast, Prince has headlined the Coachella Valley Music and Arts Festival and 2007's Super Bowl halftime show. He sold out a 21-night run at London's O2 Arena and released an album, a high-end photo book and a perfume. Most recently, he's whetted fans' appetites with sneaks of songs from three upcoming releases, first on the popular "Jonesy's Jukebox" radio program on Indie 103 and then on two websites, the now-dark MPLSound.com and the still-evolving Lotusflow3r.com.

This flurry of activity has been characterized by what might be called methodical spontaneity. Everything happens quickly, whether it's a show that takes place only a few days after its announcement or an evening interview arranged that morning. But Prince's personality seems to be governed by two oppositional impulses: the hunger to create and an equally powerful craving for control. Intense productivity battles with meticulousness within his working process. Others might not anticipate his next move, but it is all part of the chess game for him.

That's why I was there, on the eve of a holiday eve, as the mainstream music industry was enjoying a break from its ongoing plunge toward insolvency. The turn of the year is a slow time for pop, not the moment blockbuster artists usually release material. But Prince has been hinting for a while that his upcoming recordings might not be tied to a conventional label. Abandoning that machine, including its publicity arm, requires other ways of getting the word out.

Prince began experimenting with new methods of distributing music more than a decade ago, and his early efforts with the now-defunct NPG Music Club paved the way for later bold moves by Radiohead and others. Most recently he's partnered with major labels to get copies into stores. Columbia handled the release of 2006's *Planet Earth*, except in Britain, where copies were distributed free via a London newspaper, the *Mail on Sunday*.

Now Prince is about to unleash not one but three albums without major label affiliation, and talking to well-vetted writers is one part of the rollout. How well vetted? "You're blond," he said when we met. "I thought you were a redhead." (He'd done his research; I'd changed my hair color only the year before.)

When I entered the house, which has the vaguely European opulence of an upscale spa, I found Prince with designers Anthony Malzone and Scott Addison Clay, examining mock-ups for a "highly interactive" website. "It's a universe," said Malzone, showing how a mouse click could make the whole screen rotate. "There's a lyric in one of the new songs about an 'entirely new galaxy.' We took that cue, and from there on, we thought that everything would emanate from Prince."

The website, still under construction, revealed the recognizable logo of a major big-box retailer with whom Prince is finalizing negotiations to distribute the albums. The three will hit the Web and that retailer, the artist said, "as soon as the holidays are over."

I'd be hearing music from each of them.

"Let's go to my car," Prince said. "We'll listen to the first album there."

Religious perspective

Entering his garage, he ushered me into a low-slung black sports car that he's apparently named after his late friend Miles Davis. I strapped on my seat belt, but we didn't venture outside.

Instead, Prince turned serious as he brought up a recent *New Yorker* article that had spun beyond his famously controlling grip.

"I want to talk about that interview," he said, gazing seriously over the steering wheel before turning on the music. He'd felt the writer had taken certain remarks he'd made—particularly one about gay marriage that implied he was against it—out of context. (The *New Yorker* stands by the story.)

"They try to take my faith . . . ." he said, his voice trailing off. "I'm a Jehovah's Witness. I'm trying to learn the Bible. It's a history book, a science book, a guidebook. It's all the same."

Prince's understanding of religion requires him to avoid political stands, including those that concern morality. "I have friends that are gay, and we study the Bible together," he said. He did not vote for Proposition 8, the referendum to make gay marriage illegal. "I don't vote," he said. "I didn't vote for Barack [Obama], either; I've never voted. Jehovah's Witnesses haven't voted for their whole inception."

Prince, who became a Jehovah's Witness in 2001 under the guidance of veteran bassist and songwriter Larry Graham, views everything through the lens of his religion. No topic—sexuality, civil rights, his disdain for corporate pop—comes up in which it doesn't play a role. Recounting a recent meeting with Earth, Wind and Fire singer Philip Bailey, for example, he commented that that group's penchant for Afrocentric garb revealed a lost history similar to the one uncovered in the Jehovah's Witnesses' version of the Bible.

Prince's statements can sound extreme to a secular listener. Some have accused him of trying to conceal his views to avoid alienating nonbelieving (and, particularly, gay) fans. But his desire to be tolerant seems sincere. His favorite television show, for example, is *Real Time with Bill Maher*. Asked if the comedian's confrontational atheism bothers him, he harrumphed. "That's cool," said Prince. "He can be what he wants. I like arguments. Somebody saying I'm a terrible guitar player feeds me."

Prince's faith fulfills a yearning that his songs expressed long before he became devout: a need for some kind of ruling theory to explain the sorrow and violence that intertwines with life's joy. Songs as early as 1981's "Controversy" focus on a quest for God, and his catalog overflows with complex number and color systems, prophetic statements and disquiet about the fallen state of humanity. In his religion, he's found a code as inexhaustible as the one he was previously generating himself.

Which leads back to *MPLSound*, the album Prince recorded by himself at Paisley Park studios mostly last year. "People ask me, 'Why don't you sound like you used to?'" he said by way of introduction. "But that music doesn't have any wave energy to it. It'll move a party, but that's not what I'm doing here."

These tracks did sound new in some ways: electronica-based, futuristic and subtly mind-altering. They also harked back to early Prince, including touchstones like "When Doves Cry" and *The Black Album*. Some, like one about a "funky congregation," could become live show pieces. Others, like the playful "Hey Valentina," inspired by his friend Salma Hayek's baby, and the Space Age ballad "Better with Time"—dedicated to another actress pal, Kristin Scott Thomas, who costarred in Prince's 1986 film, *Under the Cherry Moon*—contained sounds that didn't seem possible to replicate anywhere but in Prince's imagination.

The key to this particular aural universe, it turns out, is the ubiquitous computer platform Pro Tools. Prince avoided the system for years. One thing he's truly moralistic about is the use of artificial vocal enhancement by subpar artists, which in his view has reduced mainstream pop to a "weak diet" of sugary junk. Yet he's unlocked new elements within the very control surfaces Pro Tools employs. Using both analog equipment and digital technology, Prince has come closer to the body-altering music he wishes to make.

"I'm interested in the inner workings of music, the effect on the body," he explained. "I'm trying to understand why we respond to beats differently." His former associate, the producer Terry Lewis, helped him realize Pro Tools might help. "Terry talked me into it. He said, 'Don't think of it as a digital machine,'" said Prince. "'Don't play by its rules.' I just took it and started flipping things."

As the music played, Prince singled out a few lyrics. "The songs we sing lift us up to heaven," he said as a song espousing "old-school ways" played. "This one's about Babylonian tricks." Then the music ended, and we moved on to the next offering—one that took us into Prince's bedroom.

Celebrating pleasure

Before the *New Yorker* piece, the biggest question about Prince's spiritual conversion concerned its effect on his own sexual expressiveness. No one in pop has written more powerfully about the transformative power of sex. His sometimes perverse, often humorous fairy tales opened up worlds of pleasure and possibility to listeners. After finding Jehovah, however, fans worried that he would denounce his most fruitful subject matter.

But a really powerful code can unlock anything. "I've studied Solomon and David now," Prince said, referring to two famous Old Testament lovemen. "[In biblical times] sex was always beautiful. You come to understand that, and then you try to find a woman who can experience that with you."

Songs on all three of Prince's new projects celebrate carnal pleasures, but the album he played in his white-carpeted bedroom explores the topic from top to bottom. It's *Elixir* [*sic*], the debut of Bria Valente, Prince's latest protegee. Valente grew up in Minneapolis and attended parties at Paisley Park as a teen, but she registered on Prince's radar in Los Angeles. A tall brunet with a smooth, delicate voice—"she knows how to use her breath like I do on my falsetto, to make it glide over the track," he said—she is Prince's collaborator, along with keyboardist Morris Hayes, in reviving the quiet storm sound.

"This might be my favorite," he said, playing a steamy ballad. "Remember those old Barry White records? A whole lot of people are gonna get pregnant off of this! I gotta call her." With that, he left me to contemplate Valente's "chill" songs, the heart-shaped mirror over his round bed and the large Bible on the nightstand.

It never became clear whether Valente is Prince's partner in more than an artistic way. Since meeting him, she has become a Jehovah's Witness. She lives just down the hill from Beverly Park, and later in the evening, she joined us at a nearby nightclub—she's a friendly young woman who held her own in conversation with the superstar directing her career.

At the club, Prince carefully sat me between himself and Valente, only touching her once, when he gestured for her to accompany him to the front of the club to check out the noisy blues band rocking the crowd. Later, she laughed when he sneaked away to play a quick keyboard solo with the band. "He's like Velcro," she said. "Stuck to the stage."

Beautiful women always have been important in Prince's life, both as musical collaborators and as prominently displayed companions. He has been married twice, separating from his second wife, Manuela Testolini, in 2006. Now he carries himself with the exacting self-sufficiency of a middle-aged bachelor. Often citing famous beauties as close friends, he never mentioned a sexual conquest.

Whether or not he needs a day-to-day companion right now, Prince does seem to require a muse. Valente's project has allowed him to make more openly sensual music than anything else he's recently produced. He even took the high-fashion-style photographs that will adorn the CD booklet.

As her album played, he spoke of other female musicians he currently admires. "Have you heard Janelle Monae?" he asked. "She is so smart. How about Sia, do you like her?" The jazz bassist Esperanza Spalding was due to spend a few days with him later in the week. The names of previous collaborators peppered his conversation: the singers Tamar Davis and Shelby J., his old companions Wendy Melvoin and Lisa Coleman.

For now, Valente is the conduit for Prince's female energy. Her music sounds contemporary but also connects to earlier Prince proteges like the Family and Taja Sevelle. Though he was quick to praise her songwriting abilities (and to point out that he helped her cement a good publishing deal), he spoke about her songs as they played, almost as if they were his own.

"The art of making records, I give it so much respect," he said as the album's final track, a New Age-flavored set piece about Valente's baptism, concluded. "But it gets trampled on for the sake of commerciality."

He led me back into the hallway. "Let's get in the limo to listen to the last one," he said.

An album's range

Lotusflow3r will likely be greeted by Prince fans and the general public as the central product of his latest creative spurt. It's a full band album with a sound that ranges from cocktail jazz to heavy rock. The first track included the lyric his Web designer had mentioned about the expanding universe, while subsequent ones referred to traveling to other dimensions and transcending race.

Directing his driver to take us for a spin after leaving to change from black loungewear into a red suit, Prince explained that *Lotusflow3r* began to emerge during the sessions for his 2006 album, *3121*. Prince selected the best of his massive output for this release, delaying its finish until he was sure every element hung together.

"The thing that unites these songs is the guitar," he said. He'd fallen back in love with the instrument after playing in Davis' backup band during a 2006 tour. He singled out a vampy solo in the samba-influenced "Love Like Jazz." "When we do this live, that's going to go on forever," he said with a grin.

Positioning *Lotusflow3r* as a rock record is a canny marketing move, given urban radio's current focus on hip-hop-defined samples and beats. This music sounds more organic, meant to be played live, and Prince is trying out players for a new band, ones who'll be able to grasp the tricky changes in the new songs. He makes decisions, he said, by "listening to the universe. If a name is mentioned to me three times, I know I need to check it out."

Whatever band he assembles will have to be able to leap from the light-stepping funk of the song simply titled "$," about "the most popular girl in the whole wide world," to the soul jazz of "77 Beverly Place," to the heavy-metal thunder of the album's title track. That song references both Carlos Santana and Jimi Hendrix, but asked about the influence of the latter rock god, Prince demurred. "I try to play guitar like singers I like," he said, later adding, "Don't you think journalists can be lazy, I mean, when they make comparisons?"

He delivered this criticism in a kind tone. Talk turned to the Internet and the need for musicians to claim a niche. "My audience is really big, though," he said. "And they're really easy to reach online. Everything has gone viral."

He continues to be firm on copyright issues—"I made it," is his simple response to those who call him a hypocrite for restricting his material online even as he uses the Web for his own purposes—but seems fairly open to trying new ways to promote his avalanche of music. "You can put in that I'd like to play the Troubadour," he said, though he hasn't made any arrangements for local club dates.

As the night wore to an end, the conversation turned free form, touching on topics ranging from Edie Sedgwick (he saw *Factory Girl*) to Ani DiFranco (he loves her) to his favorite guitar (the blue and white Stratocaster he played during the Super Bowl, named "Sonny" after an early mentor). And then the limo pulled into the driveway.

He hugged me goodnight, and I got into my mud-stained Mazda Protege. Hugging the road down Mulholland Drive, I asked myself, "Did that really happen?" So many moments would seem fantastic in the retelling.

But then, as Beverly Hills became the Valley, I realized how carefully executed this visit had been. Each listening environment had been ideal: the close confinement of the sports car for the intense *MPLSound*, the boudoir for *Elixir* [sic] and the classic rock star ride for the far-reaching *Lotusflow3r*. And though Prince had been open about many things, he's also an expert at wielding the phrase "off the record."

What I'd experienced was like a dream—a dream Prince had designed just for me. Which is what he's been doing for his fans for 30 years.

PARIS PRESS CONFERENCE

October 12, 2009 | Original Transcript

Just as *MPLSound*, *Lotusflow3r*, and Bria Valente's *Elixir* were released in spring 2009 in physical form in the United States exclusively through Minneapolis's big-box-store Target, September 2009 saw an exclusive French release through the independent label Because Music. The collection went to number fourteen and was accompanied by a digital single, "Dance 4 Me," that also charted in France. There was Prince buzz in Paris.

This press conference followed two shows at Paris's Beaux Arts architectural temple the Grand Palais and preceded a live TV appearance and a fans-only intimate show at La Cigale. This press conference is notable for a second half in which Prince reaffirms his commitment to live music (he'd quit the Internet in 2010 and release only one more album until late 2014) and claim that he's waiting to do something different after 2012 (his new band 3rdeyegirl debuted live January 2013).

The piece is also interesting for Prince's playfulness with the press corps and his obvious affection for France and Paris. This fondness was not only evident in his choice of Nice as a location for *Under the Cherry Moon*, but also in the quantity and quality of his scheduled Parisian concerts and late-night shows, in particular 2010's epic and essential 225-minute New Morning club performance. —Ed.

Prince: Did he say nice things? [*about the MC's introduction*]

Reporter: Yes. Lots of nice things.

MC: Some questions?

Reporter: What did seduce you in the Grand Palais and the glass-and-iron structure of the Grand Palais?

Prince: When I did 21 Nights in London, the sound of the audience was so powerful that I needed something better and bigger, and when I saw the Chanel fashion show—when Karl [*Lagerfeld —Ed.*] came out—there was this roar that came up, and I was jealous.

Reporter: So, you did company? You did, you signed with a French label? What didn't you dare doing yet, you know?

Prince: I'll get to it. I'll eventually do everything.

Reporter: [*Unintelligible.*]

Prince: Let's see . . . 150 shows at Bercy. [*Laughter.*]

Reporter: You fell in love with the Grand Palais, and do you fall in love often?

Prince: Well, I needed some place to stay, and that was the best he could do. He just forgot the furniture.

Reporter: And how was it yesterday? And do you plan to do other shows in France, and by the way, have you already met some fashion designers? For the show? About your costumes?

Prince: Well, I do all my own stuff.

Reporter: Own stuff?

Prince: Yeah, I have my own team. It's hard to find clothes that look like this.

Reporter: For sure. And do you plan to do other shows in the country?

Prince: We're talking about it.

Reporter: OK, great.

Prince: It's just in the planning stages.

Reporter: I saw the show yesterday. It was great and the stage was amazing.

Prince: Wasn't it! [*Laughter.*]

Reporter: It was. What did you think about this show? These two shows? How did you feel it?

Prince: That was my favorite so far. I always try to outdo different shows that I've done. This is the best. Absolutely.

Reporter: Can you define, can you explain the pleasure to be on stage and to make music?

Prince: I was telling a friend of mine recently that, like, last night I couldn't sleep and I apologized for being late. It feels like I'm in a dream. And I don't like to go to sleep anymore because the dream is never as good as real life.

Reporter: What did you think about the crowd last night and the way they received you?

Prince: Amazing. It's . . . it's actually indescribable. That much love. I can't even speak about it.

Reporter: Do French people know how to dance? In a proper way.

Prince: Some do and some don't. [*Laughter.*]

Reporter: The question is, are you planning to play in Paris—

Prince: [*Points to other reporter.*] One thing I do want to say is they're very respectful. We ask that no one use camera phones, and they honored that request, unlike Americans, who are so obsessed with technology. And we don't like to have our concerts filmed that way because it sounds so bad, and then you give all the footage to somebody like YouTube, who is run by Universal Publishing and some of those same lawyers. A lot of people don't know that. They just see the logos, but we know all the behind-the-scenes guys. So, we're just thankful that the people are so respectful, and on the quiet songs no talking, they're just . . . they're just very respectful. It's wonderful.

Reporter: What will be the next place for a next show in Paris?

Prince: Well, it's gonna be hard after last night. I gotta think about it.

Reporter: Were you planning to play in Paris and discovering the Grand Palais last minute, or was it a last-minute show?

Prince: No, we play because we don't have bands to go see. It's just rare that you see a band that you like, so we make music because we want to hear music. So it was a last-minute thing, but I had very cool musicians who would fly out at the moment, at moment's notice and . . . it was cool.

Reporter: You were just talking about Universal and how people are very attracted by new technology, saying if you were gonna label, like Because, what does that mean to you, and is it the kinda mistake you were talking about that you try to fix now that you know?

Prince: I don't think of anything as a mistake. Everything's a learning process. Life is full of ups and downs. It just depends on how you react to them. The situation with Because is similar to the one we had at Target. Target doesn't have a problem selling physical CDs, and neither does Because, so there just seems to be a problem in America with selling them. And it seems they also want to control who becomes popular and who doesn't. The radio is state controlled and YouTube and how many hits you get and all that kind of stuff—er, how many views you get, rather—and it's just a system now that is just not enticing to me. So we stick with concerts, and we can do new music that way. Might be a time in the future where technology will be advanced so that people can bring technology to the concerts and they can record the shows right then on the spot. You know, we'll just see, you know.

Reporter: About your time in Paris. This city gives you admiration or inspiration even?

Prince: It's a very erotic town, so . . . it's very inspirational.

Reporter: Do you like French food?

Prince: No. [*Laughter.*]

Reporter: Talking about erotic. In *MPLSound* you're singing "Dance 4 me, I like it when you dance 4 me." Were you thinking about somebody special?

Prince: Yeah, it is.

Reporter: Who?

Prince: I was looking in the mirror when I wrote it.

Reporter: How does it feel to be Prince today?

Prince: It's indescribable. It's impossible. Really impossible.

Reporter: You're one of the best guitarists in the world.

Prince: Ahhh . . .

Reporter: What do you think about Guitar Hero? These types of games where you become a musician all of a sudden.

Prince: Do you actually learn how to play the guitar?

Reporter: No.

Prince: Well, there you go. It took a long time to learn how to play like I wanted to. So, I respect somebody that puts that much effort into it. You think they'll have Basketball Hero one day? Takes a lot to become LeBron James. Lotta work.

Reporter: How long will you stay in Paris and what will you do in the next days?

Prince: That's the boss. I do what he tells me to do.

Reporter: You struggled a lot for your artistic freedom. Now it seems you are totally artistic freedom. How does it feel? I mean, you can play when you want, where you want, what you want.

Prince: Well, these are the days I was looking forward to. Like I say, it's hard to sleep because the options are, they're so numerous. It was worth the fight. It was worth the struggle that we went through. I advise every artist to go through it, if they can, you know. And cream rises to the top anyway. A real free music doesn't mean that you don't pay for it. It just means that there's no authoritarian figure telling you what you're supposed to do with it.

Reporter: Is Internet opening new doors for you?

Prince: It's a tool. It's not a means to an end, by no stretch. My concerts have always been dear to me, and it's almost a shame that I got so good at making records because the medium is dying now. Until something new happens and we get some laws with restrictions to how media is used and how the revenue is shared, then I'll just stick with the live stuff. And every once in a while we'll do records. I make records all the time, though. There's tons of stuff in the vault. We'll see. It will come out one of these days.

Reporter: Would you be interested in using cinema and images again to do something different with your music?

Prince: There again, we're just waiting. Maybe after 2012 we'll see. But everything's gonna change. There's gonna be different people running companies. Manuela's talking about artist-run companies, different things like that. will.i.am is a friend of mine and we talk a lot about what the future will look like and how people will actually get music, and it has nothing to do with lawyers and accountants that have nothing to say in regards to the creative process.

Reporter: How do you find satisfaction in your work, and are you a happy man today?

Prince: Very happy. More happy than ever, actually.

Reporter: You used to write "slave" on your cheek.

Prince: I did? [*Laughter.*] That wasn't me.

Reporter: But, if you had to change you name again, what would you change it for? [*Laughter.*]

Prince: I like this name. I think it fits.

Reporter: And your work is genius. Who is qualified to critique your music today?

Prince: Nobody.

Reporter: Do you listen to anyone else other than you? Are there other singers we are talking about? Maybe others?

Prince: I like will.i.am, his business sense and how he sees the world. It's very interesting. He's very technology driven, but let's remember he did write "My Humps." [*Laughter.*] So . . . I do love Anna Maurer. I love her music. I listen to that a lot. Bria Valente. I love female vocalists, mostly. Esperanza Spalding. I look forward to what she's going to do in the future. She's really talented. But, there again, she's a musician. So is Anna. They work very hard at the craft. They take care of their instruments.

Reporter: If you were to write the definition of the word "funky" in a dictionary, what would that definition be?

Prince: If you can describe it, you ain't funky.

Reporter: Is there any question that you want to be asked?

Prince: Ask me about God.

Reporter: And what do we want . . .

Prince: You need him. We all do. Thanks.

PRINCE: "I'M A MUSICIAN. AND I AM MUSIC."

Dorian Lynskey | June 23, 2011 | *Guardian*

In June 2010 Prince declared the Internet "dead." This conclusion led, in part, to his decisions to release his next LP, *20Ten*, as a free covermount on print publications in five European countries in July 2010 and to rededicate himself to live performances, which he did in the four-plus-year gap until his next album releases. Others might argue he had to give *20Ten* away for free because it's his weakest song-for-song album, one which has never received a physical release in the United States.

In this interview designed to drum up ticket sales for the cumbersomely titled Welcome 2 America: Euro Tour 2011, Prince talked with a half-dozen European reporters in the summer of 2011. In this lone UK interview, he and his interlocutor discuss numerous topics, including aging, why Prince stood out among the musical giants of the 1980s, and, even though it was off limits, his most recent thoughts on the Internet. Although he claims he's not recording, only playing live (that is, making bank), he had in fact just completed *Welcome 2 America*, which would not be released until 2021.

The big takeaway here is Prince's return to a discussion of "order," a concept based on his Biblical readings and his evolving reassessment of authority. More controversially, Prince explains that Islamic countries are "fun" because they offer order and no choices. When nudged on the topic, he claims that "there are people who are unhappy with everything." —Ed.

Prince is running late, and when Prince is running late the prospective interviewer begins to worry. I'm in the otherwise empty upstairs room of a chic Paris restaurant, its walls, carpet and banquettes all (perhaps by chance) a Prince-appropriate purple. As last trains and planes out of Paris are missed, I think of the writer in the early 90s who spent six days rattling around Paisley Park, Prince's Minneapolis nerve center, waiting for an audience, only to have to speak to him on the phone. Even a relatively modest three-hour wait can make one nervous.

But suddenly there he is, sans entourage, full of handshakes and apologies. Perching himself on a banquette, he looks impeccable. His trousers and chunky polo-neck sweater are as black as his shiny, sculpted hair. His ring, ear cuffs and huge, shrapnel-like neck chain all gleam silver. His skin, uncannily smooth, does not look like that of a 53-year-old. Charisma seems to add a few inches to his height. He orders a cup of green tea. "They don't take Mastercard here," he says with a sly grin. "Only Amex. So I'll have to wash the dishes."

You expect funny peculiar from Prince, one of the few superstars who still enjoys an old-fashioned forcefield of enigma and hence endures the rumors that enigma tends to spawn. Funny ha-ha, however, is more surprising. He often seems mysteriously amused, cocking an eyebrow and pulling a coy, wouldn't-you-like-to-know smirk, but he likes to laugh out loud, too. He is determined to be entertaining.

Asked, for example, why he doesn't appear to have aged, Prince embarks on a baroque explanation that takes in an illustration of celestial mechanics involving a candle (the sun) and a sugarcube (the Earth); DNA research; his late father's Alzheimer's disease; the reason he doesn't celebrate his birthday ("If you look in the Bible there's no birthdays"); the importance of study; God's concept of time; and the *Purple Rain* tour. "Time is a mind construct," he finally concludes, setting his candle and sugarcube aside. "It's not real."

All of this is accomplished in a tone that ranges from preacher to schoolteacher to salesman to stand-up comedian to chat-show raconteur. He very rarely talks to the press ("If I need psychological evaluation, I'll do it myself") and his ban on writers using recording devices suggests a certain paranoia, but he's surprisingly good at being interviewed.

People must be intimidated when they first meet you, I say. Do you try to put them at their ease?

"I do that pretty quick. I'm real easy-going." He stares at me for a moment. "You're not intimidated, are you?"

Not now, but definitely by your reputation.

"A lot of that comes from other people. The press like to blow things out of proportion so this person becomes bigger than they are. The sooner this thing called fame goes away, the better. We got people who don't need to be famous."

Prince misses the days "when I could walk the street without being harassed and bothered." He remembers the first time he realized he was famous, around 1979. "It happened very fast. I had some old clothes on because I was going to help a friend move house and some girls came by and one went: 'Ohmigod, Prince!' And the other girl went," he pulls a face, "'That ain't Prince.' I didn't come out of the house raggedy after that."

Prince, along with Michael Jackson and Madonna, was one of the regents of pop music in its blockbuster pomp. Unlike them, he could do everything: sing, write, play, produce, design, make movies, call all the shots. With 1984's *Purple Rain*, he could simultaneously boast the No. 1 album, single and film in the US. During his imperial phase, it felt like his only competition was himself. "I had creative control," he says proudly. "We had to fight for over a year before I even got signed. So whatever I turned in, they had to accept. They weren't even allowed to speak to me!"

Rumors circled him because he was such a defiantly outlandish presence: the pop star as inexplicable alien, with a sexuality as ambiguous as it was voracious, and so unsettlingly potent that the censorship lobby PMRC was spurred into existence by a single song, "Darling Nikki." Did he work hard to make himself as fascinating as possible? "We were very fascinating," he says. "In Minnesota it was a clean slate. It was punk rock. There were a lot of fascinating people around."

He took so many gambles, in terms of image as well as music. Did he ever worry that he might blow it? "All the time. You want an example?"

Yes please.

He chuckles. "You'll have to pay for the autobiography." (There is no autobiography.)

Does he think the atomization of pop culture since the 80s allows for another star of his stature? He thinks for a moment. "It would have to be manufactured. Michael [Jackson] and I both came along at a time when there was nothing. MTV didn't have anyone who was visual. Bowie, maybe. A lot of people made great records, but dressed like they were going to the supermarket." He thinks flamboyant showmanship is making a comeback but, he adds: "How many people have substance, or are they just putting on crazy clothes?"

What does he make of Lady Gaga? "I don't know," Prince says diplomatically. "I'd have to meet her."

Prince will happily talk about how much he adores Adele ("When she just comes on and sings with a piano player, no gimmicks, it's great") or Janelle Monáe, but he won't criticize other artists. "The new pushes the old out of the way and retains what it wants to. Don't ask me about popular acts. Ask Janelle. Doesn't matter what I say. We ain't raining on anyone's parade. I ain't mad at anybody. I don't have any enemies."

Actually he has many, but they're not fellow musicians. He is drawn back again and again to the perfidy of pretty much everybody in the music industry who doesn't make music themselves. There was, of course, that business in the 90s when he went to war with Warner Bros, changing his name to an unpronounceable symbol and marking his eventual exit from the label with a triple CD pointedly titled *Emancipation*. "A lot of people didn't know what I was doing," he says, "but it helped some people. I don't care what people think." He's not as angry now. "I don't look at it as Us versus Them. I did. But you know *The Wizard of Oz*? When they pull back the curtain and see what's going on? That's what's happened."

Now his opponents are no longer the ailing majors, but the people selling or sharing music online. He was one of the pioneers of self-financed website releases; more recently he made lucrative deals to give away albums with tabloid newspapers. But he has no plans to make a new album, even though he has hundreds of songs stacked up. "The industry changed," he says. "We made money [online] before piracy was real crazy. Nobody's making money now except phone companies, Apple and Google. I'm supposed to go to the White House to talk about copyright protection. It's like the gold rush out there. Or a carjacking. There's no boundaries. I've been in meetings and they'll tell you, Prince, you don't understand, it's dog-eat-dog out there. So I'll just hold off on recording."

His management's pre-interview list of guidelines insisted, "Please do not discuss his views on the internet," but perhaps Prince hasn't read them. "I personally can't stand digital music," he says. "You're getting sound in bits. It affects a different place in your brain. When you play it back, you can't feel anything. We're analogue people, not digital." He's warming to his theme. "Ringtones!" he exclaims. "Have you ever been in a room where there's 17 ringtones going off at once?"

Does he have a ringtone?

"No," he says, looking as offended as if I'd asked him if he drove a clown car. "I don't have a phone."

He's equally put out by covers of his songs, Glee's version of "Kiss" being the latest offender. "There's no other artform where you can do that. You can't go and do your own version of Harry Potter. Do you want to hear somebody else sing 'Kiss'?"

Next weekend, Prince is back in Europe—this interview is to promote his headlining appearance at the Heineken Open'er Festival in Poland— but he bats away an inquiry about the annual Glastonbury rumors. "They use my name to sell the festival," he glowers. "It's illegal. I've never spoken to anyone about doing that concert, ever."

Touring is where the money is these days, of course, but it also seems to be where his heart is. He describes himself as a "loving tyrant. I'm probably the hardest bandleader to work for, but I do it for love." His band have rehearsed around 300 songs, from which Prince can choose at whim, which makes playing live more fun than it used to be. "*Purple Rain* was 100 shows, and around the 75th, I went crazy," he says, "and here's why. They didn't want to see anything but the movie. If you didn't play every song, you were in trouble. After 75 you don't know where you are—somebody had to drag me to the stage. I'm not going! Yes you are! It was bloody back then. I won't say why but there was blood on me. They were the longest shows because you knew what was going to happen." Now, he says: "If there's a challenge it's to outdo what I've done in the past. I play each show as if it's the last one."

For inspiration he keeps coming back to Sly and the Family Stone, and it was that band's former bassist, Larry Graham, who introduced him to the Jehovah's Witnesses a decade ago. The faith seems to have made him calm and content, albeit at the loss to his songwriting of the anguish, combativeness and transgressive sexuality that animated some of his strongest 80s material. "I was anti-authoritarian but at the same time I was a loving tyrant. You can't be both. I had to learn what authority was. That's what the Bible teaches. The Bible is a study guide for social interaction." He puts it another way. "If I go to a place where I don't feel stressed and there's no car alarms and airplanes overhead, then you understand what noise pollution is. Noise is a society that has no God, that has no glue. We can't do what we want to do all the time. If you don't have boundaries, what then?"

Sometimes he seems a little too fond of boundaries. "It's fun being in Islamic countries, to know there's only one religion. There's order. You wear a burqa. There's no choice. People are happy with that." But what about women who are unhappy about having to wearing burqas? "There are people who are unhappy with everything," he says shruggingly. "There's a dark side to everything."

Noting my unconvinced expression, he tries to clarify, but gives up with a sigh. "I don't want to get up on a soapbox. My view of the world, you can debate that forever. But I'm a musician. That's what I do. And I also am music. Come to the show for that."

It's been over an hour, and he's starting to look restless. Does he feel most at peace when playing music?

"I can feel pretty peaceful doing other things as well," he says, with what I think might be a saucy look.

Does he ever feel nostalgic?

"I tend to dig some of the art from back then. I like putting it on shirts and bags. The fans dig it. But musically, no. Each band brings different songs out of you."

He keeps playing down his own stardom and doffing his cap to his band or God or Sly and the Family Stone, but does he ever think, perhaps midway through playing "When Doves Cry" to 30,000 people: "I'm really very good at this"?

"Well I don't think it," he smirks, raising an eyebrow. "I know it."

EVERLASTING NOW: PRINCE

Vanessa Grigoriadis | July 3, 2013 | *V Magazine*

Prince was quiet publicly most of 2012, with a brief Welcome 2 Australia tour in May and scattered US live dates in the fall leading up to the November release of "Rock and Roll Love Affair," his first single in a year. Behind the scenes, he had been assembling and then rehearsing his new band, 3rdeyegirl: bassist Ida Nielsen, who had been with him since 2010, drummer Hannah Ford, and guitarist Donna Grantis.

3rdeyegirl was unveiled on a New Year's Eve 2012 YouTube stream of a "Bambi" rehearsal (the Internet had been resurrected). The group made its thrilling live debut on January 18, 2013, on the final night of Prince's six-show "Three Nights with Paisley Park" residency at Minneapolis's Dakota Jazz Club and Restaurant. An extensive US tour rolled out in April and May, and one-off dates in the United States and Europe followed the rest of the year.

This interview took place in Anaheim in May. Prince hands over the beginning of the interview to members of 3rdeyegirl before signing a record deal for them with Kobalt Music Group (a deal which seems to have only yielded 2014's "Pretzelbodylogic" single). For the balance of the interview Prince seems a bit antsy, a dance party clearly in his sights. He talks guitars, calmness, religion, and his role as the central sun in the Prince galaxy. And it's clearly Prince's galaxy—we just live in it. —Ed.

It's no sweat for Prince to play two sets a night, as he does this evening at the 1,700-seat City National Grove of Anaheim California. He tells me that if anything he's more energized after the second show, not less. Both shows stretch to a delicious two hours, as the crowd, in blowouts and Vegas-style cocktail dresses (it's worth dressing up for Prince, even in California), screams and sings along with glee. The only tense moment comes when we file into the theater and a security guard says, "No cameras, no cellphones—don't even take them out of your pocket. Tonight, we're not asking, we're just escorting." I ask her what that means. "If we see you with your phone out, we're not going to ask what you're doing—you're just gone."

This demand might seem extreme coming from the Purple One—a very young-looking 55, with a tight Afro instead of his usual loose curls, clad in a black bodysuit with white lines that makes him look like a spider—but in fact it's not out of character.

You could argue that Prince was an early adopter of phone-text-speak ("I Would Die 4 U" and all that), but he's eschewed the PR opportunities afforded by the latest tech almost completely, refusing to put his videos on YouTube and offering new music mostly for sale on his websites. And in part by making himself so unavailable, he's remained as mysterious as ever. Prince has always refused any label the world wants to slap on him. A devout Jehovah's Witness since 2001, he writes music that is explicit about both Jesus and sexual desire. He's a black man with light skin who usually dresses in clothes that seem inspired by female icons, from Twiggy to Marie Antoinette. A heterosexual man who deeply worships sexually confident women, he nonetheless wants to dominate them. Prince keeps his private life private: he's usually either on the road or at Paisley Park, his $10 million compound in the suburbs of his hometown of Minneapolis, with multiple recording studios, wardrobe rooms, a video-editing suite, a sound stage, production offices, rehearsal areas, and "the vault," which includes his extensive library of unreleased recordings.

Tonight's show is a lot less about pop, R&B, and funk than his music has been in the past—in fact, he's playing rock, like his new song "Screwdriver," and doing guitar-heavy, stripped-down versions of his old hits, including "Raspberry Beret," "When Doves Cry," and "Computer Blue," for which the stage is suffused in blue light. For this tour he's backed by 3RDEYEGIRL, a new rock band that he assembled himself. It's made up of Danish bassist Ida Nielsen, wearing pigtails, blonde Chicago College of Performing Arts at Roosevelt University jazz performance major

Hannah Ford-Welton, on drums, and Canadian Donna Grantis, with half her head shaved, playing a wild, shredding guitar. "I'm trying to get these women's careers started, because they're all so talented," he tells me later. "It's not even about me anymore."

Playing with 3RDEYEGIRL, there's lots of room for Prince, one of the world's most celebrated guitarists, to show off his skills (though Ms. Grantis does keep up with him). The show feels like a gospel revival, with Prince as the groovy, feel-good pastor facilitating a release of energy for the crowd, which sings along and nods when he throws out lines about "compassion" or preaches "the only love we have is the love we make—we've got to take care of each other, everybody." At the end of the show he says, "Thank each and every one of you for leaving your cell phones in your pocket. I can't see your face when you've got technology in front of it." At 1:30 am, as the lights go up after the second show, two MILFs chat by the stage. "He was gorgeous up there," says one. Prince's elegant manager, Julia Ramadan, appears quickly and whisks me through a clutch of roadies and onto Prince's idling tour bus, where 3RDEYEGIRL is hanging out. I'll do my interviews here, and per Prince's usual demand of journalists, will conduct them without a tape recorder or notepad, though I am allowed to have a list of questions. When I ask him why he's required this of journalists over the past decade, he says, "People have sold my interviews."

First, I talk to 3RDEYEGIRL, who are still flushed with excitement from the shows, about their experience with Prince. Nielsen, who has played with Zap Mama, was the first one he recruited. Prince's manager found Ford-Welton. Grantis appeared when Prince told Ford-Welton and her husband to discover "the best female musician out there" (they found her videos on YouTube). We talk about what life is like at Paisley Park. "We practice all the time," says Ford-Welton—it's something like 12-hour days, six days a week. All the musicians in 3RDEYEGIRL have a background in jazz improvisation, so they're able to react quickly to Prince's lead when he's composing, but they're still astounded at how fast he is at songwriting and arranging. Grantis calls him the "best band leader in the world." Nilsson nods. "There's a special chemistry between us," she says. Later Prince will ask DJ Rashida to play a banging song for me that he wrote for Ford-Welton and her husband at the after-hours party. I ask Rashida what Prince songs he doesn't like her to play at his parties, and she says, "Well, not the ones with curse words, because he doesn't curse anymore."

Soon the door to the tour bus opens: it's the man himself. He's changed into a new outfit of flared pants with primary color stripes, a large ring with a blue evil eye at the center of his right hand ("nothing evil about it," he tells me) and a rhinestone-encrusted pimp cane in the other. The cane is just for decoration; he is clearly in amazing shape. Prince points at me and then at Richard Sanders, President of Kobalt Music Group. Richard takes out a sheaf of paperwork and puts it on the bus's kitchen table. It's the contract for the new 3RDEYEGIRL record, which has been awaiting a final signature. Prince affixes with a flourish.

"That's it," he says, turning to Grantis, Ford-Welton, and Nilsson. "You've got a record deal. Now we just have to make some songs." Everyone laughs at this joke—with Prince's prolific output as a producer, they've been recording so much for the past few months that they already have most of the album done. The women take their cue and leave the bus, with Richard hot on their heels. "Thank you so much for coming," Ramadan says to him, graciously. "Oh, please," he replies. "This is the fun part." With everyone gone, Prince and Ramadan take seats on a low-slung black leather couch. I sit opposite and throw out my first question: "I was just talking to the women about your new band, about how they met you. But what drew you to creating the band in the first place?"

Prince rests his thin, elegant hands on top of the cane and speaks quietly—he expended his voice during the shows, and now he's saving it—but never averts his gaze. Framed by thick lashes, his extremely large, liquid eyes seem to occupy half his face.

He takes a breath and then begins a long monologue: "This organization is different than most, in the sense that we don't take directions from the outside world. It's like a galaxy. The sun is in the center giving off energy, and everything revolves around it." He talks about what it would be like if instead of the sun giving of energy, energy was trying to exert its force on the sun. That wouldn't make a lot of sense. It would be, he says, like "meteors hitting a planet!" What makes much more sense is "a sun pulling everything around on its own axis, with information. The sun is information. Nobody really talks to me. Nobody talks to me a lot." He points at Ramadan. "I talk to her. She talks to you. She talks to Richard. And so on and so forth. If I trust her, then you can trust her."

Prince likes this system. "I directed a couple films and it was taxing in that people were asking me questions about their jobs." He much prefers peace and calm. "I have to be quiet to make what I make, do what I do." He takes a breath. "Another thing that's different about this organization is that time here is slowed down, because we don't take information from the outside world. We don't know what day it is and we don't care. There is no clock."

Living in the now, he says, makes the tour go by very quickly. Indeed he couldn't tell me how long he's been on tour because he only counts the hours he's actually onstage when he thinks about it. So in the last month, "I've only been on tour for two days," he says. "That's the work."

He seems to have come to the end of this thought, so I look down at my questions, unsure if I should ask the first one again. Better not. "Your shows are wonderful, obviously, but known to be very unpredictable," I say. "How do you decide what you are going to play?"

"I decide in the moment," he says. "I change the set list right then and there." He also takes into account the state of his guitar. "To play solos the way I'm playing them, the guitar goes out of tune sometimes. It's just a piece of wood."

"What happened with The Roots' guitarist's guitar, the one that you threw after your performance on *Late Night with Jimmy Fallon?*" I ask.

"What?" he says.

"Didn't you borrow a guitar from him and then throw it after your set? It was all over the news."

"No," he replies, straight-faced. "Another thing that's different about this organization is that we don't think about that," he says, pointing at the TV.

He returns to speaking about guitars. Sometimes, he says, he makes sure to include a song he can play on piano so the guitar can go off-stage and get tuned. In fact, he explains, this is why he added Gratis to the band—he needed a second guitarist for these moments. "But that guitarist had to be great," he says. "She couldn't be a punk." How does he think female and male guitarists are different? "I don't think women and men are different in that regard. Donna can whup every man on guitar, bar none."

What's the difference between men and women generally?

"Well," he says. "If we didn't have to go to a party, we could talk about that." I see him shifting around in his seat a little—he has planned an after-party in the venue's VIP lounge—and I start to think he's going to cut the interview short. So I ask my big question: "How do you, as a religious person, reconcile the religious impulse with what most of your songs are about, which is the sexual one?"

Prince bursts out laughing and points to Ramadan. "Ha!" he says. "Now we know what you're going to write about. We were waiting for your thread." He clears his throat. "First of all, do you see a difference in religions?" he asks. I say no, suggesting all religions are based on the same idea and then corrupted by their human leaders. "Then what are the wars about?" he asks, unhappy with my answer. "If one religion believes Christ is the king, and another doesn't, then there's a difference in religions." He goes on for a bit, and adds, "we are sensual beings, the way God created us, when you take the shame and taboo away from it," and continues that religion should be thought of like a force, an electromagnetic one or like gravity, that puts things in motion. Then he says, "I don't want to talk about this."

I ask him if he believes in sin. "You have to look at the origin of the word," he says. "Humans needed a language to describe a rule given from some group from . . ." He pauses, then says, and this is as I remember it: "Words are tricky. And plus these days I just talk to the folks in the outside world about music. If you were a student and I was teaching you something we could get into that. We can't do this before a dance party."

I begin madly crossing off my non-music questions and tell him I'm thinking of learning guitar so I can teach my daughter. "See," he says, "if I discussed my past, your baby would never see you. And what a waste."

We talk about how he seems to be operating on a business plan that requires him to do a lot of touring. "I love it," he says. "What, this is so terrible? I'm sooo bored of it." He gestures around his swank bus and laughs. We discuss which song in his vault he feels he should have released. "Which one of your children do you like the best?" he says. "Music comes from the same source. It's all the same thing."

What records does he listen to now? He mentions Lianne La Havas, KING (a female trio he's worked with), Janelle Monáe, and Esperanza Spalding. "I listen to my friends' records before they come out," he says. "Feel me. A record nowadays comes out a year after it's made. When we make music, we want it to come out right away. Because we're going to have some new stuff right away."

What does he feel about the return of vinyl? "It never left," he says. "Think about a young person listening to Joni Mitchell for the first time on vinyl. You know how fun that is? Whoa, we gonna be here a minute."

I ask how tech-averse he really is; does he have an iPhone? "Are you serious?" he says. "Hell, no." He mimics a high-voiced woman. "Where is my phone? Can you call my phone? Oh, I can't find it." He talks about people who come to his concerts all the time, akin to the Deadheads. "People come to see us fifty times. Well, that's not just going to see a concert—that's some other mess going on. This music changes you. These people are not being satisfied elsewhere by musicians, you feel what I'm saying? It's no disrespect to anyone else, because we're not checking for them. But we don't lip synch. We ain't got time for it. Ain't no tape up there."

He stands up, planting his cane on the floor. I ask how the music that he's playing now, with 3RDEYEGIRL, has changed him. "I'm calmer now," he says. "I'm rougher with men. I bring my tone down with women. If they make a mistake, I don't look at them and go, 'Seriously?!'" He talks about Ford-Welton missing a cue on one of their songs and how he simply gestured to her and told her just not to do it next time. "I explained that she had to pay attention. Stay in the moment." Then he smiles. "Let's go to the party."

THE BLACK INTERVIEW

Miles Marshall Lewis | June 2016 | *Ebony*

Prince and 3rdeyegirl sandwiched multiple one-off shows around a brief European tour in late spring 2014. After a four-year gap, the collaborative 3rdeyegirl LP *Plectrumelectrum* was finally released in September 2014, the same day as the Prince solo LP *Art Official Age*. Both were distributed through a mended-fences deal with Warner Bros. Records. Without fall 2014 interview support, but with a decent amount of marketing, the 3rdeyegirl LP reached number one on Billboard's rock charts and the solo LP hit the top of the R&B charts.

Prince didn't undertake an official tour in 2015 but played a few dozen live shows. The two most significant performances were the May 10 Rally 4 Peace in Baltimore, arranged in response to Freddie Gray's death in police custody and subsequent protests, and a June 13 appearance at Barack Obama's White House to celebrate African American Music Appreciation Month.

In September, Prince released the slightly experimental *Hitnrun Phase One*, which was followed in December by the more traditional funk of *Hitnrun Phase Two*. He supported these releases, sort of, with his first solo tour, Piano & a Microphone. The tour kicked off with a pair of gala events at Paisley Park on January 21 and wended through Australia and New Zealand before hitting the United States and Canada for eight spring dates before his untimely death on April 21.

Prince promoted the final LPs with a few one-on-one interviews and a quasi–press conference with five European journalists. One of the latter pieces is incorrectly credited in the book *Prince: The Last Interview and Other Conversations* as "the last interview." At the time of this writing, the last interview appears to be a too-brief e-mail exchange about the Down Under leg of the Piano & a Microphone tour with reporter Kathy McCabe that appeared February 7, 2016, in the *Sydney Telegraph*'s Sunday supplement *Insider*.

This *Ebony* interview is among the richest and most personable of Prince's career. Writer Miles Marshall Lewis gives Prince the space to discuss his latest distribution schemes (primarily Tidal) but also gets Prince to talk about his past in considerable detail during a first listen to *Hitnrun Phase Two*.

Lewis was Arts & Culture editor of Ebony.com when a small portion of this interview was published on August 28, 2015, a week before the Tidal-exclusive debut of *Hitnrun Phase One*. After the second album was officially released, *Ebony* revisited the August interview with an expanded December 22 article. This was quickly removed from the publication's website at Prince's request.

After Prince's death, portions of the December article were reprinted in the June 2016 print edition of the magazine, a version preceded by a Lewis memorial essay that touches on Prince's unappreciated and often unacknowledged contributions to Black communities. With Lewis's guidance, the version here offers the April 2016 memorial and article introduction accompanied by a comprehensive compilation of the complete 2015 interview.

This isn't Prince's last interview, but it's among his best and most important. —Ed.

When an icon such as Prince Rogers Nelson transitions, he becomes a torch for both nostalgia and the power of music to unite, proving an artist could transcend race. To be sure, Prince—with songs that included "Controversy" ("Am I Black or White? Am I straight or gay?")—messed around enough with the grays. The myth of his mixed-race identity even foregrounds his cinematic breakthrough with *Purple Rain*. But Prince's choices were concessions to the prejudices of the marketplace, not the lived realities of race.

In ways that reflect his upbringing as a working-class Black kid from the American Midwest (an AFL-CIO statement after his death revealed he was a 40-plus-year member of labor unions), he was always a race man.

Prince came of age as an artist and celebrity in an era when the entertainment industry, if not American society in general, was still deeply ambivalent about Black male sexuality. If Teddy Pendergrass represented the apex of potent Black male sexuality in the mainstream in the late 1970s, it's notable that the men who vied for that throne in the early '80s were alternately more flamboyant and subdued. While Rick James, Michael Jackson and Prince all sought to be Black men who regularly adorned the bedroom walls of teenage American girls, Prince's persona was the one that pushed nontraditional boundaries around gender, sexuality and race.

But as Dave Chappelle and Charlie Murphy made clear a few years ago on *Chappelle's Show*, we shouldn't let Prince's ruffles obscure the fact that in art, business and philanthropy, he kept an investment in the Black aesthetics and communities that provided him with both his voice and vision.

Many have cited Prince's 2015 recording "Baltimore" as proof of his Black Lives Matter bona fides, as well as his May concert that year in support of both the city and organizers protesting the police killing of Freddie Gray. But nearly 20 years earlier, Prince recorded "We March," written with Marvin Gaye's daughter, Nona, in support of the symbolic goals of the Minister Louis Farrakhan–organized Million Man March. Less remembered is the artist's 2011 cover of the Staple Singers' "When Will We Be Paid," which, over a decade before Ta-Nehisi Coates's celebrated essay in *The Atlantic*, was a strident call for Black reparations in the popular realm.

Prince's concern about reparations was the by-product of a musician with a keen sense of the exploitation often experienced by performers, particularly Black artists. Prince's most pronounced public "statements" on race came via his dispute with his label, Warner Bros. Records, over control of his music catalog and ownership of his master recordings.

In the mid-1990s, Prince scrawled "slave" on his cheek and responded to queries about its appearance with the quip, "If you don't own your masters, your master owns you."

In referencing his lack of ownership of this literal physical product of his music, he echoed a dilemma confronted by entertainers dating back to Black blues musicians such as Lead Belly, whose music was transcribed by enterprising Whites for their own profit, and early soul artists including Sam Cooke, Ray Charles and others, who fought for ownership of their music publishing rights.

Ever aware of historic ironies, when Prince independently released his No. 1 song "The Most Beautiful Girl in the World" on his own NPG Records in 1994, the single was distributed by Al Bell's Bellmark Records.

Bell is well-known for his successful efforts to rebuild the iconic Stax label in the early 1970s, after the death of Otis Redding and the loss of much of its catalog to Atlantic Records, who distributed their albums. It was under Bell's stewardship that Stax embarked on an ambitious attempt to "give back" by underwriting a day-long free concert at the Los Angeles Coliseum in 1972 that was known as Wattstax.

Prince's relationship with Bell underlines the late musician's own philanthropic efforts and his interests in exploring alternative platforms for his music. Many of his monetary gifts remained anonymous during his life, including a financial donation to Trayvon Martin's family. Like his rival Michael Jackson, Prince was a supporter of the United Negro College Fund, donating profits from his 1992 single "Money Don't Matter 2 Night" to the organization.

The talented singer/songwriter/musician was known as an early adopter of the Internet as an artist platform, even as he later challenged the delivery models established by digital streaming services that continued the exploitation of artists. Prince's philanthropy and interests in emerging technologies intersected with his support of #YesWeCode, a San Francisco Bay Area organization that aims to train 100,000 Black and Latino youth in coding. As fans sought to play Prince's music immediately after his death, many were surprised to find it was unavailable on the major streaming services, with the exception of Tidal. When Prince reclaimed his master recordings, he eventually chose Tidal as his streaming service of choice, in part because of their enhanced royalty rates for artists.

Prince was that shining example of a Black person who had won his freedom on a number of levels. In the early 19th century, the groundbreaking musician might have been referred to as a "free man of color." Today, we can remember him as the race man in purple.

In December 2015, Prince requested that this interview, one of his last, be removed from EBONY.com. In light of his untimely death, EBONY has chosen to unlock his words for the sake of history.

Last August, word went out from Paisley Park Studios that I was being summoned. Prince wasn't aware I spent my teenage years on an out-of-tune upright piano in my bedroom with his sheet music practicing "Raspberry Beret," "The Beautiful Ones," "Sometimes It Snows in April," "The Cross," "God," and others. He didn't know I once jetted past security at the New Morning club in Paris at 2:00 a.m. to see him play an unannounced show for four hours. Or all the bootleg cassettes I poured over in college. None of that. He's seen a piece I'd written online about his 1980s jazz band Madhouse (Prince on every instrument save saxophone) and wanted me to interview Joshua Welton, producer of his latest album, *Hitnrun: Phase One.*

Which I did, for 10 minutes on Aug. 24, 2015, at Paisley Park. But then Prince entered Studio B, gave me a warm hug (visualization works!) and started a two-hour conversation. We spoke of Vanity, Morris Day, and Bruce Springsteen, of Beyonce, D'Angelo, and Taylor Swift. I asked every question I'd been holding on to since the age of 13. He let me play his grand piano. Our exchange ended in his Cadillac sports car, *Hitnrun: Phase Two* (an already completed album he hadn't announced yet) on the stereo.

Part of my Q&A ran on EBONY.com August 28. I'd kept a more detailed transcription of our extensive talk for a future cover story, one that never materialized. So when *Hitnrun: Phase Two* dropped as a surprise release in December, we at the EBONY site decided to run with it. Hours after its posting, Prince's team asked that it be removed. It was suggested Prince felt portions of it were off the record (I had stopped writing each time he said something was). And with that, it disappeared.

Prince, my hero since forever, didn't approve. Famously hyperaware of his image, perhaps he felt he'd revealed too much. "You really got further than any other journalist had done," Questlove commented on my Facebook page. "It was a great piece, let's hope it can return to the light of day," added Alan Light, author of *Let's Go Crazy: Prince and the Making of Purple Rain.* Twitter exploded. The value of this singular interview was clear immediately. But I never meant to cause him any sorrow. So we deleted the post. Like *The Black Album*, my interview was gone.

Now, however, in view of its historical value, our original interview follows.

Prince asked me to keep some secrets. I may still have a few, truth be told. This past summer, a call went out to a few music journalists to visit the purple rock, Paisley Park Studios in Minneapolis. Joshua Welton, 25, had a few words to share about producing his first Prince project, *Hit N Run*. The operative word being "few." After 10 minutes of talk, Prince himself entered Studio A and took over the conversation for two enlightening hours, discussing everything from Jay Z's TIDAL streaming service to the origins behind "Purple Rain" and "The Beautiful Ones," and the reformation of The Time. Bob Seger, Esperanza Spalding, Kendrick Lamar and beyond.

Our couple of hours raced by faster than the accelerated voice of Camille. Then Prince disappeared, pulling up later in front of Paisley Park in a Cadillac sports car to play his already finished, secret follow-up to *Hit N Run*. On December 12, *Hitnrun Phase Two* arrived on TIDAL for streaming and digital download. So now you know. The following is a feverish transcription of more of our August convo from the summertime, previously unpublished. There may be more; Prince is full of secrets.

EBONY: Do you ever see yourself writing a memoir?

PRINCE: You ever heard of checking your list to see who's naughty and who's nice? I just let people talk. I was talking to somebody about "The Beautiful Ones." They were speculating as to who I was singing about. But they were completely wrong.

If they look at it, it's very obvious. "Do you want him or do you want me," that was written for that scene in *Purple Rain* specifically. Where Morris [Day] would be sitting with [Apollonia], and there'd be this back and forth. And also, "The beautiful ones you always seem to lose," Vanity had just quit the movie. To then speculate, "Well, he wrote that song about me?" Afterward you go, "Who are you? Why do you think that you're part of the script that way? And why would you go around saying stuff like that?"

So we just let people talk and say whatever they want to say. Nine times out of 10, trust me, what's out there now, I wouldn't give nary one of these folks the time of day. That's why I don't say anything back, because there's so much that's wrong.

EBONY: But you could set the record straight.

PRINCE: There's too much! They get down to, "See, what he was thinking at that specific time was . . . His mindset at the time . . . " They psychoanalyze you.

There was one engineer who said that their sole purpose in life was to get the stuff out of the vault, and get it copied so it wasn't lost to the world. I'm trying to figure out if that's illegal. Should I fear for my safety that you might need some medical attention? You want to come up in my vault and you feel like that belongs to you and that's your purpose? You better find something to do. That's scary.

EBONY: What made you decide to move your catalog to TIDAL and away from the other streaming services, and why is *Hitnrun* about to be exclusively available on TIDAL?

PRINCE: TIDAL is a new company, it's brand new. They're just getting their footing, and I think when there's a company like that, or the OWN network—situations where we finally get into a position to run things—we all should help. It's been a lot of fun.

We've changed the format of how our music appears. Where it would normally say "RELATED" and have a bunch of random stuff pop up—I love D'Angelo but he's just getting started, he came *way* after—what we did is we changed that to INFLUENCES. Then all these black and white pictures come up and you can go back and look at all the people who influenced me. Then in each one of those situations, TIDAL allowed us to go and work on *those* pages.

That's the problem with these formats is that there's a lot of laziness out there. They have to do so much, so a lot of times it's just a program. It's an algorithm. I didn't want to be a part of that.

EBONY: Many initial media reports wanted to count out TIDAL.

PRINCE: With 1 million-plus subscribers. Spotify has 10. So if you imagine a million people in front of you? That's a lot of people. So you gotta talk to them, and you getting ready to drop something, and all of 'em are gonna get it. What do you wanna say? How are you gonna move all of 'em? Oh, now it gets interesting. It's always going to be the peanut gallery and that's all right.

My thing is this. The catalog has to be protected. And some of our fans were actually disingenuous. Taking the time to get their playlists together, and yeah, it's gone. Now you got to actually go subscribe to get the music that you lost on Spotify. Spotify wasn't paying, so you gotta shut it down.

EBONY: I talked to people about switching from Spotify to TIDAL who didn't want to recreate their playlists all over again.

PRINCE: That's the line in the sand. That is exactly what I'm talking about. When you make issue of those things, that is exactly what ownership means. It doesn't mean that you just get pimped by somebody. And none of our kids should be subject to this.

You can't give away Google. You can't give away the country. Nobody can just come up and just start selling the Statue of Liberty—stuff like that. So the Prince catalog now—and again, I don't want to sound like a megalomaniac—but I have to manage it, that's Americana now. You gave the Beatles $400 million and then tried to squash the news? That's why Apple held out. I had more albums than they did.

EBONY: What is your perfect model of the music industry? You've been vocal about the changes it needs to make for decades now.

PRINCE: Technology is getting all of humanity to the point where we're gonna be able to dial up our own experience here. So I may have a version of it, and Jay Z may have a version of it, and Kendrick Lamar may have a version of it. There isn't gonna be one size fits all. You could see that with hip-hop, really. They didn't say "courtesy of," they just jumped on people's records when they felt like it. You're talking about grown men asking another grown man permission to sing. So yeah, there is no perfect.

Different situations call for a different approach, a different set up. The *Musicology* Tour for example, when we bundled the record with the tour, it was perfect for that time.

EBONY: Did you hear the last album by The Time, *Condensate*?

PRINCE: No. You know, it was Morris playing drums and me on the bass. That's how we would make the basic track. Naked. Just like that, and nobody would know. And then when you put the keys on it and the guitar, then that's what The Time was. And it was perfect. Going through it now, I can hear all that stuff. Like "The Walk." I hadn't heard "The Walk" in ages. It's like you can't believe that you did it. I don't even know how it's possible. I don't. I do but I don't. That can never be duplicated again. It was a time period. His son [Derran Day] sings now, and look just like he did. So it should be like Steph and Dell Curry. Let's do this. The Time can still be alive, he just needs to do it. I'm gonna see him in a minute anyway to work together. Musicians I'm cool with. But other folks standing around talking about they gon' take out the vault? Boy . . .

EBONY: Will you be remastering the catalog?

PRINCE: Hopefully, yeah. A new *Greatest Hits*. Because I never had anything to do with [*The Hits/The B-Sides*]. But put great liner notes in it to explain what record came from what and why. Explain the backstory of it. Somebody said "Purple Rain" was inspired by Bob Seger! I said, call him in. "Sit down, man. Y'all got to have everything, huh? Bob Seger?! You gon' put that in the ether? OK." [*Laughter.*]

EBONY: Let's talk about horns in your music. The lore is that you went to a Bruce Springsteen concert and saw how much Clarence Clemons brought to winning his crowds over. And then you incorporated horns into your live shows afterwards, with Eric Leeds on the *Purple Rain* Tour.

PRINCE: How do you get "Hot Thing" from "Born in the USA?" 'Cause that's where Eric shines, on "Hot Thing." But how do you get Madhouse from "Dancing in the Dark?" I have a lot of respect for Bruce and everything he's done. He's one of my favorite bandleaders of all time. But he wouldn't even say that.

But seriously, here's the thing. There's half of me that understands that. Because I don't talk about it, they have to fill in the gaps because there's nothing. There's nobody saying anything about it. So they gotta say something. But what I notice is that they keep naming names that there's no connection. Clarence Clemons don't play funk. There's nothing about Clarence that's funky. He plays old '50s saxophone that was on those types of records, Frankie Valli and that type of stuff.

If you notice when Eric showed up, it was during the *Purple Rain* tour. And I was the only soloist in the band if [Matt] Fink wasn't soloing. And he had his solos that were planned out. He didn't improvise. There's the channel and then there's the practiced, technical way that somebody plays. And Fink, he's incredible at that: something he's practiced.

No Doubt, you know that group? Friends of mine. Came in here and jammed together. They don't know how to jam. They don't know nothing about that. You get them to play one of their songs? They'll pound you in the ground. Girl jumping on top of tabletops and all of that, all kinds of stuff. But you get them to do anything other than what they done practiced at the house, they don't know where they are. You know what I'm saying? Esperanza Spalding, that's a different story. She's gonna actually lead.

So there was no other soloist in the band. So Eddie M., one of the horn players, and Eric was brought in. But Clarence Clemons, that's just a sideman. One of the greatest sidemen in history, and he's a star in his own right. Them two was nothing like that. C'mon, man. That's a whole different thing. Clarence'll smile and you'll forget every solo Eric ever did. Like Louis Armstrong. Beautiful dude. Aura was huge.

And you can't copy Bruce. I would never mess with somebody whom I respect and who was actually gigging at the same time.

EBONY: I've read "The Beautiful Ones" was based on Susannah Melvoin.

PRINCE: Any ballad like that, you know it's not going to be about anything, uh, what's the word? Carnal. It's not gonna even be based in flesh. Regardless of what I'm singing about, it's all spiritual. This is a channel. I'm trying to do "Somewhere over the Rainbow." It's not about somebody human that I'm looking at right now. It wouldn't have worked if it was. This was literally for that character. And that's why it worked. Everybody thinks the song is about them. "This song's about me and the other one's about Bob Seger." [*Laughter.*]

[*Prince leaves Paisley Park Studios, pulls up later in a sportscar, and plays* Hitnrun Phase Two *in his Cadillac. Plays "Stare."*]

This bass is wicked, you understand? That's why none of 'em will come to the gig anymore. They'll just stand in the back, because they know what they said. Making up all these names about people and giving credit where credit ain't due. Kendrick [Lamar], this is his year now. I asked him to come up here just to visit. This is related: I told him, "You got the whole year. Don't worry about it. Ain't nobody gonna bother you."

EBONY: I interviewed him for the June cover. He said he came to Paisley Park, but he wouldn't talk about the conversation.

PRINCE: We talked about a lot of stuff. Listen. A lot of times I don't talk about the past because you can't do it without naming names. I'm not bitter by no stretch of the imagination. But I grew up poor, so I'm used to something: if it's mine, I'm used to it being mine. If somebody takes it from me, it's taken. It's taken a lot to get used to that. That, OK, you're somebody else. But I'm like, that's my coat that's in Hard Rock Café. They're not supposed to have that. Get that outta there. And second of all: how did they get it? And then they'll say, "well, a bandmate." I say, "Oh really? Go get the band member and bring him to me." And then they sit down and come in with their head down. I ain't gonna say who it is, but that's what I'm talking about.

"Why? What do I say to your wife now?" "I came on hard times, I don't know what to tell you." Now in my heart, I forgive them. But like I said, it's like, you won't hear from him anymore. See, back in the day, he was making some comments too. We've all had to deal with it, but I just, wow.

I didn't wanna go this far, because it's about *Hit N Run* and Josh and all that, but this is where "Baltimore" is. It starts this whole album. Check this out.

[*Plays "Baltimore."*]

And it goes right into this.

[*Plays "Rocknroll Loveaffair."*]

EBONY: How close is this to being . . . ?

PRINCE: It's done.

EBONY: It's done! My man . . . [*Plays "2 Y. 2 D."*]

PRINCE: They say that stuff when I ain't around. Ain't nobody else heard this. [*Plays "Look at Me, Look at U."*]

EBONY: Are you feeling more oriented to the bass lately?

PRINCE: Yes. I spent years on the guitar, so. [*Plays "Groovy Potential."*] This came out briefly on a file on SoundCloud or something, but never been on an album. You know the sequencing is perfect into this one. This is driving music.

EBONY: You've never had a producer. What made you choose Joshua Welton for *Hit N Run: Phase One*?

PRINCE: His faith in God really struck a nerve. And you know how you can just feel that something's gonna work and it feels right, it's a good fit? I knew the band was going to work, I knew the relationship with him was gonna work. I check people out now to see how faith-based they are and how real they are about it. That goes a long way, I gotta tell you. Because I can trust them. I can give him the key and don't have to worry.

EBONY: You produced this album [*Hit N Run: Phase Two*]?

PRINCE: Yeah. Josh did the other one. And just so you know, where Josh is to me, he's like me, younger. But I'm trying to get him to cut through all the junk that I had to learn on my own. I'm trying to throw it all on his desk at once. Because he can grasp it. He's learning quickly. Mixing is the thing that he appreciates. It'll float. It'll literally levitate when you find the right spot for it. When he hears it, I see his light bulb go on. If his light bulb didn't go on, I wouldn't waste the time. I would say, maybe he'll be a beat manufacturer or something like that. But to do the whole thing, you need to learn how to make stuff float. And it's hard. It doesn't work all the time.

Paisley Park is an academy any which way you look at it. Musicians have gone through here. We've jammed, we've shared with one another. And ultimately there's now a storehouse of great music to learn from, productions and arrangements you can study. And we pride ourselves with working with the best people. Eric [Leeds] and those guys were some of them, but not the only ones. And so what people can't do is say, "Oh, well, that team was better than any." Please. It's actually just getting better. I'm not saying that 'cause it's us. I just hear it. [*Plays "When She Comes."*]

Recording like Al Green. I don't need no words. I don't need nothing. You know, Doug E. Fresh told me—we used to hang out when he was touring with us—he said, "Man, Prince, Rakim is so bad, Prince, he don't have no friends. Just no friends." I said, "Why?" "Nobody wanna be around him, they just feel small." And that's why I always know I'm doing alright: nobody comes around. Be quiet around here. I love it just like this.

EBONY: Did you do all the instruments on this?

PRINCE: No, no. Keyboards a little, just parts. I'm getting in the habit of that now. I did it on one album a long time ago. I love schooling musicians on just one track. "You are gonna do a masterpiece today. You just gotta listen." And when they get it, it's so fun, because you see them go through what I go through. It's magic, you know? You gotta feel that you did something magical. It all blends, and you get everybody to calm down and listen to when they're playing and get outside of themselves, like they're listening to the record rather than playing it. [*Plays "Black Muse."*] This is the oldest one on here, and I loved it so much I just saved it.

EBONY: I like this album better than *Hit N Run: Phase One*. No disrespect.

PRINCE: *Hit N Run* sounds like today. TIDAL is sinking money into it, and they need it. And my heart is always on because I want them to do well. [Beyoncé and Jay Z] have taken a lot of abuse, their family has. A historic amount of abuse between the two of 'em. And when we win on this, none of us'll gloat. He's not the gloating type anyway. He's slick with his. He says to brush the dirt off your shoulder. "Y'all just need to stop. Just calm down! Everybody calm down! There ya go."

When this does well, nobody gloats, we go about our business. But we'll do another one. And this is a way for Josh to step up. 'Cause he's not gonna stay around here forever. So I gotta work with him while

I can. And you remember: Teddy Riley was under somebody before; Pharrell was under somebody before. Jimmy [Jam] and Terry [Lewis] were under me.

EBONY: "America" is my favorite Prince 12-inch, an extended version over 20 minutes long. Those 1980s Prince singles weren't remixes.

PRINCE: It blew my mind too. I brought them "I Hate U" and I thought it was one of the greatest records I had ever done in years. And they said, "Yeah man, this is dope. Now we gonna have Puffy do the remix." Like, I was in shock. "OK, I'm out." That wasn't the reason; that was just another compound to the thing.

All the musicians that played on this, they go, "He just records and he puts it in the vault." All of them have stories. "He's recording stuff you would not believe. He just threw it away." I didn't throw it away. It just has to be on the right project. And all of these fit together now. It reminds me of this time period. I can see all of their faces. And this is probably the last record I'll do with Shelby J. She's all in here too. And Andy Allo's singing background here too.

EBONY: Shelby's a powerhouse.

PRINCE: So's Liv Warfield. Watch this though. [*Listening to a song transition.*] You know, where else would it go except there? But before, I had that whole song starting another album sequence. And it didn't work. So now, where it's placed, it's right where you wanna be at that point on the album. [*Plays "Revelation."*]

EBONY: "Housequake" really starts with the end of "Play in the Sunshine." It's not the same without that interruption.

PRINCE: When I was doing that, there'd be no way I could hear this. Now I think this is the best stuff. This is "Revelation." That's Marcus Anderson on soprano.

EBONY: That moody keyboard effect works.

PRINCE: When I did the track, it was about an hour and a half of just messing around with the groove. He just kept messing around with programming. When he got that one, it sounded like "U Got the Look."

I said: "That! Stop!" Then he didn't have to play that much on the key-board. That's why this song has the sex appeal it does.

Those types of records you can't make unless you had a hit prior to that, you get what I mean? You do it out of confidence. "I can do any-thing now." So then you try anything. And that's what this is.

And that's when faith comes into it. [*Listening to the end of "Revelation."*] What that's about is Moses. Remember they said he put his hand into his cloak and pulled it out and it was white? [Exodus 4:6] What color was it before he put it in? So now we can start talking about that stuff. We couldn't do that until you had a [Black] president. Couldn't do that until hip-hop.

Hip-hop is its own force now. It took a minute. And that's why Jay has to succeed. Our entities have to succeed. Baby and Lil Wayne ain't supposed to be fighting. That's supposed to be where cooler minds sit down and say, "Check this out fellas: For all of us, stop. 'Cause we said so. Everybody's gonna calm down." Rap ain't gonna be a ghost town. Nobody's gonna shoot nobody.

I'm saying: now we can start talking about this stuff. And without faith . . . I was telling a friend of mine who was here was that I wouldn't have met Josh if it wasn't for faith. We wouldn't have had nothing in common. He'd have thought I was crazy, and vice versa.

Religion, when used properly, actually is like a health regimen. And they're finding now that people who have faith live longer. I mean, it says so in the book. That's what it's supposed to be. You ain't supposed to die. If there's God, then that's what God would be.

EBONY: What do you say to people who are more spiritual than religious?

PRINCE: That's OK. Because eventually they're gonna get more respon-sibility. And that's where religion will come into it. Because you have to have some sort of glue that's gonna keep people honorable. Even if you're thieves. And that's what religion is. It's order. Just think about it like that. The word's been muddied. We forget what it was in the begin-ning. Did you see Tut?

EBONY: No.

PRINCE: It was interesting. 'Cause that's the way it was in the beginning. And it's all explained out there. Remember: all of that was African. If you just look at it for its African properties, then everything's straight. It's all in there. Every story is based upon that story, the story of Tut and his father. They just keep retelling it in different ways. And the Bible is just the same story, that story, told different ways in several different parts in the Bible. Once you know that, then you don't get overwhelmed by what's in the Bible. That's if it's taught properly. You don't get overwhelmed by it, and there's nothing to fight about.

Like, this supposed to be like wings. Take you up higher. Now do your work from a higher place, get more done, cover more ground, and whoop your competitors. Comparisons with this, that, and the other, we never thought of ourselves as having competition with anybody.

EBONY: We've got this rare audience with you. What would you most like to express to the EBONY readership at the moment?

PRINCE: I've always made it a point when I've spoken with EBONY to encourage ownership. Because we can look at situations, with TIDAL for example. Apple, Pandora, Rhapsody, Deezer, when you give them your record, you might get paid six months later. Beyoncé, her last album came out, $18 million went into the kitty the very next day. She didn't get that money. She got paid on a royalty scale, just like all the other artists. That's what I'm talking about.

LeBron James, his deal is a completely designer deal, completely different than any other basketball player. So that's what we need for the future. To stay afloat, it's gonna need the Kanye Wests and the Kendricks and people like that who can make product and get people excited about stuff. And they're going to dictate what the deal is gonna look like. And that's what's fun about the times now.

ABOUT THE CONTRIBUTORS

Mick Brown is a British journalist who has freelanced for numerous publications, including the *Guardian, Rolling Stone,* and *Crawdaddy.* He contributes to London's *Telegraph* magazine and the *Daily Telegraph* newspaper and has authored six books, including *American Heartbeat: A Musical Journey Across America from Woodstock to San Jose* and *Tearing Down the Wall of Sound: The Rise and Fall of Phil Spector.*

Robert L. Doerschuk was a writer and editor with the Country Music Association's *Close Up CMA*, an executive editor at Allmusic.com, and editor with *Musician* magazine. His books include *Playing from the Heart: Great Musicians Talk About Their Craft* and *88: The Giants of Jazz Piano.* He is retired from the music industry.

Bilge Ebiri is a writer and editor for *New York* magazine and has written for the *Village Voice*, the *New York Times*, and the Criterion Collection among other media outlets. He wrote and directed the 2003 dark comedy film *New Guy.*

Ben Edmonds was an editor of *Creem* magazine and longtime contributor to music publications in the United States and United Kingdom. He was an A&R executive at various labels, signing Mink DeVille while at Capitol Records, and a manager of the post–Jim Morrison Doors. He died in 2016 at the age of sixty-five.

Dimitri Ehrlich is a *Huffington Post* blogger whose writing has appeared in the *New York Times, Rolling Stone,* and *New York.* He's written two music books, including *Inside the Music: Conversations with Contemporary Musicians About Spirituality, Creativity and Consciousness*. He's also a former MTV VJ and multiplatinum-selling songwriter, with songs recorded by Moby, Westlife, and Kim Wilde.

Electrifying Mojo (Charles Johnson) is a disc jockey who has been on the radio in Detroit and the American Midwest since the mid-1970s. He is known for his disregard for genre-based music programming, lengthy deep-dives into artists' catalogs, and influence on the Detroit Techno sound and scene.

Gary Graff is a multimedia journalist with Detroit's MediaNews Group. He's written for *Billboard*, the *Boston Globe*, the *New York Times*, and many other publications and was a columnist for *Guitar World*. He founded and edited MusicHound's "Essential Album Guide" series and has written multiple music books, including *The Ties That Bind: Bruce Springsteen A to E to Z* and *Neil Young: Long May You Run: The Illustrated History*.

Barbara Graustark is the art editor for the *New York Times*. She was a writer at *Newsweek* in the late 1970s and early 1980s, securing one of the last interviews with John Lennon. She freelances for publications such as *People* and *Musician*, and wrote and directed the 1984 documentary *Yoko Ono: Then & Now*.

Vanessa Grigoriadis is a contributing writer for *Vanity Fair* and the *New York Times*, a National Magazine Award winner, and author of the book *Blurred Lines: Sex, Power, and Consent on Campus*. She cofounded the podcast company Campside Media, cocreating *Chameleon: Hollywood Con Queen*, which was named one of 2020's best podcasts by Spotify, Stitcher, and *Rolling Stone*.

Robert Hilburn was a music writer for the *Los Angeles Times* from 1966 to 2005, serving many of those years as music editor. He hosts a weekly radio show on Los Angeles's KCSN and has written multiple books, including *Johnny Cash: The Life* and *Paul Simon: The Life*.

Barney Hoskyns is a former US correspondent for *MOJO* magazine who has contributed to *Vogue*, *GQ*, *Rolling Stone*, *Spin*, *Uncut*, and countless other periodicals. He is the author of numerous books, including *Hotel California: Singer-Songwriters and Cocaine Cowboys in the LA Canyons* and the Tom Waits biography *Lowside of the Road, Trampled Under Foot*. He is the cofounder and editorial director of the essential rock-music database Rock's Backpages.

Dennis Hunt worked as a pop music writer for the *Los Angeles Times*, an entertainment writer for *USA Today*, and video/DVD columnist for the *San Diego Tribune*.

Steven Ivory was a regular contributor to *Soul* magazine in the 1970s before becoming editor of the popular teen magazine *Black Beat*. He's written for a multitude of major publications, including *Vibe*, *Essence*, the *Los Angeles Times*, and the *Source*. In 1984 he published one of the first Prince biographies (*Prince*), and he has written a Tina Turner biography and the autobiographical *Fool in Love: One Man's Search for Romance . . . or Something Like It*.

Gene Kalbacher was music writer best known for his 1982 cofounding of *Hot House*, a then-monthly, now-online guide to the New York City jazz scene. Kalbacher died in 1999.

Minneapolis native **Neal Karlen** was an associate editor for *Newsweek*, a contributing editor for *Rolling Stone*, a regular contributor to the *New York Times*, and an on-air essayist for CBS News and National Public Radio. He has published nine books including *Babes in Toyland: The Making and Selling of a Rock and Roll Band* and *This Thing Called Life: Prince's Odyssey, On and Off the Record*.

Nick Krewen is a Canadian journalist who has contributed to many publications including the *Toronto Star*, the *Arizona Republic*, and the *Vancouver Sun*. He's written numerous LP liner notes, including Klaatu's *3:47 E.S.T.*, FM's *Black Noise*, and Glass Tiger's *The Thin Red Line*, and coauthored *Music from Far and Wide—Celebrating 40 Years of the Juno Awards* in 2011.

The work of **Miles Marshall Lewis** has appeared in multiple publications, including *GQ*, the *Washington Post*, and *Wax Poetics*. He's been deputy editor at *XXL*, music editor at *Vibe*, deputy music editor at BET

.com, and arts and culture editor at Ebony.com from 1998 to 2015. He has published three books, including *Promise That You Will Sing About Me: The Power and Poetry of Kendrick Lamar* and the 33⅓ series entry for Sly and the Family Stone's *There's a Riot Goin' On*.

Dorian Lynskey is a regular writer for the *Guardian*. He has contributed to publications including *Q*, *Word*, *Spin*, *Empire*, and *Blender*. He is the author of *The Guardian Book of Playlists* and *33 Revolutions Per Minute: A History of Protest Songs*.

Adam Mattera was the editor of *Attitude* magazine, winning Best Men's Magazine editor at the British Society of Magazine Editors awards in 2005. He has been a frequent popular culture commentator on UK television and has contributed to numerous publications including the *Sunday Times*, *Time Out*, *Out*, and the UK Black-music monthly *Echoes*.

Jesse Nash is the cofounder and director of Cricket Public Relations. He has had a long career in the media, including podcast and online programming with The AftershockXL Network.

Ed Ochs was one of the first rock critics, serving two stints with *Billboard* and writing the columns "Soul Sauce" and "Tomorrow," which were the most widely read weekly features in the music business from 1968 to 1972. In 1970 he was honored by the National Association of Television & Radio Announcers for "Soul Sauce" and his contributions to Black music. He has published three novels and coauthored a Stevie Nicks biography.

Ann Powers is an American music critic who works for National Public Radio (NPR). She was the top popular music critic for the *Los Angeles Times*, a pop critic at the *New York Times*, and an editor for the *Village Voice*. She is the author of *Weird Like Us: My Bohemian America* and *Good Booty: Love and Sex, Black & White, Body and Soul in American Music*, and coauthored *Piece by Piece* with Tori Amos.

Chris Salewicz was the senior features writer for *NME* from 1975 to 1981 and has written for *Q*, *The Face*, and the *Sunday Times Magazine*, among other publications. He was part of the team that set up MTV Europe and subsequently presented the weekly film program *Kino*.

He has written several books, including biographies of Jimmy Page, Bob Marley, and Joe Strummer.

Jeff Schneider was a writer for Minnesota's *Insider* magazine in the late 1970s.

J. Randy Taraborrelli is a longtime print and television journalist and author of twenty books, fifteen of which have made the *New York Times* bestseller list. His musical biographies include works on Madonna, Michael Jackson, Diana Ross, and Beyoncé.

CREDITS

I gratefully acknowledge the help of everyone who gave permission for material to appear in this book. I have made every reasonable effort to contact copyright holders. If an error or omission has been made, please bring it to the attention of the publisher.

"Prince: A Touch of Magic," by Jeff Schneider. Published May/June 1978 (No. 3, Vol. 11) in *Insider: The Midwest Magazine of Music News, Arts and Lifestyles*. Publication owner is deceased.

"That Mysterious Prince: He Talks About Himself!," by J. Randy Taraborrelli. Published March 1980 in *Soul Teen*. Reprinted with permission.

"Prince: More Than Just a 'Dirty Mind,'" by Dennis Hunt. Published December 21, 1980, in *Los Angeles Times*. Copyright © 1981 by *Los Angeles Times*. Reprinted with permission.

"Prince in the Afternoon," by Gene Kalbacher. Published February 25–March 4, 1981 (Issue 356) in *Aquarian—Night Owl*. Reprinted with permission.

"Prince: Mom's Favorite Freak," by Ed Ochs. Published June 1981 in *Rock & Soul Songs*. Reprinted with permission.

"Strutting with the New Soul Monarch," by Chris Salewicz. Published June 6, 1981, in *New Musical Express*. Reprinted with permission of Rock's Backpages.

"The Renegade Prince," by Robert Hilburn. Published November 21, 1982, in *Los Angeles Times*. Copyright © 1982 by *Los Angeles Times*. Reprinted with permission.

"Mixed Emotions: Prince on the Music," by Robert Hilburn. Published September 1983 in *Musician*.

"Prince: Strange Tales from Andre's Basement . . . And Other Fantasies Come True," by Barbara Graustark. Published September 1983 in *Musician*.

"Prince Talks," by Neal Karlen. Published September 12, 1985 (Issue 456) in *Rolling Stone*. Copyright © 1985 by *Rolling Stone* LLC. All Rights Reserved. Reprinted with permission.

Radio interview by Electrifying Mojo. Broadcast June 7, 1986, on WHYT 96.3 Detroit.

"Prince Invites Black Beat to Paisley Park!," by Steven Ivory. Published January 1992 in *Black Beat*. Reprinted with permission.

"New Gold Dream," by Adam Mattera. Published March 11, 1995, in *Echoes*. Reprinted with permission.

Prince press conference at Paisley Park, Chanhassen, MN, November 12, 1996. Public domain.

"Portrait of The Artist as a Newly Free Man," by Nick Krewen. Published November 20, 1996, in *Hamilton Spectator*. Reprinted with permission.

"Portrait of the Artist: The Sound of Emancipation," by Robert L. Doerschuk. Published April 1997 in *Musician*.

"18 Questions for The Artist (Still Generally Known as Prince)," by Ben Edmonds. Published August 1998 in *MOJO*. Reprinted with permission of Rock's Backpages.

"The Artist Formerly Known as Prince . . . An Exclusive Interview," by Jesse Nash. Published October/November 1999 in *OCA Magazine*. Reprinted with permission.

"♀: Portrait of the Artist as a Free Man," by Dimitri Ehrlich. Published December 1999 in *Notorious*. Reprinted with permission of the author.

"An Interview with the Prince Formerly Known as The Artist," by Barney Hoskyns. Published March 2000 in *MOJO*. Reprinted with permission of Rock's Backpages.

Prince press conference, New York City, May 16, 2000. Public domain.

"Prince: The Y-Life Interview," by Bilge Ebiri. Published June 2001 in *Yahoo! Internet Life*. Reprinted with permission.

"Prince of Paradox," by Mick Brown. Published June 12, 2004, in *Daily Telegraph*. Reprinted with permission of Rock's Backpages.

"Where's My Interview?," by Gary Graff. Published September 12, 2004, in *Gallery of Sound*. Reprinted with permission.

"My Night with Prince," by Ann Powers. Published January 11, 2009, in *Los Angeles Times*. Copyright © 2009 by *Los Angeles Times*. Reprinted with permission.

Prince press conference, Paris, October 12, 2009. Public domain.

"Prince: 'I'm a Musician. And I Am Music.'" by Dorian Lynskey. Published June 23, 2011, in the *Guardian*. Reprinted with permission of Rock's Backpages.

"Everlasting Now: Prince," by Vanessa Grigoriadis. Published June 3, 2013, in *V Magazine*. Reprinted with permission.

"The Black Interview," by Miles Marshall Lewis. Published June 2016 in *Ebony*. Reprinted with permission.

INDEX

All songs and album titles by Prince unless otherwise attributed.